Contents

READ IT ... GIVE IT AWAY ...

Annie Porthouse
Hayley DiMarco
Elizabeth Goudge
Abidemi Sanusi
Anne Atkins
Josh Harris
Peter Greystone
Ruth Valerio
Rev Andrew Body
Stuart Briscoe
Selwyn Hughes
Tony Anthony with Angela Little
David Adam
Francine Rivers
David Aikman
Simon Ponsonby
R.T. Kendall
Max Lucado
Nick Baines
Leith Anderson
Jonathan Aitken
Joel Osteen
Stormie Omartian
Joyce Huggett
Steve Chalke with Anthony Watkis
John Maxwell
Hugh Rayment-Pickard
Lee Strobel
Dave Roberts

Copyright © 2005 SAM BOOKS

First Published in 2005 by SAM BOOKS

Permission has been granted by the following publishers:

Baker
Church House Publishing
Continuum Books
Darton, Longman & Todd
Harvest House
Hodder & Stoughton
IVP
Kevin Mayhew
Kingsway
Lion Publishing
Monarch Books
Navpress
SCM – Canterbury Press
Scripture Union
SPCK
St Andrew Press
Thomas Nelson
Tyndale House Publishing
Zondervan
Authentic Media
The Good Book Company
CWR

Full Copyright details are included at the beginning of each chapter

11 10 09 08 07 06 05   7 6 5 4 3 2 1

British Library Cataloguing in Publication Data
A catalogue record for this book is available from the British Library

ISBN 1-90083-666-1

Cover Design By Jeremy Bye
Typeset by GCS, Leighton Buzzard, Bedfordshire UK
Print Management by Adare Carwin
Printed and bound by Haynes, Sparkford, Yeovil, Somerset, UK

Foreword

One of the greatest joys of my life is the reading of books which have a spiritual message. I started this habit during my prison sentence when I was searching for a right relationship with God.

What began partly as an antidote to the boredom of being locked up in a cell for many hours a day grew into a serious hunger for spiritual study and refreshment. After my release this same hunger took me to Wycliffe Hall, Oxford, where I read theology for two years.

Since then I have continued to drink deeply at the well of Christian reading in my daily quiet time and in my leisure time. This is the inspiration for my prayer life and the fuel for my professional work as a Christian author. Without this love of books my spiritual journey would not have made much progress.

Good books are rather like good friends. Sometimes they are familiar and relaxing companions. At other times they are more like teachers or guides as we cross life's deserts, climb mountains, or descend into difficult valleys. We need them in our hearts and on our bookshelves.

I don't suppose I will get around to reading each and every one of the books on this year's World Book Day list but I already know several of the selected authors. Their books, and the books whose authors I do not yet know, are sure to provide me and others with many marvellous hours of reading in the years ahead.

Jonathan Aitken, 2005

Dear Bob

Annie Porthouse

Jude Singleton is about to face the biggest challenge of her life … she is looking for a man. On the way to finding 'Bob' she has to deal with those annoying distractions of university life, broken toes, waterproof curtains and driving instructors with dubious breath. Oh and she is not sure whether there is, or isn't a God.

Scripture Union
£9.99
PB/1 8599.9633 7

Dear Bob

Annie Porthouse

First Published in 2003 by Scripture Union UK, 207-209 Queensway, Bletchley,
Milton Keynes, MK2 2EB

A Freaky Start

Dear Bob

Fri 17 Sept

Dear Bob

Arrggghhhhh!! Just come round after v freaky dream – scared the pants off me (not that I tend to wear undergarments in ... sorry, too much info, swipe that).

Dream took me to youth group, where Jim (leader) was giving farewell chat (was deserting us to work for Geriatric Goats for God Ltd in Uganda, or whatever). He began like this:

'God isn't real ...'

In true dream-like fashion the church hall began to sway – everything drifting into slow motion. Wanted to scream/cry/hide.

He went on to apologise for 'misleading' us over the past couple of years (hey – no probs Jim). Said he'd changed his mind about Uganda – was now off to spend year at 'New-Holistic-Enlightening-Centre' to 'find himself'.

Am having MAJOR freak-out. Like ... think of it from my angle, Bob – there I was ... the (almost) perfect Cn (Christian) girl (woman?) knowing exactly what (whom) I believed in (God) and what it meant for me in my life ... church, lots of Cn pals, reading Bible every day (almost), knowing all Matt's songs off by heart (Redman) ... even the guitar cords, and don't even PLAY the thing (amazing what you pick up being a page-turner) ... and then, in a matter of seconds, someone I'd respected big time announces is all off coz:

'God isn't real'
in a dream! A stupid, insignificant dream (prob due to over-heating
in sleep, due to dodgy radiator that can't suss out ... always have
nightmares when get too hot and sweaty ... or is it that always get
hot and sweaty due to nightmares ...? hmmm ...).

8:22 pm Not that am sweaty person in general, please note.

8:30 pm Apart from when do extreme amounts of aerobic exercise...
which (fortunately) is about as often as bother to have eyebrows
'tidied' (never).

Sat 18 Sept

5:47 am

Dear Bob,

No, is not insignificant (the dream).

Arrgghhh ... brain hurts now as used multi-syllabic words before
breakfast ... nooooooo ... did it again! How come am even up at this
time of ... day/night?

Has sunk in deep: Jim...Mr Ace-Cn,

Mr Happy-to-lead-the-worship,

Mr Moving-in-the-gifts,

Mr Cool-youth-group-leader...

denied the existence of God,

albeit (good word) in a dream.

Has caused me to doubt/question/pace up and down (doesn't
take long in here ... am convinced humans were never designed to
live in such TEENY spaces).

Not sure what's going on – am v messed up. HELP! Need
emotional (and spiritual?) 1st aid.

Am lost.

8:45 am

Just had ½ packet Pringles for breakfast (SC&Onion). Great. Now lost … AND obese.

Sun 19 Sept

3:32 pm

Dear Bob

Another freaky dream last night. Not as profound as last one tho. This time was Pooh (Winnie the) in story where he gets stuck in entrance to Rabbit's den coz he's eaten too much honey. Except in MY case, Pooh (me) had eaten too many Pringles.

Was stuck tight, buttocks wedged in den and head poking out in the sun … a multitude of friends/family gathered around and started lecturing me (Pooh) on dangers of eating too many Pringles. But THEY were munching away on pack after pack (of varying flavours).

'Give them up Judith darling,' said Mum in ghost (+ball+chain) like voice. 'You'll only get addicted and have to be delivered from the Spirit of … the Pringle … ' she sang whilst stuffing a large handful (SC&O) down her own gob.

Arrgggghhhhh! Felt a billion times fatter.

Couldn't even pray for comfort in hour of need as not sure what to think about God.

Tweenies usually does the trick when am blue (for a bunch of pre-schoolers, their sense of harmony is pretty fab) … it's on now … but failing to turn me into a less depressing colour.

Last day of Freshers' Week today. Shame. Has been v cool. Quite forgotten am here to study … 3 years of Freshers' Weeks would surely be more fun.

Mon 20 Sept

6:12 pm

Dear Bob

1st ever lecture today. Should you learn details, you'd spontaneously combust (love that phrase!) due to boredom overload, so won't share them.

Really did have high expectations re lectures. They always sounded so grown-up ... much more sophisticated than 'lessons'. Are nothing to write home about tho (saying that, included all details in last email to Mum, who'll find them riveting, no doubt).

Got quite distracted (not unusual) thinking how it would be real cool to BE a Tweenie. As in someone who prances around in loud costume and solves moral dilemmas in under 20 mins.

Would be Fizz ... or Jake ... tho Milo's quite fun ... not Bella for sure ... who'd want to be THAT bossy cow? Wonder what they get paid ... perhaps will enquire if whole degree thing doesn't work out.

Don't ask why I chose psychology – am not too sure of reason. Need psycho-analysis/counselling/general help myself at the mo. To be honest, am scared.

11:45 pm

Actually, not Fizz, as doubt could get voice to go that high ... unless in extreme pain ... like in style of having legs waxed ...

Wed 22 Sept

10:13 pm

Dear Bob

Just seen *Silence of* the *Lambs* with Libs (someone she knows got it out on video) – did NOT contribute in a positive way to current state of mind. (Libs = Liberty Young, lives: floor above me, studying: psychology, same as me, but she's good at it, status: single, and non-Cn.)

Always been scared of scary stuff, like scary films. You know, the ones with baddies, killing, torture, war, torture …
esp torture.

Was always me who was convinced (on fairly regular basis) there was evil burglar downstairs in early hours of morning. Would wake up Mum – send her down to check. Reasons for this:

1 *Waking Dad would take all night, and most of following day, and*
2 *one glimpse of Mum in flowery 70s nightie would scare Mr Burglar away, pronto … trust me.*

Was me who spent hours surfing net for info re nuclear bombs/ biological warfare, and after effects, so would know what to do (esp since 9/11).

But pre-JimDream, could talk to God about such stuff, and read a multitude of comforting verses to regain 'my peace'. Could chat with Jim – have him pray for me … but has all vanished now … down drain like manky washing-up water.

Bit of a bummer this should happen in 1st week of uni.

Things aren't exactly going to plan.

Thur 23 Sept

2 pm

Dear Bob

Just back from another yawnyawn lecture. Interesting bit: watching Prof Carr's wig slip further and further backwards off head each time he got over-excited (which he did A LOT). Was willing it to fall off altogether …for him to be revealed for baldie that he is, but twas not to be.

11:32 pm

just been for drink at Fir and Ferret with Libs. Told her what was on mind re dream and God and all that. Her reply:

'Jude honey ... stop farting around with all this God crap ... come and have some FUN ... hick ... live the life ... go on the pull ... get wrecked ... hey babe, it works for me ... hick!'

(After 4 pints Dry Blackthorn – I was counting.)

It does too (work for her). She seems happy with who she is and with life, yet has no faith in God to account for it.

Lost her just after last orders – she went up for ANOTHER pint Dry B (how DOES she do it ... my legs and brain go jelly-like after just 1). Went looking for her after a bit. Found her chatting to this guy ... well, eating his ear. He looked all smug and slimy AND blew smoke directly in my face. Left without her.

Haven't heard her come back yet. Guess she'll be out for few more hours ... if she comes back at all tonight.

Mum wouldn't approve of Libs. Can hear her now:

'Darling, you mustn't spend too much time with ...

with the ...

those who ...

NON-Christians.

They might lead you astray.'

Lead me astray from WHAT? To WHAT? Huh.

Is it poss that I'd never really believed in God in the 1st place?

Yeah, course I'd believed in God ... well, think so ... hmmmm. Maybe. Probably. Oh ... sorry ... goodnight.

12:07 am

Can't sleep. Getting quite cross (understatement of the millennium) with several people, all at once. Going to invent some emails to help me ... errr ... organise my thoughts (vent my anger) ...

To: ma&p@@cityofboredom.com
Subject: Brainwashing
Mum & Dad why did you brainwash me into becoming a Cn, and not let me decide for myself?

To: jim@indrivingseat.com
Subject: Dictating
Jim why did you dictate my feelings and beliefs to me, without letting me stop to think it all through?

To: homechurch@wackyland.com
Subject: HUH?
Pastor Vic all that leaping up and down and speaking in tongues and stuff you encouraged me to participate in what was that all about? God? Me? The church? Loonies Anonymous?

To: libs@wildchild.com
Subject: Chucking up & chucking in
Libs why are you expecting me to chuck it all in and follow you in your quest for lads and liquor? How do you expect me to cope with more than 1 Dry B per evening?

To: profcarr@baldiesanon.com
Subject: Lack of hair
Yo Prof why do you wear that stupid wig? Why do you get excited about the selfish gene theory? NO ONE gets excited about that. Get some help mate.

Am going to eat just 1 Pringle (BBQ) for medicinal purposes (to induce sleep) …

12:15am

Well, maybe just a couple more, now tube's been opened …

V v late: Almost asleep when sudden extreme banging at door … twas Libs, who'd clearly been leaning v hard on door, coz when I opened it she fell right into me, mumbling,

'Shooo-d … wassupshooodbabe … wan nasleepienowshoood … nightie nightie … hick … shooooood!' etc.

Steered her in direction of HER room – tucked her in her bed, as she slipped into a blessed state of unconsciousness. Honestly ... should charge for such a service.

Fri 24 Sept

10:32 am

Dear Bob
Questions:

1 *Who broke into room last night and finished off* ALL *BBQ Pringles? Couldn't* POSSIBLY *have been moi.*
2 WHY *are curtains waterproof? Remind me of Nat's w proof sheet under his regular one, in case he pees in his sleep* (Nat = *my nephew, he's* 2).
3 *Do they think we're gonna* PEE *on said curtains? Guess Libs might find it a tad hard to locate loo after trillionth Dry B, but even* SHE *would prob avoid curtains.*

Just gonna check what wrote to you last night.

Ah, yeah, sorry bout that. Feel guilty now. Do actually love parents v much, and Jim and Libs (tho only known her a week) ... but hold fast to feelings re Prof Carr.

Ought to be starting essay today:

'To what extent can evolutionary theories account for human behaviour?

Critically discuss with reference to Darwin's theory of evolution by natural selection and Dawkins' selfish gene theory.'

But will leave til tomorrow, when 'peeing on curtains' query has eased off a bit.

Hope Libs has elephant-sized hangover today and feels v guilty about last night ... but doubt this to be the case. Do her parents even KNOW what she's like? (One thing have noticed – she never talks about her parents ... always changes the subject ... odd.)

Have banned myself from Pringles. Felt like huuuuuuuge BBQ monster, all day.

Mon 27 Sept

3:40 pm

Dear Bob

1st ever driving lesson just over. A snippet for you:

Him: Now, Miss Singleton, I actually just requested that you turn left at the next junction. Do you mind telling me what your indicator lights are currently suggesting to the surrounding traffic?

Me (in head): Yes I do mind, you stupid snotty instructor-guy who insists Christian names are obsolete.

ME (out loud): Errr … oh, yeah, right, I'll just change it to … there we go.

(Head): Why didn't you just SAY I was indicating the wrong way, like any normal human being?

Him: That's better. We don't want any nasty accidents now do we?

Me: Nooooo, we don't.

(Head): How OLD do you take me for – 5? Don't patronise me you old git!

(Swearing was not part of upbringing, and is not part of my nature, but generously allow myself to use certain semi-swear/slang words … 'git' is one of them.)

He has a tendency to tap his pencil on his clipboard – does it every time he tells me off. Guess is sort of threat … 'You do that one more time Miss Singleton and I'll ram this pencil up your nose … REALLY HARD.' (Or could just be nervous habit.)

Not sure if I was cut out to drive. Never even seen *Top Gear*.

So here's me – 18, still a virgin (this is no lie) and have never even experienced *Top Gear* … is this normal?

6:03 pm

Haven't had any Pringles all day – am cured, hurrah!

Might just pop to kitchen tho, to see what other snack can devour – a healthy fat-and-calorie-free one if at all poss … like juicy lettuce leaf/stick of crispy crunchy celery …

6:14 pm

Arrrrggghhhhhhhh!! Entered kitchen and some guys were sat around table, tucking into PRINGLES (Cheese&Onion/S&Vinegar). Don't they KNOW it's my weakness? Can't they see how HIPPO-like those things are making me every time see/smell them? They offered me some – couldn't refuse – would have looked odd, and want to 'fit in' as much as poss. (Had to go for C&O...even tho they make breath sim to that of d instructor, who has stilton breath, they are surely far better than nasty old S&V.)

Not sure who I was trying to kid … don't even HAVE above mentioned green salad-type food-stuffs in my cupboard, that is white, and has a lock (in case that is in any way relevant).

Also … MISS … SINGLETON … LOVES … PRINGLES!! There. Said it. Feel better now.

10:56

Yeah, tis an unfortunate surname to own…feel free to have a chuckle at my expense…everyone else does. Was bad enough already, but made 3 million times worse when old Bridget Jones showed up and decided it was the name belonging to ALL those who were without partners. Have considered changing my name to something more sexy, like Law (get it?!) or Halliwell (as in Geri). Course, if you turn up in the not too distant future, and we tie the knot, will be rid of it forever, AND won't be single … hurrah!

Huh … ought to sue Ms Jones for damages.

Hmmmmm, there's an idea … will rally round all those in country who share my surname, and start class action suit against her … yeah … that's a comforting thought … might help me sleep tonight. (Lib's HorrorMovie-Pal is doing law, and I read one of her textbooks during worst bits of *Silence of the Lambs* … thus my unlikely knowledge of such things as 'class action suits'.)

Tue 28 Sept

10:47 pm

Dear Bob

Didn't do much today.

Listened to Libs drone on about bloke she went out with last night:

'He was sooooooooo DULL. Duller than dull, like the dullest person you could imagine … like duller than Carol Vorderman.'

Couldn't help thinking twas ME who was by far dullest person on planet … I blame the 'borrrrrrrrring' genes inherited from Ma&Pa … can't even roll my tongue! Why is she hanging around with ME?

What's WRONG with Carol anyway?

'He kept on and on about his BEEEP Audi TT convertible – how it does 0 to 60 in 6.5 seconds … who cares? Not ME babe, that's for sure … he didn't even PAY for my BEEEP Big Mac … I had to cough up myself!'

A tough cookie she sure is … a feminist she is not.

Felt it was a good time to tell her about my longing/yearning/deep-rooted desire for a bloke. She seemed vaguely interested, so explained how was after more than just ANY old bloke, but one of the marrying sort. Can hear myself now …

Me: Ummm … I just wanna find Mr Right. Mr Divinely-chosen-just-for-Jude Right. I long to tell 'him' … well, what's on my mind – my deepest thoughts. Not just that though … all the stupid mundane stuff too, like what really pees me off, and what my fave food is, and … yeah … so I've started writing to him, sort of like a diary I guess, but just for him.

Libs: Uh-huh? And then, when you finally meet your hubbie-to-be, you'll lock him in a cell and force him to READ all these BEEEP letters, filled with your deep thoughts, your boring thoughts … and your dietary requirements?!

She always makes my plans look feeble. It's a special gifting she has. If she belonged to my home-church she'd be known as 'the girl blessed with the gift of discouragement'.

Wed 29 Sept

11:23 am

Dear Bob

Am really hoping you're into food shopping in a big way, as think have just made 1st and last visit to local Tesco:

TillGirl 'Keri': (*Sounding bored with her job, and life in general.*) That'll be twenty-two pounds fifty-nine please.

Me: (*Panicking as had planned to spend £5 on extra/yummy food a week – max.*) Errr ... really?

Keri: (*Wondering what possessed the Planet Dork to let me out for the day.*) Yeah, really.

Me: Ummm ... but I thought that ... twenty-two fifty-nine? You don't mean FIVE fifty-nine do you ... per chance?

Keri: (*Now super-unimpressed.*) NO, I don't. Look at your receipt if you like, it's all there.

Me: Oh, no, it's OK ... I'm sure you're right ...

Keri: (*Getting pee-ed off.*) Yeah, people generally think so, as a rule.

Me: Well, can I pay by Visa card then, as I don't have that much cash?

Keri: (*Relieved we were getting somewhere at last.*) Yes. Do you want cashback?

Me: Huh?

Keri: (*Back to Planet-Dorh-type-thinking.*) It's a debit card ... DO-YOU-WANT-CASH-BACK?!

Me: Urrr ... no, probably not. (*Made mental note to ask Libs what 'cashback' was.*)

Keri: And do you have a clubcard?

Me: (*Help – more foreign Tesco-ese.*) Well, no ... should I? Do I need one? How much are they?

Keri: (*Taking pity at this point, fortunately.*) Errrrrrrr ... no worries – but ask at Customer Services if you want one.

Me: Oh, yeah, thanks, I will. (*A Mount Everest-sized lie ... was going to* LEG IT *out of there as soon as was through.*)

Bob, please don't write me off as hideously immature and useless.

Is just that had only ever used my Visa card a couple of times before, and knew NOTHING about cashback, and as for a clubcard ... Mum always shopped at Asda, and never took me (as never wanted to go ... surprise surprise) so tis not my fault, honest. Ah well ... it can only get easier. Can't it? Please say yes.

Felt a bit panicked re Keri. (Why not 'Kerry'? what's so evil about the letter Y all of a sudden?) Made me worry again about coping in big wide world (of uni). Hadn't thought it'd be a doddle, but then had initially been thinking that God and his angels would be looking out pour moi, stopping my feet trampling on stones, or whatever that bit in Psalm 91 says (know you'll have good Bible knowledge, Bob, so won't insult you by looking it up to put in correct verse).

9:14 pm

Or WILL you have any knowledge of the Bible at all? Here's me, doubting my faith, when am weirdly still assuming you will hold the SuperCn-of-the-decade award ... hmmm. But, if ...

God isn't real (Arrrgghhhh ... there it is again!),

then his angels are about as real as Santa (come on – a big boy like you should know he's your Dad + 2 cushions + cotton-wool beard, by now) ... so how am I gonna cope with things even HARDER than shopping in Tesco, like drugs and errr ... other dangerous stuff people say happens at uni?

Oh Bob – come and take me away from all this ... soon.

Fri 1 Oct

8:42 pm

Dear Bob

Another smelly d lesson today.

Times told, 'The mirror is your friend!' – 7

Times told to turn one way and managed to indicate the other – 4

Times told, 'Miss Singleton, what does the speedometer say?' – 5

Times thought that if speedometer could 'say' anything it would be a darn sight MORE interesting than StiltonBreath – 3,000,000

Doesn't he know he's dealing with someone who got 33 out of 35 for their theory test? (Passed it today – whoo-hoo!)

In case you were wondering, was being chastised for driving too slow, not too fast. Thing is, if have to drive past a granny walking on pavement, can't help but imagine her suddenly deciding to leap into road, shopping trolley and all … so automatically slow down, just in case.

My emergency stops could currently be described as maybe-will-just-bring-the-car-to-a-gradual-halt stops.

So tis clearly safer for me to drive slowly, but StiltonBreath can't see it that way … insists I do 30 in 30 zone, not 20. If EVERYONE drove at 20, world would be a safer place … fewer horrible accidents, tho might take ages to travel long distances … motorway would become car park … hmmmmmm …

As pavements fairly chocka with people (inc aforementioned grannies) sense is only right to go slowly. The one who mings of stilton doesn't care about people like I do – obviously not a Cn.

But then am I really a …

and there I go again.

Sat 2 Oct

11:34 pm

Dear Bob

CU today (why is on Sat when I will be at parties etc?). Twas 'an introductory informal drink' at F&Ferret … is called BURP (Bymouth Uni Revival Plan – whoever christened it that needs SERIOUS help).

Know what you're thinking Bob: 'Why is she going to that, when she's not even sure he's really there (God)?' Thing is, knew 1st question all pals back home would ask, after: 'How's the talent?' (or 'How often does your room get cleaned?' from Mum) would be:

'How's the CU?'

Could hardly say, 'Dunno, don't go ... not sure I believe in all that any more.'

Had got to know quite a few of them in Freshers' Week – about 100 of them in total ... 100 WHAT? Cns? Believers? Losers? Nutters? Hmmm. Anyway, am pretending to be one of them until suss it out (life, God etc). Shouldn't be too difficult ... have been one pretty much all my life, til now.

Had heard so much about CUs from student friends, so had really looked forward to going, being in the centre of things, and even ... wait for it ... getting on the committee ... the ultimate goal for every Cn student ... well, it was in my case. Huh.

They're a mixed bunch. At CU at old school, we were all sort of from the same mould ... same type of church (raving charismatic) same style of clothes, same taste in music etc. But here ... didn't know you could get Cn chess-playing geeks, Cn goths with multiple piercings, Cn hippies, Cn designer-clothes freaks ...

Oh yeah ... REALLY hot bloke at BURP called Reuben. Is in a class all of his own. V cool, like at least as cool as naked chef (watched every show and not even HINT of nakedness ... shame).

Is just my type ... long blonde hair (tied back in ponytail, but in manly-stud fashion, as opposed to girlie-Barbie). Sort of hippy/ surfer dresser, bound to be fab Cn ... perfect ... Reuben ... If he doesn't turn out to be you, will edit this bit, if you see what I mean (Reuben that is, not old Jamie). Reuben ... the man who saved his bro from death ... Reuben ... come and save me from my miserable eternal state of being a Singleton. Hmmmmmm ... R ... E ... U ... B ... E ... N ...

Mon 4 Oct

8:46 pm

Dear Bob

Hmmmm ... how shall I describe myself? Well, picture this (just in case we meet over internet and I have to email these letters to you, and only actually meet you on day of wedding, or something bizarre like that).

5ft, 6.

Female-star-of-Friends-style figure.

Long brown curly-ish hair, shampoo-ad-style.

A cute face, dead symmetrical.

Not a blackhead in sight.

OK, the girl you are picturing ... is my sister ... and I look NOTHING like her.

Actually, people say we do look alike, so I smile and say, 'Oh, do you think so?' then add under my breath, 'Yeah, right, if I was slimmer, taller, prettier, had great hair and no zits and all, we'd be twins for sure.'

Anyway, am thinking about my sister because visited her today (she's about 20 mins away on bus). She is pregnant.

Remind me not to get pregnant, or at least not to be seen in PUBLIC when am pregnant – couldn't cope with feeling/looking any huger than already am (size 14/height 5 ft, 8 inch) ... in case that means anything to you, or you thought I had trouble squeezing into lifts.

Abby reminds me of Monica off *Friends*, lost in Obsessive-Compulsive Disorderland. Don't get me wrong, do love her, in a sisterly sort of way, but find it difficult to be HER sister.

Was pondering on this thought earlier today, as watched Nat use a yellow crayon to add Laa-Laa to the lounge wallpaper design. Recalled once overhearing Mum say to her: 'Abigail, you're a clever girl ... you can do ANYTHING you put your mind to.' She's never said that to me.

Laa-Laa clones were appearing all over the wall when Abby came in the lounge, shrieked (in a controlled fashion) and set to work on their elimination. No wonder she never asks me to babysit.

Oh, she's also married to a perfect guy – Amos. They're one of those couples that you assume were matched at birth – Abby n

Amos. Like Romeo n Juliet (without the tragic ending of course) or Posh n Becks (would kill to look like Posh). Went to their church once (Abby and Amos's, not Posh and Becks's) and it was instantly clear that they were loved by all, as was Nat. The perfect family. The perfect Cn family. Huh.

He is Kenyan … she met him over there when she was … oh, enuf of them … got to go, meeting Libs@F&Ferret at 9 pm, which now observe was 9 whole minutes ago!

Tue 5 Oct

9:38 am

Bob

Just had hour long shower. Bliss! (Room is en-suite – whoo-hoo!) Feeling the need to make the most of new freedom … at home, showers involved setting timer for 10 mins!

Got d lesson later – at least one of us will smell fresh!

10:15 am

Oh. Just remembered. A weird and disturbing thing occurred during yesterday's visit to Abby's. Was using upstairs loo, as downstairs loo occupied by Nat, who is coming to terms with using the toilet instead of the potty (aren't you glad you get all these details?!) and overheard phone convo of Amos's:

'Hi – it's me … how's you? Uh-huh … no, I haven't told her yet … it's not the right time … I know I said I would … sorry … (*Pause.*) Not sure, maybe … maybe next week … Look, (*Voice raised slightly.*) look Kate (*Voice lowered again, don't think he wanted to be heard from downstairs.*) this means a lot to me – it's got to be done right, my life won't be the same again, give me TIME to … no … yes … no … uh-huh … OK … yeah … I know … yeah … OK. Must go – dinner's ready … yeah … bye.'

He's quite a hot guy really, for a bro-in-law. He and Abby could well model together on the front of *Happy Clappy Families* or some such yet-to-be-published magazine. But he's NOT kind of guy to mess around with other women. No doubt he prays loads, loves every man/woman/crawling insect … knows the Bible so well you'd think he was involved with the editing in some former life (not that believe in former lives … do I?).

Hmmmm. A bit worrying. Perhaps is nothing though. Yeah, like Kate could be … err … his … long lost identical twin sister … and … she has just come to this country … but he can't tell Abby coz … coz … she would be freaked out by it … and he doesn't want this to upset her as she's pregnant … and …

Hmmm … OD'ing on *Hollyoaks* has polluted my mind – many apologies.

Wed 6 Oct

12:04 pm

Bob

Do you ever feel that no one understands you? Am feeling like this right now. Maybe this is reason am writing all this to you, in this bizarre probably-need-to-see-shrink-rather-than-become-one way.

Right, am going to stop waffling and start essay … RIGHT NOW!

12:15 pm

Well, got as far as lining up books on bed, all THIRTEEN of them … how on earth am I gonna SKIM through that lot and extract exact info needed? Come back A levels … all is forgiven.

Anyhow, just been distracted by another thought …

In the past, have seen pals 'lose their faith' due to something dramatic in their lives (death in family, getting ill themselves, whatever). Had sometimes wondered if something like that would do the same to me, but doubted it. Held fast to the many (many many) books that tell the story of Cns who find an even deeper faith through tragedy. But never thought that something as stupid as a DREAM would knock me so hard. Suddenly feel more lost than before.

On that bright note, will leave you alone and go WRITE THAT ESSAY!

4:46 pm

OK ... know what you're thinking ... the slacker hasn't done a single thing re essay ... well that's where you'd be wrong, my dear Bob ... had written all of 29 words ... (errrrr, including title) when Libs materialised. Decided to share above 'lost' feelings with her ... big mistake. She laughed in a way that enabled her to shower me with the Big Mac she was in the process of consuming, and congratulated me on my discovery that each and every one of us is 'well-lost'.

She practically lives on Big Macs ... if the diet of personkind was reduced to only Big Macs and Dry Bs, she'd be a happy bunny.

6:03 pm

Am beginning to think the Big-Mac-gal might just be right. Are we ALL lost? IS God real?

If he's not, then what are we here for anyway? To enjoy ourselves and have a laf? Maybe. Why not do whatever pleases ME, instead of what I feel I OUGHT to do? Wow ... never had such non-Cn thoughts.

Have notched up a good few hours over several years at church, 'serving', 'doing', 'helping' for no money (and often no thanks whatsoever). Was ready to start that all over again here, at BURP ... but not sure if can be arsed now (sorry, correct spelling of 'arsed' currently unknown ...).

So is it OK now to go out with/sleep with guys – a whole ARMY of Bobs, and some Marks, Grahams and Jons – just for fun ...?

Please reply: 'Whoooah there Jude ... this is getting WAY out of control!' Thing is, do I care enough about God (or the possibility of him existing) or myself, or others, to stay all squeaky-clean and ... boring?

Are you following all this?

Will probably edit out such trash before you read this, but will leave in for now – getting all my thoughts down is kinda helping ... and, to date, you're a good listener.

Now, where are my Pringles?

Mean Girls

Hayley DiMarco

Sugar and spice and all things nice? Not quite. You have probably been a victim of a mean girl once or twice, the kind that loves to spread rumors, fight over the smallest things, tease, and torment. Let's face it. Sometimes girls can be just plain mean. But here's a way to end the cycle of mean once and for all.

Baker Publishing
£8.99
PB/0 8007.5913 3

Titles by the same author

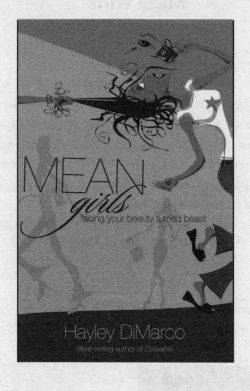

Published by Fleming H. Revell a division of Baker Publishing Group PO Box 6287,
Grand Rapids, MI 49516-6287

Mean Girls

My Story

If you have a Mean Girl in your life, I understand more than you might know how horrible you feel right now. You hate getting up in the morning because you know that as soon as you get to school or work, she will be there. Leering at you, laughing at you, thinking about you, *talking* about you. You don't know what she'll do next or where she will be. Oh yes, I know that feeling all too well because my high school years were plagued with Mean Girls.

In my class of 40 people, I was the victim of choice for the popular crowd. For 4 years I hated going to school. I sat in class day in and day out and watched them plot and plan to hurt me. I tried to make friends, but in the end even they turned against me in one way or another. The kiss of death for me (which might have some of you rolling your eyes) was that all the boys liked me. I was really shy and so I guess kind of mysterious. I also wasn't a sexually active girl, so, boys being boys, they all wanted to get the virgin. (News flash: They never did!)

I was continually the subject of all kinds of plots. If I was dating a guy, they wanted to get him from me. If I had a nice car, they wanted to ruin it. If my mom trusted me, they wanted her to stop trusting me. One day a pair of panties was placed in our mailbox as if someone was returning them to me after a night of passion. What a joke. Torturing me was quite a sport for them, though. Every day when I left school I would find a big wad of spit on the hood of my car. Every day, without fail. I hated walking out to my car as they all laughed at me. I can remember being afraid to go to the bathroom because I might meet one of them in there alone, and that would be devastating.

When I started dating a guy that one of them wanted to date, they not only TP'd his house but also spray painted his driveway with bad things about *me*. They were bent on making me look bad. When our Sadie Hawkins dance (girls ask guys) came along, one of the girls asked my boyfriend before I could (of course, he was a stupid boy for saying yes, but that's beside the current point).

I thought I had found sanctuary in those friends I told you about, but they soon turned on me as well. Why is it that girls think that boys are more important than their friends? My friend made out with my new love the day after he and I got together. I was shocked, but I guess I shouldn't have been. After all, friends aren't as important as boys. Ugh!

All this meanness finally culminated in one horrible act that freaked me out and made me fear for my safety. One day in my senior year I went to my locker, and as I opened it I saw a small noose with something hanging from it. It was soft and slimy like a dead finger. A note that hung from the rope said, "Beware the DOA." Needless to say, it totally freaked me out. I slammed the locker and ran to the school office. This was too much. Until that time I hadn't said anything to anyone, but this looked like something that should be taken more seriously.

When the principal went back to check my locker, she found that what was hanging there was a peeled carrot, carved like a person. Apparently it had been left in the freezer overnight so that now it was cold, clammy, and limp. Pretty ingenious girls!

I was devastated that their hatred of me had gone that far. I don't know for sure why the girls decided that I was archenemy number one, but I was. Was it because I was shy? Was I aloof in my shyness?

I'll never know, but my high school years were tainted by the treatment of a handful of angry teenage girls.

I always thought they had no idea what they were doing to me – until years later when I found out the truth. I was at a party with a bunch of friends from high school, and one of the Mean Girls was there too. She pulled me aside and said, "We treated you really bad in school and did some really mean things. I'm sorry about what we did." I thought that was a really nice and noble thing to do, so I smiled and said, "Oh, don't worry about it. We were young; it's okay. I forgive you." She looked at me in shock, her mouth open, and said, "Oh, great. Why'd you have to be so nice even now? It would have been much easier if you would have been mean about it!" Even then, my kindness was killing her. Maybe that's what they mean by "kill 'em with kindness."

I didn't learn to trust girls for years after high school. I spent most of my college and adult years, until a few years ago, only being close to guys. I just couldn't handle the "girl scene," as I liked to call it. "They are just so catty and mean. I don't like 'em. Guys are easygoing, not vindictive or petty. I prefer guys," I used to say. But now that I have healed from my experiences and started to see the truth, I can say that I love girls. In fact, I *need* girls. If it weren't for girls, I would be really messed up. Let's face it, we need each other. Guys are great, sure, but they are different, and you can't really connect with a guy the same way you can connect with a girl.

Now I can sit up all night with my girlfriends, talking about guys. I can talk their ears off and never feel like I'm boring them. I can shop all day with my girlfriends. I can share clothes with them. Tell my secrets to them. Confide in them. And nurture them. Girls bring out the girl in me, and that's pretty cool. Because when you get right down to it, it's the girl in you that guys are attracted to, not the guy in you. I didn't understand that till many years after high school. I was so busy trying not to be like the Mean Girls that I became like a guy and totally gave up my girlyness. And it wasn't until I decided I really wanted a man and was ready to think of the "M" word that I found out I really needed girls.

See, my dears, guys will never replace girls. They weren't meant to. Most guys don't need to talk as much as girls, so we need backup friends to use all our words on. Guys, on the whole, don't like shopping as much either, so we need girls to fill that void. And most guys definitely don't like sharing all their hopes, fears, and emotions with us all the time like we want to, but girls do, and I thank God for that. My mom always told me, "Hayley, whenever you start dating someone, don't stop seeing your girlfriends. You need them. If you dump them and expect him to take their place, you'll be in big trouble. He just can't do it. He's a guy. Save all your girl emotions and traumas for girls who get it. And just enjoy the guy." Women who are wise know that even after you get married, keeping your girlfriends is essential. Guys and girls both need "me" time, and a girlfriend is a good sounding board and confidante for your emotions and dreams.

So don't give up on girls just yet. We are fun. We have fun together. We bond in ways guys never can. And besides, you need someone to get your back, to tell you when your jeans are too short or your belt doesn't match your shoes or, worse yet, when you have something in your teeth. Ah, girls. They are great. Don't let a few mean ones taint it for the rest of us. Find a girlfriend or two and make a good relationship that will last a lifetime.

When I was a teenager, my spirit was imprisoned by fear, maybe like yours is right now. I had no sense of the greatness of God or the power of his hand in my life. I couldn't see life from his point of view, only from my weak little place on the planet. I didn't understand a bigger picture because I had not yet discovered Christ and his teachings, his Spirit, and his love. I didn't come to understand that until after college. If I had known *then* what I know *now,* maybe those girls would have ended up my friends or at least left me alone a little bit. No one ever told me how to handle them, what to say to them, or how to be around them. Instead I was just plain scared of them. I lived a lot of my life in fear, and it didn't have to be that way. How sad that no one was there to tell me about the amazing truth of godliness with love. Now that I have come through years of fighting with the Mean Girl and of not knowing how to avoid her or get rid of her, I have a new understanding of how I am supposed to react to her, even if I can't get rid of her.

I wrote *Mean Girls* to help you better understand who you are so that you can stop the Mean Girl cycle. This book will help you to find your destiny and live in it as a graceful spiritual girl. *Mean Girls* will help you face the beauty in the beast of your Mean Girl and maybe even find a way to change a generation of Mean Girls from the inside out. What you learn in this book might shock you. It might even tick you off, but don't stop. If you want to get to the bottom of your pain, then you have to power through. On the other side is hope and a life filled with peace and love. Mean Girls might be around you forever, but they might never affect you again if you follow the principles in this book and remain honest with and true to yourself.

The Beast

The Mean Girl. The beast. The one who tears at your flesh and devours your heart. She growls when you walk by. She hisses as you leave. She probably drools over you in her sleep. She's a beast all right, plain and simple. It's evident in all she is and all she does. So what do you do with this beast in your life? Can you find a hint of hope, or are you destined to spend your life running in fear from this rabid female? Oh, my dear, the answer is near. Come with me on a journey through the bizarre. Join me in scrutinizing the female psyche and follow me to a land of freedom and hope.

Girls have become the most catty, manipulative, emotional people on the planet, and you are at their mercy. Or are you? At one time I didn't see a way out, so weak was my faith. But now I do. I believe that the Mean Girl can be a thing of the past. I believe that her power over you will diminish and that your victories will be many. Your bruises will heal and your cuts will mend. *Mean Girls* is a call to spiritual strength. A call to stand firm. It is a call to face the beasts in your life head-on and with faithful resolve. And it is the answer that you've been looking for. Mean Girls … shall we attempt to find the beauty in your beast?

Why This Book Works

This book is full of some powerful stuff that is guaranteed to help you with the Mean Girls in your life if you are willing to live by it.

This isn't for the faint of heart.

It isn't self-help for the brave or the strong.

It's about a way of life based on the truth offered by a bestselling book called the Bible.

Conquering the mean in your life is only going to work if you have a power bigger than yourself working alongside you, above you, and in you. And I hope that by the end of this book you will know a little bit more about this life-changing power that tramples mean.

Warning: You might find some tips and tricks in here that make perfect sense, and you might try them and find that life gets a little bit better – but without faith in a God who can change lives and change hearts, any change will only be temporary.

So let's dive into the realm of mean
                                    and see if we can't find real beauty.

Do You Have a Mean Girl Problem?

Answer the following to find out.
1. When you walk down the hall, most of the time you are:
    a. alone
    b. with your gang
    c. with your best bud

2. Sometimes you:
   a. get laughed at by other girls
   b. make fun of the not-so-popular girl's clothes
   c. hang with your friends and have so much fun you forget it's
      time to go
3. You know how it feels to:
   a. be gossiped about
   b. make someone look bad so you look good
   c. care for a friend who is hurt
4. You spend hours:
   a. worrying about how not to be seen by other girls
   b. thinking about how to get even with someone
   c. helping your friends through tough times
5. When you go to school, you are:
   a. afraid to go to the bathroom alone
   b. lovin' life
   c. counseling your friends about all their problems
6. Your parents:
   a. would say you worry a lot about going to school
   b. know that you are happiest when you are with your friends
   c. taught you how to care for others
7. At least once a week:
   a. another girl laughs at you or picks on you
   b. you talk about another girl in a way that puts her down
   c. you try to make your friend feel really good about herself
8. You have cried at school:
   a. many times
   b. only occasionally when a guy is a jerk
   c. not really at all, because you save that for your bedroom

Now add up your scores:
   A = 3
   B = 2
   C = 1

18–24: MG problems. You probably have to deal with at least one girl who is out to get you. This book will help you learn more about her and how to handle yourself when she freaks out on you. Don't worry, this won't last forever. This trauma you are living in has an end. Keep the faith.

11–17: MG. Did you ever think that you might be the Mean Girl of someone's nightmares? This quiz isn't a perfect diagnosis, but you might want to read on to find out who you are when others are looking.

8–10: No MG for you. You probably are the one helping the victims of MGs. You see the pain they cause but have mostly stayed free from their attacks. You'll be in a great place if you can learn more about them so you can help more than you do right now. You are the key to solving the troubles between these girls. Never stop being faithful.

The Little White Horse

Elizabeth Goudge

Maria Merryweather, a stranger to Moonacre, is fascinated by the mysterious story of the long lost Moon Princess and the magical little white horse. Before long she is determined to restore peace and happiness to the valley and Maria usually gets her way

Lion Publishing
£4.99
PB / 0 7459 4578 3

ELIZABETH GOUDGE

The Little
White Horse

'I absolutely adored
The Little White Horse'
J.K. Rowling

Published by Lion Publishing plc, Mayfield House,
256 Banbury Road, Oxford OX2 7DH

Chapter 1

1

THE carriage gave another lurch, and Maria Merryweather, Miss Heliotrope, and Wiggins once more fell into each other's arms, sighed, gasped, righted themselves, and fixed their attention upon those objects which were for each of them at this trying moment the source of courage and strength.

Maria gazed at her boots. Miss Heliotrope restored her spectacles to their proper position, picked up the worn brown volume of French essays from the floor, popped a peppermint into her mouth, and peered once more in the dim light at the wiggly black print on the yellowed page. Wiggins meanwhile pursued with his tongue the taste of the long-since-digested dinner that still lingered among his whiskers.

Humanity can be roughly divided into three sorts of people – those who find comfort in literature, those who find comfort in personal adornment, and those who find comfort in food; and Miss Heliotrope, Maria, and Wiggins were typical representatives of their own sort of people.

Maria must be described first, because she is the heroine of this story. In this year of grace 1842 she was thirteen years old and was considered plain, with her queer silvery-grey eyes that were so disconcertingly penetrating, her straight reddish hair and thin pale face with its distressing freckles. Yet her little figure, small as that of a fairy's child, with a backbone as straight as a poker, was very dignified, and she had exquisitely tiny feet, of which she was inordinately proud. They were her chief beauty, she knew, which was why she took, if possible, a more burning interest in her boots than in her mittens and gowns and bonnets.

And the boots she had on today were calculated to raise the lowest spirits, for they were made of the softest grey leather, sewn with crystal beads round the tops, and were lined with snow-white lamb's-wool. The crystal beads, as it happened, could not be seen, because Maria's grey silk dress and warm grey wool pelisse, also trimmed with white lamb's-wool, reached to her ankles, but she herself knew they were there, and the thought of them gave her a moral strength that can scarcely be overestimated.

She rested herself against the thought of those beads, just as in a lesser degree she rested herself against the thought of the piece of purple ribbon that was wound about her slender waist beneath the pelisse, the little bunch of violets that was tucked so far away inside the recesses of her grey velvet bonnet that it was scarcely visible, and the grey silk mittens adorning the small hands that were hidden inside the big white muff. For Maria was one of your true aristocrats; the perfection of the hidden things was even more important to her than the outward show. Not that she did not like the outward show. She did. She was a showy little thing, even when dressed in the greys and purples of the bereaved.

For Maria was an orphan. Her mother had died in her babyhood and her father just two months ago, leaving so many debts that everything he possessed, including the beautiful London house with the fanlight over the door and the tall windows looking out over the garden of the quiet London Square, where Maria had lived throughout the whole of her short life, had had to be sold to pay them. When the lawyers had at last settled everything to their satisfaction, it was found that there was only just enough money left to convey her and Miss Heliotrope and Wiggins by coach to the West Country, a part of the world that they had never seen, where they were to live with Maria's second cousin, her nearest living relative,

Sir Benjamin Merryweather, whom they had never seen either, in his manor-house of Moonacre in the village of Silverydew.

But it was not her orphaned state that had depressed Maria and made her turn to the contemplation of her boots for comfort. Her mother she did not remember, her father, a soldier, who had nearly always been abroad with his regiment, and who did not care for children anyhow, had never had much hold upon her affections; not the hold that Miss Heliotrope had, who had come to her when she was only a few months old, had been first her nurse and then her governess, and had lavished upon her all the love that she had ever known. No, what was depressing Maria was the wretchedness of this journey and the discomfort of country life that it surely foreboded.

Maria knew nothing about the country. She was a London lady born and bred, and she loved luxury, and in that beautiful house looking out on the London Square she had had it; even though it had turned out at her father's death that he really oughtn't to have had it, because there had not been the money to pay for it.

And now? judging by this carriage, there would not be many comforts at Moonacre Manor. It was an awful conveyance. It had met them at Exeter, and was even more uncomfortable than the stage-coach that had brought them from London. The cushions on the seat were hard and moth-eaten, and the floor had chickens' feathers and bits of straw blowing about in the icy draughts that swept in through the ill-fitting doors. The two piebald horses, though they had shining coats and were obviously well loved and well cared-for, a fact which Maria noticed at once because she adored horses, were old and stout and moved slowly.

And the coachman was a wizened little old man who looked more like a gnome than a human creature, clothed in a many-caped greatcoat so patched that it was impossible even to guess at its original colour, and a huge curly-brimmed hat of worn beaver that was so much too large for him that it came right down over his face and rested upon the bridge of his nose, so that one could scarcely see

anything of his face except his wide toothless smile and the grey
stubble upon his ill-shaven chin. Yet he seemed amiable and had
been full of conversation when he tucked them up in the carriage,
covering their knees tenderly with a torn and tattered rug, only
owing to his lack of teeth they had found it difficult to understand
him. And now, in the thick February mist that shrouded the
countryside, they could scarcely see him through the little window
in the front of the carriage.

Nor could they see anything of the country through which they
were passing. The only thing they knew about it was that the road
was so full of ruts and pits that they were jolted from side to side and
flung up and down as though the carriage were playing battledore
and shuttlecock with them. And soon it would be dark and there
would be none of the fashionable new gas-lamps that nowadays
illumined the London streets, only the deep black awful darkness of
the country. And it was bitterly cold and they had been travelling for
what seemed like a century, and still there seemed no sign of their
ever getting there.

Miss Heliotrope raised her book of essays and held it within an
inch of her nose, determined to get to the end of the one about
endurance before darkness fell. She would read it many times in the
months to come, she had no doubt, together with the one upon the
love that never fails. This last essay, she remembered, she had read
for the first time on the evening of the day when she had arrived to
take charge of the motherless little Maria, and had found her charge
the most unattractive specimen of a female infant that she had ever
set eyes upon, with her queer silvery eyes and her air, even in
babyhood, of knowing that her Blood was Blue and thinking a lot of
herself in consequence. Nevertheless, after reading that essay she
had made up her mind that she would love Maria, and that her love
would never fail the child until death parted them.

At first Miss Heliotrope's love for Maria had been somewhat
forced. She had made and mended her clothes with grim determina-
tion and with a rather distressing lack of imagination, and however

naughty she was had applied the cane only very sparingly, being more concerned with winning the child's affection than with the welfare of her immortal soul. But gradually all that had changed. Her tenderness, when Maria was in any way afflicted, had become eager; the child's clothes had been created with a fiery zeal that made of each small garment a work of art; and she herself had been whipped for her peccadilloes within an inch of her life, Miss Heliotrope caring now not two hoots whether Maria liked her or not, if only she could make of the child a fine and noble woman.

This is true love and Maria had known it; and even when her behind had been so sore that she could scarcely sit upon it, her affection for Miss Heliotrope had been no whit abated. And now that she was no longer a child but a young lady in her teens, it was the best thing in her life.

For Maria from babyhood had always known a good thing when she saw it. She always wanted the best, and was quick to recognize it even when, as in the case of Miss Heliotrope, the outer casket gave little indication of the gold within. She was, perhaps, the only person who had ever discovered what a dear person Miss Heliotrope really was; and that, no doubt, was why Miss Heliotrope's feeling for her had become so eager.

Miss Heliotrope's outer casket was really very odd, and it just shows how penetrating were Maria's silvery eyes, that they had pierced through it so very soon. Most people when confronted with Miss Heliotrope's nose and style of dress stopped there and could not get any further. Miss Heliotrope's nose was hooked like an eagle's beak, and in colour was a deep unbecoming puce which aroused most people's instant suspicions. They thought she ate and drank too much and that that was why her nose was puce; but, as a matter of fact, Miss Heliotrope scarcely ate or drank anything at all, because she had such dreadful indigestion.

It was the indigestion that had ruined her nose, not over-indulgence. She never complained of her indigestion, she just endured it, and it was because she never complained that she was so misunderstood by everyone except Maria. Not that she had ever mentioned her indigestion even to Maria, for she had been brought up by her mother to believe that it is the mark of a True Gentlewoman never to say anything to anybody about herself ever. But Miss Heliotrope's passion for peppermints was in the course of time traced by the discerning Maria to its proper source.

So distressing was Miss Heliotrope's nose, set in the surrounding pallor of her thin pale face, that the great beauty of her forget-me-not-blue eyes was not noticeable, nor the delicate arch of her fine dark eyebrows. Her scanty grey hair she wore in tight corkscrew ringlets all round her face, a mode of hairdressing which had been suitable when she had adopted it at the age of eighteen, but was not very becoming to her now that she was sixty.

Miss Heliotrope was tall and very thin, and stooped, but her thinness was not noticeable because she wore her old-fashioned dress of purple bombasine over a hoop, and winter and summer alike she wore a black shawl over her shoulders and crossed over her chest, so that she was well padded. Out of doors she always carried a large black umbrella and wore a voluminous shabby black cloak and a huge black poke bonnet with a purple feather in it, and indoors a snow-white mob-cap trimmed with black velvet ribbon. She always wore black silk mittens, and carried a black reticule containing a spotless white handkerchief scented with lavender, her spectacles and box of peppermints, and round her neck she wore a gold locket the size of a duck's egg, that held Maria did not know what, because whenever she asked Miss Heliotrope what was inside her locket Miss Heliotrope made no answer. There was not much that Miss Heliotrope denied her beloved Maria, if what Maria wanted was not likely to injure her immortal soul, but she did consistently deny her a sight of what was inside her locket … It was, she said, a matter that concerned herself alone … Maria had no chance to have a look on the sly, because Miss Heliotrope was never parted from her locket; when she went to bed at night she put it under her pillow. But, in any case, Maria would not have looked on the sly, because she was not that kind of girl.

Maria, though decidedly vain and much too inquisitive, was possessed of the fine qualities of honour and courage and fastidiousness, and Miss Heliotrope was entirely made of love and patience. But it is difficult to draw up a list of Wiggins's virtues ... In fact impossible, because he hadn't any ... Wiggins was greedy, conceited, bad-tempered, selfish, and lazy. It was the belief of Maria and Miss Heliotrope that he loved them devotedly because he always kept close at their heels, wagged his tail politely when spoken to, and even kissed them upon occasion. But all this Wiggins did not from affection but because he thought it good policy. He was aware that from Miss Heliotrope and Maria there emanated all those things which made his existence pleasant to him – his food, always of good quality and served to him with punctuality in a green dish to which he was much attached; his green leather collar; his brush and comb and scented powder and soap. Other mistresses, Wiggins was aware from the conversation of inferior dogs met in the park, could not always be relied on to make the comforts of their pets their first consideration ... *His* could ... Therefore Wiggins had made up his mind at an early age to ingratiate himself with Maria and Miss Heliotrope, and to remain with them for as long as they gave satisfaction.

But though Wiggins's moral character left much to be desired, it must not be thought that he was a useless member of society, for a thing of beauty is a joy for ever, and Wiggins's beauty was of that high order that can only be described by that tremendous trumpet-sounding word 'incomparable'. He was a pedigree King Charles Spaniel. His coat was deep cream in colour, smooth and glossy everywhere upon his body except upon his chest, where it broke into an exquisite cascade of soft curls like a gentleman's frilled shirt-front. It was not then the fashion for spaniels to have their tails cut, and Wiggins's tail was like an ostrich feather. He was very proud of it and carried it always like a pennon in the wind, and sometimes when the sun shone through the fine hairs it scintillated with light to such an extent that it was almost dazzling to behold.

The only parts of Wiggins that were not cream-coloured were his long silky ears and the patches over his eyes, that were the loveliest possible shade of chestnut brown. His eyes were brown, too, and of a liquid melting tenderness that won all hearts; the owners of the said hearts being quite unaware that Wiggins's tenderness was all for himself, not for them. His paws and the backs of his legs were most delicately feathered, like those of a heraldic beast. Wiggins's nose was long and aristocratic, and supported fine golden whiskers that were always well under control. His nose was jet black, shining, and cold, and his beautiful rose-pink tongue was never unpleasantly moist. For Wiggins was not one of those emotional dogs who let themselves go with quivering whiskers, hot nose, and dribbling tongue.

Wiggins was aware that excessive emotion is damaging to personal beauty, and he never indulged in it ... Except, perhaps, a very little, in regard to food. Good food did make him feel emotional, so intense was his delight in it, so deep his thankfulness that the good fairies who at his birth had bestowed upon him an excellent digestion had also seen to it that over-eating never seemed to impair the exquisite slenderness of his figure ... That dinner that he had had at the inn at Exeter had really been excellent, the chop, greens, and baked potatoes that had really been meant for Miss Heliotrope, but which she had not felt equal to ... Thoughtfully his beautiful pink tongue caressed his golden whiskers. If the food of the West Country was always going to be as good as that meal at Exeter he would, he thought, be able to put up with cold mists and draughty carriages with calm and patience.

Presently it was quite dark, and the queer old coachman got down, grinned at them and lit the two antique lanterns that swung one on each side of the box. But they did not give much light, and all that could be seen from the coach windows were the drifting mist and steep precipitous banks covered with wet ferns. The road grew narrower and narrower, so that the ferns brushed against the carriage upon either side, and bumpier, and bumpier and more and more precipitous, so that they were always either crawling painfully uphill or sliding perilously down what felt like the side of some horrible cliff.

In the darkness Miss Heliotrope could no longer read, nor Maria contemplate her boots. But they did not grumble at all, because True Gentlewomen never grumble. Maria clasped her hands tightly inside her muff, and Miss Heliotrope clasped hers under her cloak, and they set their teeth and endured.

2

Perhaps in spite of the cold, they all three dozed a little from sheer weariness, because it was with a shock of complete surprise that they discovered that the carriage had stopped. And it must have been that between their loss of consciousness and its return they had come a long way, because everything was completely different. For one thing, the mist had gone and the moon was shining, so that they could see each other's faces quite plainly.

Their depression had completely vanished and their hearts were beating fast with a sense of adventure. With the eagerness of small children Miss Heliotrope and Maria let down the carriage windows upon either side and leaned out, Wiggins pushing himself in beside Maria that he might lean out too.

The fern-covered banks that had been on each side of them had disappeared, and in their place, close up against the windows of the carriage, were walls of solid rock of a beautiful silvery grey, and in front of them, too, completely blocking their passage, was solid rock.

'Can we have come the right way?' asked Miss Heliotrope.

'There's a door in the rock!' said Maria, who was leaning so far out of the window that she was in danger of falling headlong into the narrow lane. 'Look!'

Miss Heliotrope also leaned out at a perilous angle, and saw that Maria was quite right. There was a door of weathered oak set in the rock, so old that it was of the same colour as the stone and hardly distinguishable from it. It was very large, big enough to admit a carriage. Close beside it there hung a rusty chain that issued from a hole in the wall.

'The coachman is getting down!' ejaculated Maria and with eyes shining with excitement she watched the gnome-like little man as he scurried to the rusty chain, seized hold of it, lifted both legs off the ground, and swung there like a monkey on a stick. The result was a deep hollow clanging somewhere within the recesses of the rock. When there had been three clangs the coachman dropped to the ground again, grinned at Maria, and climbed back upon the box.

Slowly the great door swung open. The coachman clucked to the old piebald horses, Miss Heliotrope and Maria sat down again, and they moved forward, the door closing behind them as noiselessly as it had opened, shutting out the moonlight and leaving them once more with no illumination but that of the flickering lantern light gleaming upon the wet moss-grown walls of an underground tunnel. It gleamed also, Maria fancied, over some sort of shadowy figure, but of this she could not be sure, because the carriage moved forward before she could get a proper look.

'Ugh!' said Miss Heliotrope, not quite so happy as she had been, for it struck very clammy and cold, the tunnel seemed to go on for a very long time, and the echoing of the coach wheels made a roar like thunder. But before they had time to get really frightened they were out in the moonlight again, and in a place so beautiful that it seemed hardly to be of this world.

It was all silver. Upon each side of them the trunks of tall trees rose from grass so silvered by the moonlight that it glimmered like water. The trees were not thickly planted, and beautiful glades opened between them, showing glimpses of an ebony sky set with silver stars. Nothing moved. It was all quite still, as though enchanted under the moon. The silvery tracery of twigs and branches above the silver tree trunks was so delicate that the moonlight sifted through it like a fine film of silver dust.

But there was life among the trees, though it was life that did not move. Maria saw a silver owl sitting on a silver branch, and a silver rabbit sitting up on its haunches beside the road blinking at the lantern light, and a beautiful group of silver deer ... And for a fleeting instant, at the far end of a glade, she thought she saw a little white horse with flowing mane and tail, head raised, poised, halted in mid-flight, as though it had seen her and was glad.

'Look,' she cried to Miss Heliotrope. But when Miss Heliotrope looked she could not see anything.

They drove on for a long time, over a thick carpet of moss that deadened the sound of the carriage wheels, until at last they found themselves driving through an archway in an old grey wall; not natural rock this time but a man-made wall crowned with battlements. Maria had just time to notice the battlements with a throb of excitement, and they were within the walls and the beautiful park had given place to a formal garden, with flower-beds and paved walks surrounding a water-lily pool, and yew-trees cut into strange fantastic shapes of crowing cocks and knights on horseback.

The garden, like the park, was all silver and black under the moon, and a little tremor of fear seized Maria as they drove through it, for it seemed to her that the black knights and black cocks turned their heads to look very coldly at her as she went past. Wiggins, though he was down on the floor and couldn't see the shadowy black figures, must have felt a bit queer too, because he growled. And Miss Heliotrope also must have felt not altogether happy, because she said in quite a quavery voice, 'Aren't we nearly at the house?'

'We *are* at the house,' rejoiced Maria. 'Look, there's a light!'

'Where?' demanded Miss Heliotrope.

'There!' said Maria. 'High up behind that tree.' And she pointed to where an orange eye of light was winking at them cheerfully through the topmost branches of a huge black cedar that towered up in front of them like a mountain. There was something wonderfully reassuring about that wink of orange, set like a jewel in the midst of all the black and silver. It was a bit of earthliness amongst so much that was unearthly, something that welcomed and was pleased to see her in place of those cold black shadows who had not wanted her to come.

'But it's right up in the sky!' ejaculated Miss Heliotrope in astonishment, and then the carriage took a wide sweep round the cedar-tree and they knew why the light was shining so high up. For the house was not the sort of modern house they were accustomed to, but a very old house, almost more of a castle than a house, and the light was shining in a window at the top of a tall tower.

Miss Heliotrope let out a cry of dismay (quickly stifled, because only the ill-bred cry out when confronted by an alarming prospect), thinking of mice and spiders of both of which she was terrified; but Maria gave a cry of delight. She was going to live in a house with a tower, like a princess in a fairy-tale.

Oh, but it was a glorious house! It towered up before them, its great walls confronting the shadowy garden with a sort of timeless strength that was as reassuring as the light in a window of the tower. And though she had never seen it before, it gave her a feeling of home. For Merryweathers had lived in it for generations, and she was a Merryweather. She was ashamed of her previous dread of coming here. This was home, as the London house had never been. She would rather live here austerely than in the most luxurious palace in the world.

And she was out of the carriage almost before it had stopped, and running up a flight of stone steps that were built sideways against the wall and led up to the great oak front door, and beating upon it with her fists to be let in. Neither her light feet nor her small fists made much sound, but someone inside must have been listening for the sound of the carriage wheels, for the great door opened almost at once, revealing the most extraordinary-looking elderly gentleman Maria had ever set eyes upon, standing upon the threshold with a lighted lantern held high in his hand.

'Welcome, Cousin,' he said in a deep, rich, fruity voice, and held out his free hand to her.

'Thank you, Sir,' she replied, and curtsied and put her hand into his, and knew that she would love him from that moment on for always.

But her cousin was really very odd to look at, and once she started looking at him she found it very difficult to leave off: He was so tall and so broad that he seemed to fill the big doorway. His face was round and red and clean-shaven, and his big hooked nose put Miss Heliotrope's entirely in the shade. He had three double chins, a large smiling mouth, and twinkling eyes of a warm tawny-brown, almost lost beneath bushy white eyebrows. His clothes, most scrupulously cared for, were very old-fashioned and most oddly assorted.

He had a huge white wig like a cauliflower on his head, and his double chins were propped by a cravat of Honiton lace. His waistcoat was of pale-blue satin embroidered with yellow roses and crimson carnations, and was so beautiful that it contrasted oddly with his faded and patched riding-coat and breeches and the mud-splashed top-boots. He was slightly bow-legged, as men are who have spent most of their life in the saddle. His hands were big and red like his face, with palms as hard as leather from much holding of the bridle, but beautiful lace fell over the wrists, and on one finger was a ring with a great ruby in it that flashed like fire.

Indeed, everything about Sir Benjamin Merryweather was warm and glowing; his round red face, his smile, his voice, his tawny eyes, his ruby ring. After he had taken Maria's hand he looked at her very attentively, as though he were asking himself some question about her. And she trembled a little under his scrutiny, as though she feared herself lacking in some quality he looked for; yet she looked steadily up into his face and did not blink at all.

'A true Merryweather,' he said at last in his deep rumbling voice. 'One of the silver Merryweathers, straight and arrogant and fastidious, brave and the soul of honour, born at the full moon. We shall like each other, my dear, for I was born at midday; and your moon Merryweathers and your sun Merryweathers always take a fancy for one another ...'

He broke off abruptly, suddenly aware of Miss Heliotrope and Wiggins, who by this time had got themselves out of the carriage and up the steps, and were standing behind Maria.

'My dear Madam!' he cried to Miss Heliotrope, after subjecting her to one long keen glance. 'My dear Madam! Allow me!' And bowing very low he took her hand and led her ceremoniously over the threshold. 'Welcome, Madam!' he said to her. 'Welcome to my poor unworthy home.'

And his words rang out like a note that strikes true. He did really and truly think his home unworthy to house Miss Heliotrope.

'My dear Sir!' cried Miss Heliotrope, all of a flutter, for owing to her unattractive appearance gentlemen seldom bestowed upon her these flattering attentions. 'My dear Sir, you are *too* kind!'

Maria, picking up Wiggins, who was snorting disagreeably because no one was paying the least attention to him, pushed the great door shut and turned to follow her elders with a sigh of content. For she was aware that Sir Benjamin had seen at a glance of what fine stuff her dear Miss Heliotrope was made ... They were all going to like each other.

But no, perhaps not, for a low disagreeable growl from under her arm, where she had Wiggins, was echoed by a rumble like thunder from the hearth of the great log fire which was burning in the stone-paved raftered hall into which Sir Benjamin had led them.

An animal of sorts, a rather alarmingly large animal, whose body seemed to stretch the length of the hearth, had raised a huge shaggy head from his forepaws and was gazing at Wiggins's exquisite little face peeping out from beneath Maria's arm. He sniffed once loudly, got the aroma of Wiggins's character, thought apparently little of it, blinked once contemptuously, and laid his head back on his paws. But he did not go to sleep. Through the cascade of reddish hair that fell over them, eyes like yellow lamps shone disconcertingly upon the assembled company; disconcertingly because they were so terribly penetrating.

If the eyes of Sir Benjamin had seemed to see a good deal, the eyes of the shaggy creature on the hearth saw infinitely more. What sort of a creature was he, Maria wondered. She supposed he was a dog, and yet, somehow, he wasn't quite like a dog . . .

'The dog Wrolf,' said Sir Benjamin, answering her unspoken question. 'There are those who find him alarming, but I assure you that you need to have no fear of him. He is an old dog. He came out of the pine-wood behind the house on Christmas Eve more than twenty years ago, and stayed with us for a while, and then after some trouble in the household he went away again. But just over a year ago – also on Christmas Eve – he came back, and has lived with me ever since, and never to my knowledge harmed even a mouse.'

'You have mice?' whispered Miss Heliotrope.

'Hundreds,' boomed Sir Benjamin cheerfully. 'But we keep 'em down with traps, you know. Traps, and Zachariah the cat. Zachariah is not here just now. Now, dear ladies, you must see your rooms and lay aside your wraps, and then you will come down to the hall again and we will eat together.'

Sir Benjamin took three large brass candlesticks from a table beside the fire, lit their candles, handed one each to Miss Heliotrope and Maria, and led the way with his into an adjoining room that Maria guessed was the parlour, though in the dim light she could scarcely see anything of it.

He opened a door in the wall, passed through it, and they were on a turret staircase. The steps were of stone, worn in the middle because so many feet had trodden them during the centuries, and wound round and round the central newel in a fashion that poor Miss Heliotrope found most dizzying; though Sir Benjamin, going on ahead with his candle, mounted them as merrily as a boy, in spite of his age and bulk, and Maria, bringing up the rear, stepped up them with the agility of a happy monkey.

Six hundred years old,' said Sir Benjamin cheerfully. 'Built in the thirteenth century by Wrolf Merryweather, armour-bearer to King

Edward I, and the founder of our family, on land ceded him by the king in gratitude for Wrolf's valiant bearing in battle. In our family, Miss Heliotrope, we spell Wrolf with a W, for we are of Viking ancestry, and great fighters.'

'Yes,' sighed Miss Heliotrope. 'When Maria was little, I had great trouble in getting her to eat rice pudding.'

'Did you call the dog that came out of the pine-wood after that Wrolf?' asked Maria. She had hesitated a little before she spoke of that great beast down in the hall as a dog, because she still somehow could not think that he was.

'I did,' said Sir Benjamin. 'For tradition has it that Wrolf Merryweather was auburn-haired, and Wrolf the dog, as you may have noticed, has a reddish mane.'

'Yes, I noticed,' said Maria.

Sir Benjamin had stopped outside a door. 'Here, ladies, I leave you,' he said. 'This is Miss Heliotrope's room, over the parlour. Maria's is higher up still, right at the top of the tower.' And he bowed to them and went away down the stairs with his candle.

Miss Heliotrope, who had thought that perhaps she would have to sleep on a straw pallet on a rush-strewn floor, gave a gasp of relief upon seeing her room. It was a fair-sized room, and its oak floor was almost entirely covered by a crimson carpet. It was a very shabby carpet with large holes in it, but it was a carpet and not rushes.

There was a big four-poster with a flight of steps leading up to it, and crimson velvet curtains to keep the draught out. There was a bow-fronted mahogany chest of drawers, a huge mahogany wardrobe, a dressing-table with a chintz petticoat, and a winged armchair with a foot-stool for her feet. The stone walls had been panelled in warm dark wood, and the window was closely shuttered, with chintz curtains covering the shutters. All the curtains needed mending, but the furniture was well polished and it was all scrupulously clean.

And someone, it seemed, had been giving much thought to her comfort, for a log fire was burning brightly on the hearth, candles were burning on the chest of drawers and the dressing-table, and there was a warming-pan between the sheets. And their luggage was already here, piled neatly at the foot of the four-poster.

But Maria did not linger in Miss Heliotrope's room. She waited only to see that she was happy, and then she went quietly off with her candle and pursued her way up the turret stairs, up and up and round and round for quite a long way. A room of her own! She had never had a room of her own before. She had always slept with Miss Heliotrope and, loving her as she did, she had not minded that; but yet, just lately, she had thought it would be nice to have a room of her own.

3

The turret stairs ended at a door so small that a large grown-up could not possibly have got through it. But for a slim girl of thirteen it was exactly right. Maria stopped and gazed at it with a beating heart, for though this little, narrow, low door was obviously hundreds of years old, yet she felt as though it had been made especially for her. For if she had been able to choose her own door, this was the door she would have chosen. It was more like a front door than a bedroom door, like the door of her very own house. It was of silvery grey oak studded with silver nails, and it had a knocker made of the smallest, daintiest horseshoe Maria had ever seen, polished so brightly that it shone like silver. At sight of it Maria thought instantly of the lovely little white horse she had thought she had seen in the park and that she had pointed out to Miss Heliotrope … only Miss Heliotrope hadn't been able to see it … The door was opened by a silver latch that clicked in a friendly sort of way, when Maria lifted it, as though it was welcoming her.

She went in, latched the door behind her, put her candle carefully down on the floor, leaned back against the door and gazed and gazed, with her lips parted and her usually pale face glowing like a pink rose, and her eyes like stars.

No pen could possibly do justice to the exquisite charm and beauty of Maria's room. It was at the top of the tower, and the tower was a round one, so Maria's room was circular, neither too large nor too small, just the right size for a girl of thirteen. It had three windows, two narrow lancet windows and one large one with a window-seat in the thickness of the wall. The curtains had not been drawn across the windows, and through them she could see the stars. In each of the windows stood beautiful silver branched candlesticks with three lighted candles burning in each of them.

It was the light from one of these, Maria realized, that she had seen from outside shining through the branches of the cedar-tree. The walls had not been panelled with wood, as in Miss Heliotrope's room, but the silver-grey stone was so lovely that Maria was glad. The ceiling was vaulted, and delicate ribbings of stone curved over Maria's head like the branches of a tree, meeting at the highest point of the ceiling in a carved representation of a sickle moon surrounded by stars.

There was no carpet upon the silvery-oak floor, but a little white sheepskin lay beside the bed, so that Maria's bare toes should meet something warm and soft when they went floorwards of a morning. The bed was a little fourposter, hung with pale-blue silk curtains embroidered with silver stars, of the same material as the window curtains, and spread with a patchwork quilt made of exquisite squares of velvet and silk of all colours of the rainbow, gay and lovely.

There was very little furniture in the room, just a couple of silvery-oak chests for Maria's clothes, a small round mirror hung upon the wall above one of them, and a stool with a silver ewer and basin upon it. But Maria felt that she wanted no more than this. Heavy furniture such as Miss Heliotrope had, would have ruined this exquisite little room. Nor did she mind that the fireplace was the tiniest she had ever seen, deeply recessed in the wall. It was big enough for the fire of pine-cones and apple wood that burned in it, filling the room with fragrance.

But when Maria started to explore her room she found that it was not without luxuries. Over the fireplace was a shelf, and on it stood a blue wooden box filled with dainty biscuits with sugar flowers on them, in case she should feel hungry between meals. And beside the fireplace stood a big basket filled with more logs and pine-cones – enough to keep her fire burning all through the night.

It was all perfect. It was the room Maria would have designed for herself if she had had the knowledge and skill. For she realized that very much knowledge and skill had gone to the making of this room. Fine craftsmen had carved the moon and stars and fashioned the furniture, and an exquisite needlewoman had made the patchwork quilt and embroidered the curtains.

This way and that she stepped, putting her pelisse and bonnet and muff away in one of the chests, smoothing her hair before the mirror, washing her hands in the water that she poured out of the little silver ewer into the silver basin, touching all the beautiful things with the tips of her fingers, as though caressing them, saying thank you in her heart to the people who had made them, and whoever it was who had arranged them. Was it Sir Benjamin? But it couldn't have been, because he couldn't have got through the door.

A knock on the door, and the startled voice of Miss Heliotrope outside, reminded her that her governess, with her height and her hoop, would not be able to get through the door either, and in spite of her love for Miss Heliotrope she felt a little thrill of glee … This room was indeed her own … When she opened the door there was a mischievous dimple in her left cheek that had never been there before.

'My dear! My dear!' lamented Miss Heliotrope, who had now removed her outdoor garments and was wearing her mob-cap and her black shawl folded across her chest, 'what a ridiculous little door! I shall never be able to get inside your room!'

'No!' giggled Maria.

'But what shall we do when you're ill?' asked poor Miss Heliotrope.

'I shan't *be* ill,' said Maria 'Not here!'

I certainly think that the air here is salubrious, agreed Miss Heliotrope, and then her eyes fell upon the inside of Maria's room and widened with horror. 'What an extraordinary little place! So very odd! Oh, my poor darling Maria! However are you to sleep in a place like this? It'll give you the creeps!'

'I like it,' said Maria.

And Miss Heliotrope, looking at Maria's rosy cheeks and sparkling eyes and that entirely new dimple, could not doubt that she spoke the truth. And looking again, more attentively, at the extraordinary little room, she saw that it suited Maria. Standing there so slender and straight in her grey dress, her room seemed to curve itself about her like the petals of a flower about its heart; they completed each other.

'Well, well!', said Miss Heliotrope. 'So long as you are happy, my dear. And now, I think, we should go down to supper.'

Carrying their candles, and with Wiggins following them, they made their way down the winding staircase again.

'I wonder,' said Miss Heliotrope, 'who does the work of this house? I have seen no sign of a maidservant, and yet everything is scrupulously neat and clean. A darning needle is wanted everywhere, as no doubt you have observed, but apart from that I have no fault at all to find, so far, with the household staff ... But where are they?'

'Perhaps they'll wait on us at supper,' said Maria.

Kemi's Journal
of Life, Love and Everything

Abidemi Sanusi

Welcome to Kemi's world – slice of zany London life as only a twenty-something born-again believer might see it. Meet the cast: Kemi's friend-with-all-the-answers Vanessa and Vanessa's perfect fiancé Mark; Kemi's marketing company boss Amanda and colleague Robert, who conduct a whirlwind office romance; Pastor Michael and the Sanctifieds – not a boy band but Kemi's friends at church. And Zack, Kemi's boyfriend from life BC (Before Church). Jesus is very much there, too, as Kemi's friend and confident. And the Bible, which inspires and freaks her out by turn.

Scripture Union
£6.99
PB/1 8442.7092 0

KEMI'S
JOURNAL
of life, love and everything
ABIDEMI SANUSI

Published by Scripture Union, 207-209 Queensway,
Bletchley, MK2 2EB, UK.

Kemi's Journal
of Life, Love and Everything

Wednesday March 6

... seek first his kingdom and his righteousness ... (Matthew 6:33).

I have decided to keep a diary this year. You know, kind of like a spiritual diary. Never mind the fact that we're already way into the New Year. Everyone tells me about the utmost importance of doing this. OKAY... maybe not everyone. Triple S People (Spiritual Super Stars) tell me it's vital to keep track of what God is doing in my life.

Personally, I don't know what the big deal is about the New Year, anyway. Sure, I do distinctly recall kneeling by my bed at the year end, praying in my desires. But, as far as I can see, nothing's changed. It's hard to live for God and make the heavenly kingdom my concern when my life is a glitzy advertisement for Boring Inc.

Mum called today. *Was I alright?*

'Of course I'm alright,' I squelched down the phone.

'Just checking,' she said. 'It's just I worry about you. You're not getting any younger, you know. You're 28 and you don't have any fun. All that going to church. When was the last time you shook your boogie and really enjoyed yourself?'

Shook my boogie?

'Mum, I'm fine. Stop worrying. You know, if you would come with me to church one day, you might just enjoy it.'

'Not me. Why you waste your time with those holy rollers, I'll never know. Filling your head with nonsense. Absolute nonsense! Got to go. Love you. Byeee.'

Love you too, mother.

Promised myself that the next time I would have the last word. Though she does have a point about my life – or lack thereof.

Hey! What am I thinking? I'm a born again Pentecostal Christian!

Same day, that afternoon

Had a call from Zack, the boyfriend from life BC (Before Church). I'm sure Mum called him. I must be the only woman blessed with an ex-boyfriend who can do no wrong as far as her parents are concerned. Anyway, I don't know why he bothers. You would think a year's long enough for anyone to understand that you're not interested in them. Anyone but Zack, it seems. He just doesn't seem to get the message.

Zack rocks though.

Dear God, there must be more to this Christianity stuff than going to church, prayer meetings and conventions. I'm turning into the person I promised myself I would never be – the boring church girl who needs to get a life.

Thursday March 7

Have mercy on me, O Lord, for I call on you all day long (Psalm 86:3)

Dear Lord, I need all the help I can get. Feel like I'm slipping.

The day didn't start too well. Spotted a fine-looking specimen at the bus stop this morning. Didn't realise I was staring until the woman beside him screeched, 'What are you looking at?' I ignored her. Didn't want anyone thinking we were both crazy. But the bloke winked at me as he got on the bus. I ignored him and took out my Bible. You never saw a smile disappear so fast.

Then Zack called me. As if I wasn't stressed out already. The devil sure knows how to pick his agents. Wanted us to meet for lunch. Refused. It's that time of the month. Don't trust my hormones. I just wish he would leave me alone. Thinking of the Bible verse for the day from my daily devotional comforted me somewhat. If the Psalmist could feel like that, then I guess it's okay to feel like this. And like him, I'm calling on you, God, to steady me. I'm starting to feel like church is stealing my joy.

There's a prayer meeting tonight. Not sure I really want to be there. All that noise. One would think God was deaf.

Still three hours to 5.30. I'm in the toilet writing this. I'm not cut out for work. Or maybe it's just marketing I'm not cut out for.

Vanessa, my perfect best friend, just sent a text. She wants us to go shopping after work. I just don't know if I can face hearing more about her perfect fiance, Mark. Then she'll turn to me and say, 'Don't worry. God is faithful. If I can be engaged, then God can do the same for you.'

At home, that evening

Had a lovely time with Vanessa. She really cheered me up. Zack called when I got home. We're going to Smollensky's jazz club this weekend. Will definitely cancel. I know God definitely tut-tutted when I said, 'Yes!' At least I have a date other than meeting up with Vanessa. I really must make more of an effort with relationships. Tell you what, I'll go evangelising. What better way to make friends?! (Or enemies?)

Lord, what am I going to wear to Smollensky's? I saw the bus-stop guy again on my way home. Minus girlfriend. He didn't smile at me. As if I care. *I'm going to Smollensky's!*

Friday March 8

I can do everything through him who gives me strength (Philippians 4:13)

Thank God it's Friday. Tomorrow, I'm going to pop into the gym, head down to the hairdresser's and afterwards get a pedicure. I'm still planning to cancel with Zack. But, there again, what's wrong with wanting to go and hang out with a friend at a jazz club?

But he's an ex.

That doesn't mean anything.

You still have feelings for him.

Feelings don't matter. I'm strong. Like the apostle. I can do everything through Christ who strengthens me. Except keep my eyes focused on getting ready for work. MOVE IT GIRL!

Actually Zack called late last night. I saw his number on caller ID. I didn't pick up. I just knew he was going to make a big deal about our date – or rather our get-together (that's better). That boy needs prayer.

And I need deliverance. It's a soul tie thing. And I need to break it. Can I imagine myself going to my pastor? 'I need to break soul ties with my ex so I can be free to move on.'

I pictured the pastor laying hands on my head, tilting it, and holding it back at an awkward angle with the confidence of a man used to exercising authority over devils.

'In the name of Jesus! Break free! Free! Who the Son sets free is free indeed! May the blood of Jee-esus cleanse you from demonic ties …'

Yes, think I'll take a rain check on that.

Don't want to go to work though. Think I should call in sick?

Lunch break

I just knew I shouldn't have come in today. The one weekend I have a date (sorry, get-together) and I have to go to Paris for the weekend.

'Why can't Robert do it?' I asked Amanda. She's the Executive Marketing Director and my boss. And Robert sits at the desk next to me, which is unfortunate because he's got a pretty bad body-odour problem.

'You're going and that's that. Don't be difficult,' she said. She's the one that's so difficult. An agent from Beelzebub himself. I get all the dumb campaigns. It was me who got the water-inflated bras. And the organic spring water. And the revolutionary new lawn mower. And the assertiveness training weekends in Bognor Regis. And now it's the musical nappies. What a daft idea. God, why am I doing this job? OH GOD! I HAVE TO CALL ZACK AND CANCEL OUR DATE

(GET TOGETHER)! He'll definitely hate me, for sure. He'll probably think I'm lying.

3pm

Had a word with Amanda. Told her I wasn't feeling well.

'I don't care if you're the living dead,' she said. 'You're going and that's it. It's only a weekend, for Gawd's sake!' Now I know what my mission is: to pray for that woman. Don't know why I missed it before. Smollensky's doesn't matter. I haven't had a date for a year. I haven't had a social life for a year either. But who cares! I have Jesus!

So why do I feel like I can't be bothered with my faith anymore? It suddenly came to me! I'm under spiritual attack from the Evil One. But I can do all things through Christ. I'm strong. I'm a born again demon-kicking, Spirit-filled Pentecostal believer! Beat that, devil!

Checked my email. My cousin Foluke will be in London next month. She has issues. I used to describe her as neurotic but I was being politically correct. She's not neurotic. She's an absolute nutter.

5pm

Home. Called Zack and started to tell him about things and he hung up on me. Great! Paris won't be so bad really as I won't be working all the time – just a couple of hours tomorrow and Sunday thrashing out the client's advertising campaign. Don't know why Amanda couldn't have sorted this out a long time ago. Can I fit in a manicure tonight before I get the Eurostar?

Saturday March 9

When you walk through the fire, you will not be burned; the flames will not set you ablaze (Isaiah 43:2b)

Didn't get my nails done. Zack came round just as I was closing my front door to go out. I ran back into the flat when I saw him but he threatened to break the door down if I didn't let him in, so I had to really. It felt sort of nice that he thought it was so important.

What am I thinking?!

Anyway, he came in, sat on my sofa and put his head in his hands. He's got lovely hands. He said, 'Why did you cancel?'

I tried to explain. 'I have to go to Paris. Sorry.'

'Bit sudden, isn't it?'

'You know what Amanda's like. Anyway, I just have to go.'

'Where're your bags?'

'I'm popping out for a quick manicure first.'

'Are you or are you not going to Paris?'

'I am. But first I need a manicure. Please leave! I don't want to be late.'

'If you didn't want to go out with me, all you had to do was say.' He left.

I felt so low. Can't believe the guy still has the power to affect me like this even after a year of not being with him. If he was a Christian, we would sail into the marital sunset but no, he doesn't see the point of my faith. And what's the point of getting involved with someone who isn't interested in the most important thing in your life? Just wished he wasn't so... so *perfect* though.

I didn't have the manicure after all. Felt so despondent after Zack left, I cried and totally indulged in a reassuring bout of self-pity. For ages. I'm boyfriendless. Unlike all my friends. Plus my faith feels unreal. Plus I can't stand my job and my boss is Beelzebub's daughter. With all these pressures, is it any wonder I'm cracking up?

I kept thinking, if I could just see Jesus in person, I would be okay. It really would make all the difference. I'm just not a good advertisement for this faith thing. Maybe if I had a fantastic testimony about seeing Jesus or angels or heaven, maybe I wouldn't struggle so much. Not much point in walking through fires à la today's Bible verse when I would rather be delivered from them.

But I digress.

Self-pity marathon lasted 30 mins which left me another 30 mins to pack my bags and get myself to the station to catch Eurostar. By the time I was stuffing too much into my overnight bag I was starting to panic and worry about Friday night traffic big time. Then my phone rang.

'I thought you were going to Paris?' It was Zack.

'Yes, but I'm late and there's just no way I'll get to Waterloo on time.'

'I'm outside. I'll take you to the station. Sorry about being such a pain. I knew you were telling the truth. It's just that I was really looking forward to Smollensky's.'

'No problem,' I said, before flying out of the flat. Thank You Lord!

2pm

Late lunch break. Meeting going OK. I think. There's Windy CEO – he passes wind relentlessly – from Singing Diapers UK subsidiary and his equally smelly Head of Marketing. (His particular problem's more in the area of nervous body odour, even worse than Robert's.)

The diapers are going to be launched in a few weeks and we don't even have the beginning of an advertising campaign. How did this happen? What was Amanda thinking? Most importantly, will I get any sleep in the next couple of weeks bearing in mind the advertising situation (or lack thereof) for this product?

Windy CEO has been coming up with the most ludicrous ideas.

'Aliens! What if we feature the diapers as friendly aliens from outer space who tell toddlers when they're wet?'

Smelly bobs his head feverishly. 'Fantastic!'

'Or we could come up with a cartoon with the diapers as the lead characters. Sort of diapers with minds.'

'Wonderful. Yes, wonderful!' More frantic bobs from Smelly.

I *determined* to bring this under control.

'What if we go for a simpler advertising campaign? You, know... research shows that mothers are tired of gimmicks. If we just market the diapers for what they are without insulting people's intelligence, then surely, that would sell more, wouldn't it?'

Silence. Then Windy CEO asked, 'What do you have in mind?'

'Well, these are the diapers that alert parents by playing musical notes when toddlers have wet themselves. No more guesswork for harassed, busy parents. After all, it's the parents who buy diapers – not the toddlers.'

Windy CEO claps. 'Wonderful!'

Smelly starts bobbing, then gets a crick in his neck.

All in all, a very satisfactory ending. Nothing to it really. Diapers should be marketed as diapers. Marketing them any other way would be stupid. It's times like this that I really appreciate my job. It's about helping people. Giving them choices and making their lives that much easier.

6pm

That serpent, Smelly! The whole weekend's ruined. Just had a phone call from Amanda. She was livid. Said Smelly said I wasn't cooperative and that I'd practically forced my idea down everybody's throat! And that the CEO had changed his mind and was sticking to the Martian concept.

Tried to defend my approach but couldn't get a word in.

Thing is, there's a dinner with Smelly et al this evening. Lord, re today's Isaiah promise feel free to douse this fire with water at any time. Just in case you hadn't noticed, I'M IN TROUBLE!

Sunday March 10

Give thanks to the LORD, for he is good; his love endures for ever (Psalm 118:1)

On Eurostar heading home. Prayed after my last entry. Don't know if 'prayed' is the right word. More like I flung myself at God and bawled for wisdom. Then calmed down and went to dinner. What do you think? Windy CEO came right up to me as I arrived, said he'd changed his mind again, that he preferred my idea. Said I was right, that we should target the people with purchasing power. Asked me to head their next campaign, too. Spied Smelly glowering at me from the corner of my eye. I smiled at him. Sweetly. Not sure how Amanda will feel about me grabbing the next campaign. Don't want her to think I'm trying to wrestle her job from her... which I am, of course.

Tuesday March 12

... be strong in the Lord and in his mighty power (Ephesians 6:10)

Amanda's still not speaking to me. Office atmosphere rather uncomfortable. As if I *asked Windy* CEO to give me the next product campaign. He's insisting I head it – not Amanda. As if my life wasn't complicated enough.

Saw bus-stop man again today. Minus girlfriend. Wonder what's happened? I said hello to him and took out my Bible as we both sat down on the bus. He was seated directly opposite me. Saw him look at me when he thought I wasn't looking.

Vanessa called. Wants to come round after work. Told her I was having a manicure. 'Me too!' she said. Guess I'm stuck with her. I just want some time to myself. Is that too much to ask?

10pm

Guess what? We bumped into Mum at *Tutti Beauty* having her nails done. She's so well preserved it's disgusting. We went for coffee, ate too many chocolate chip muffins and had a lovely time actually – three women just chilling out. I love my Mum. She's cool. Dad's cool too. They're both cool. Vanessa sometimes gets on my nerves, though. Mark's been elevated to god status.

Friday March 15

I will sing to the LORD *all my life; I will sing praise to my God as long as I live. May my meditation be pleasing to him, as I rejoice in the* LORD *(Psalm 104:33,34)*

Thank God for Fridays! I'm going to go home, get changed and go to the prayer meeting. I've missed God so much! What with Zack, Paris and Amanda, he's been pushed onto the back burner.

Midnight

Thank you, Jesus, for your love and peace. The minute I walked into the prayer meeting, I was just... you know... aware of you. Thank you for your free gift of salvation. I know I'm not the most perfect Christian in the world but your presence in that room showed me you did love me even if I'm not perfect. The best Friday present ever.

Sunday March 17

... all things are possible with God (Mark 10:27)

Pastor Michael preached on *Settling for Second Best*. That's it. I'm going to hand in my resignation tomorrow. Amanda et al can all jump, as far as I'm concerned. I knew the job wasn't what God ordained for me. I'm destined for better things. I'm meant to soar like an eagle.

(I'm also meant to get a mortgage on a five-star studio flat and get married – to Zack preferably – in a Tiffany dress... but I digress again.)

I'm going to go for it. I'm going to go out in the streets and evangelise. The whole world shall know of the saving power of Jesus Christ. Even Zack? Yes, even him! Even though it's a damp spring and freezing outside. The whole point is this: I don't ever have to settle for second best because God sent his very best to die for me. Why should I settle for scraps?

Monday March 18

... no weapon forged against you will prevail, and you will refute every tongue that accuses you (Isaiah 54:17)

Amanda called me into her office and apologised for her behaviour last week. 'You should be sorry,' I wanted to say. 'You messed up the Singing Diapers account and when you couldn't fix it, you sent me along to Paris but God delivered me and you couldn't hack it.'

But I didn't. Instead I smiled sweetly and said, 'It's okay.' I didn't know what else to say so I left her office. Tad uncomfortable actually.

Wednesday March 20

Ask and it will be given to you; seek and you will find; knock and the door will be opened to you (Matthew 7:7).

Mum's in hospital. She's had a stroke.

Wednesday March 27

… do not worry about tomorrow, for tomorrow will worry about itself. Each day has enough trouble of its own (Matthew 6:34)

What a week since I last wrote in my journal!

My Dad (he's called Femi) is not taking this very well. He's a bank manager. Mum (Gail) manages a local charity shop. They've been married for 30 years. They got married when they were both 16. Dad's black and Mum's white. To explain a bit: my grandfather on my mother's side was a colonial officer in Lagos, Nigeria. My father's mother was a maid in their house. My parents were playmates who woke up one morning and decided to get married. Naturally when they got to the registry office, my mother's father was alerted. Needless to say, my mother found herself on the next plane to England. My father wasn't the kind to give up easily. Beatings and threats notwithstanding, he stole into a ship destined for England. He was found at Liverpool, emaciated and an inch from death. He appeared in the newspapers the next day, which was how Mum tracked him down.

They got married two weeks later. Mum was disowned by her family but she didn't care. It was the 70s and they were having fun. Romantic or what? I am the result of that beautiful union, and now Mum's had a stroke. I don't know how Dad will cope. God, why this? Why now?

Friday March 29

Therefore keep watch, because you do not know the day or the hour (Matthew 25:13).

Mum's okay. Her condition's stabilised. Had the church prayer team come and pray for her. Pastor Michael even laid the dreaded hands on her. Dad didn't complain. I guess he was too desperate. He's aged. We both have this week.

Monday April 15

He has made everything beautiful in its time. He has also set eternity in the hearts of men; yet they cannot fathom what God has done from beginning to end (Ecclesiastes 3:11)

Lord, how merciful art thou! Thank you for sparing my mother. I've done a lot of thinking over the last few weeks, even though I somehow didn't get around to writing it down. It wasn't so much the fact that I faced life without my mum that terrified me. It was the knowledge that I could face the *next* life without her that drove me to my knees to pray some pretty desperate prayers.

It's true. One minute you're here and the next you could be gone like the wind.

Mum's doing okay now. She's back home, thank God. She told me she sensed our prayers when she was in hospital. 'But I'm still not coming to your church,' she added. When I started talking to her about Jesus, Dad rushed me out of the room with the words, 'I will not let you kill your Mum after the doctors have delivered her.' But he winked at me. I smiled. My parents are back.

But so is Zack.

He's been great the last couple of weeks. I honestly don't know what I would've done without him.

I tried so hard to keep him away. Lord, you know how weak I am. Actually, Dad called him about Mum and asked him to keep an eye on me! He didn't know he was sending his daughter to the lion's den. I tried, Lord. I really tried to keep Zack away. Thing is, I'm still in love with him. He came round two nights ago. Vanessa had just left. The strain of it all was too much and I just burst into tears.

He just held me and told me everything was going to be okay and the next thing I know, we're kissing. And then we slept together.

The phone's ringing. It's Zack. His number's on caller ID. I don't want to talk to him. I need to think. *Focus, Kemi, focus.*

I've just yanked the phone out of the socket and switched off my mobile. The noise was driving me crazy. Maybe he'll get the message.

I will not think about God. *Mustn't.*

Child Rearing for Fun

Anne Atkins

It is not professionals, shrinks or parenting writers who know best how to bring up our children. It is we, the parents. Our instincts are better than any expertise, our love far more powerful than any mercenary motivation. Parenting is simple, satisfying, and above all fun.

Zondervan
£8.99
PB / 0 3103 5417 5

for the amateur parent

Child Rearing for fun

Trust Your Instincts and Enjoy Your Children

Anne Atkins

Published by Zondervan, Grand Rapids, Michigan 49530

Relationships

'There are two things I care for: people and music. Work, achievements, money, all the normal things that people worry about, are only useful if they enrich your relationships with people. Or enable you to buy music. There's not a lot of point in working all your life, if you don't have time to spend with people.'

Alexander

'Hang on, Alex, what about your cat?'

Serena

'That counts. People means relationships. Girls and cats and suchlike. And music means any of the arts, anything beautiful or aesthetically pleasing. You know, girls again.'

Alexander

In the end all human life comes down to this. The happiness of our existence largely lies in the happiness of our relationships. (Unless you are a hermit living alone on the windswept slopes of a Tibetan mountain. In which case the mind boggles as to how you got hold of this book ... and *why*.) Health and wealth, fame and success are great as far as they go. As my mother says, 'Money can't make you happy. But it can allow you to be miserable in comfort.' Relationships, however, bring genuine contentment.

The story is told of a contraceptive campaign in India, presumably funded by some do-gooding Western aid agency or other. The idea was to put out an advertisement illustrating the attractions and advantages of having fewer children. The poster showed two families side by side. One followed the model of the prosperous, developed-world nuclear unit: mother and father and pigeon pair of offspring surrounded by material trappings, fridge, television and so on (this was some years ago). The other showed parents with half a dozen tumbling children and no possessions at all. The advertisement backfired spectacularly. Why? Because when the targeted people saw the pictures, they interpreted riches in terms of relationships, not possessions: they saw the poverty of the couple with only two children, and the wealth of the pair surrounded by offspring, and commented on the good fortune of the second family compared with the first.

They were absolutely right. Money is like vitamins. If you genuinely don't have the minimum requirement, you will find yourself fairly wretched. Try to survive without enough iron and you will feel tired, lethargic and lacking in energy. (Yes, I know iron is not a vitamin, but you know what I mean.) As soon as you start taking your daily supplement, however, your health quotient shoots up and everything is fine again. Your iron level is back to normal. You might be tempted to think that, as one pill has made you feel so much better, two pills will make you feel twice as good, and five make you almost supersonic. But this is not the case. Ten iron pills will give you no more of a feel-good factor than one. And you will end up very constipated.

Money is similar. If you don't have the basic minimum to survive comfortably, life is pretty grim. Constantly worrying whether you can afford to go to the supermarket for food or buy the next pair of shoes for your children is no joke. If the Lotto fairy were to visit in the night and top up your income to the amount you need for food, clothing and a few other essentials, your quality of living would increase exponentially. Research and common sense both tell us, however, that after that, increasing your wealth further does not make a great deal of difference. From poverty to subsistence is a vast and important step; from subsistence to wealth far less so. (Consequently, lottery wins of several million do very little for the sum total of human happiness.)

So, provided we have enough money to live off, enough health to get up in the morning and meaningful work to do, our sense of wellbeing is likely to be measured, largely, by the welfare of our relationships. Conversely, it doesn't matter how successful someone is: if his relationships are not functioning well, you can be sure he will not be happy.

And the place where relationships happen first and foremost is the family. This is why it is so important.

Parents teach their children all sorts of things: how to read and write, or ride a bike; how to play the violin or sail a catamaran. My mother even – goodness knows why – taught us how to knit. But above all, we teach our children how to relate. This is one of the reasons why it makes so much difference when parents stay together. Why are children of stillmarried parents more likely to stay married themselves? Or, to put it another way, why did the Princess of Wales fail in the one overriding ambition of her life, to have a happy marriage? Her own parents having separated when she was small, she presumably never had the chance to copy and practise the necessary skills. In forging our own relationships, our primary resource is the relationships we were brought up with. If we don't have a role model of marriage to draw on, it is much more difficult (though of course not impossible) to stay married ourselves.

Nor does the family we grow up in just teach us how to understand families. It enables us to relate to the whole world. Are you finding your boss impossibly aggressive and superior? Your brother was surely worse, wasn't he, that Christmas when he settled on becoming a surgeon and amputated your new Barbie doll at the knee? You miraculously refrained from stabbing him in the eye with his fifteen-blade Swiss army knife then. That early restraint has given you hidden resources.

After all, in learning how to relate to other people, the most significant people in your child's life next to you, her parents, are usually her siblings. (If she has any. If she hasn't, and never will have, you might want to skip this next section ... though you never know, you might change your mind.)

Siblings

'I think if you have children you should have lots. You have to have siblings because they are your best friends. And to stop your parents driving you around the bend.'

Bink

'Er, Bink. Why is it better if it's your sister driving you around the bend?'

Alexander

Important though our children's relationship with us is, in some ways their relationships with each other are even more so. After all, they will usually last longer. Long after we are gone, we hope, our children will still have one another: we want them to establish something that will outlast us. In addition, they are equals: it is right that they should be able to enjoy confidences with each other that they might not want to have with us. Most important of all, it is essential that children sense that their parents' love for each other takes primacy even over their love for the children themselves: you will inevitably have things that you share only between the two of you. I have almost no secrets from my children at all; nevertheless, I wouldn't want them to overhear every conversation Shaun and I have together. Some things are properly private just between the two parents.

This being the case, it stands to reason that we should want our children to be closer to one another even than they are to us. Siblings can sometimes help an ill or disabled child in a way that their parents never can. They can say 'no'. We, her parents, instinctively put a sick child's welfare even before our own, if necessary allowing our work or health to suffer in order to care for her. After all, if we didn't want to make sacrifices we wouldn't have had children in the first place. But her brothers and sisters should not do this. They have their own lives to live. So they can challenge without threatening and help without patronizing.

I am constantly amazed at the potential that is neglected when it comes to siblings. I often see parents going to considerable trouble to find playmates for their children, ignoring the fact that they have provided them with a permanent playmate at home. It is as if the estrangement between the generations that we now take for granted in Western society has extended even to children two or three years apart. So, for instance, a neighbouring mother to us, with girls aged six and eight, expected her nanny to organize friends to come and play with each of them, separately, after school several days a week. When I asked her whether her two daughters didn't enjoy playing together, she sighed and said, 'I wish. No, they don't spend much time with each other.' Well, of course they don't, if you keep shipping in other playmates for them instead.

Children pick up how they are supposed to behave from their parents' expectations. Adults who believe that children are interesting, well-meaning creatures usually find that they are. New mothers who expect their babies to sleep easily and put up with noise and bustle tend to have babies that do; others who think their newborns will be sensitive and liable to cry at the tiniest disturbance will also usually find their expectations fulfilled. It is the same with sibling relationships. It works in subtle ways. If you believe that your children will be each other's best friends, you will not feel the need to provide alternative companions for them. They will turn to each other. If you expect them to find sustenance from one another, you will encourage it in all sorts of ways, subconscious as well as conscious.

But we can go further and institute a positive policy. We had a rule that our children were not allowed to exclude one another from games. I vividly remembered my sister having a friend to play (who, ironically, was my age not my sister's; and later became, and remains, my closest friend) and the two of them always used to cut me out. I found it such an upsetting experience that I was determined my children should not do it to each other, and never allowed it. So because their birthdays are all at the same time of year, they had joint birthday parties when they were small. As they have grown older and have had individual parties for one event or another, they have always been organized at times when they could all be there.

I have been hugely gratified when, as teenagers, they have stood by each other. On one occasion they were all invited to a birthday party in a pub. Their teenage hostess had not worked out that, at thirteen, Benjamin was not allowed in, and when he was asked to leave Serena left the party too and sat outside on the pavement with him for the rest of the evening while the other guests were inside. I was proud to be her parent. That, I thought, is real friendship.

Her boyfriend recently told us of the first date he ever took Serena on, two and a half years ago. He invited her to the cinema, thought he had scored bingo when she accepted and, being an organized sort of chap, bought two tickets. But when he went to pick her up she said Benjamin was particularly interested in the film too. Not only did he have to pay for her younger brother to go on his first date with her, but he also had to sit at the back of the cinema on his own because he could no longer get three seats together. (I suppose he ought to be grateful that she didn't simply send Ben in her place.) It is over a week since he recounted this story, and I'm still laughing …

All of which begs the question, how many children is the optimum number? Of course there is no right answer to this. Most people either know how many they want, or have no choice in the matter. Some want large families and find they can't have them. Some stop at one, and are blissfully happy pouring all their energies into an only child who grows up with all the initiative and energy that so much adult attention gives. Others want lots, and are surrounded by noise and chaos for two or three decades. Some have one or two more children and a rather noisier house than they really intended.

If you have already played your innings and drawn stumps, undoubtedly you will have chosen the right number for you; if you had no choice, assuredly you will be grateful for what you have. Nevertheless, many couples are often unsure, or not in agreement, or wondering whether to have more, or still deciding. If this is true of you, here are a few things to bear in mind.

I concede that many parents have small families, either through choice or necessity, and it works extremely well. I know a couple whom I admire enormously, who stopped after one child because the mother suffered severe postnatal depression. I have no doubt they made the right decision. Their child is one of the most charming I have ever come across. And it is said that most of the world's greatest leaders have been either eldest children or only children, while families with only two children are invariably tidier, more organized and certainly quieter than larger families. They also have more time for homework and other achievements, because they don't invest so much time in relationships.

Nevertheless, I have a number of friends who have regretted not having a bigger family. I have never yet met any parents who wished their families were smaller.

Kathryn and George had already been together for some time before they considered having children. George had always resented not being well off as a child, and was determined to have enough money before having children of his own. He eventually estimated that they could afford one, so they had Toby. By the time I knew them, when Toby was about five, they had a house worth a million pounds and two good incomes. And still only one child.

'I wish we'd had more,' Kate confessed a few years later.

'Why don't you now?' I asked her.

'I'm too old,' she said. 'It's too late.'

It was said with such wistfulness that I could never forget it.

I also know a number of people who have restricted themselves to two children because they 'couldn't afford any more'. What is interesting is that they are all, without exception, comfortably off. So presumably what they mean is that they couldn't easily afford private schooling, Mediterranean holidays, summer camps, and debt-free university for more than two children. I rate education very highly, but I've never yet come across a school that could make as much difference to anyone's life as having another sibling (or certainly not in the West, where everyone is educated anyway).

In vivid contrast to Kate's, Jenny's story is familiar. I don't know her well, but I have several friends who have had similar experiences. All of them had four children already, and had always planned to stop at four. All of them, like Jenny, became pregnant by mistake with a fifth.

'I was beside myself,' Jenny told me, 'throughout my pregnancy. It was the last thing I wanted, I had no idea how I was going to cope, and I became quite depressed.'

'And now?' I asked her.

'It's the best thing that ever happened to us,' she glowed.

I don't take offence easily, but I confess I find it offensive when people ask whether a child was a 'mistake'. No child is ever a mistake. God plans them, even when we don't. And sometimes the ones he plans in spite of us are the ones who give the most pleasure. (Our family, of course, was meticulously planned: Shaun planned the first, I planned the last, and the ones in the middle seem to have planned each other.) Having said that, I have frequently wondered, during more than one of my pregnancies, what on earth we were doing and why, and whether the whole *idea* of having children was a mistake, even if that particular child wasn't. Pregnancy can be a terrifying time, and I can understand why some women feel they can't go through with it. But I have never known any who have regretted it once they have. (And if there is a stable marriage, enough money to live on and no ill health, I can't imagine the woman who would.) Being reminded of it again so recently, seeing the way everyone's eyes light up as soon as Rosie grins at any of us, the laughter she gives us all, the therapeutic effect on the illness we were coping with, the fun one child can bring to so many, I find it inconceivable (so to speak) to think of any child – even one the parents might have been unsure whether or not to have – as being a mistaken idea.

So if you are in doubt, have more not fewer. If you are not in agreement, go with the parent who wants more. It is not uncommon to wish you had more children when it is too late; it is unthinkable that you would ever wish you had fewer. My brother-in-law once said to me, 'Your sister wanted four, I wanted two, so we compromised and had four.' That's what I call a compromise.

Many years ago I read a magazine article interviewing families of all different sizes, from one child to ten. Obviously it was a tiny sample, and the findings hardly representative. But I found it so striking I have remembered it since, so I repeat it here for what it's worth. The children of families with fewer than four children tended to want to have more children themselves: the only children, and the children from families of two or three, all said they would like large families, or certainly larger than they Part II: Building the Househad grown up in. But children in families that were larger than four had mostly decided to have fewer when they grew up. So the child who was one of six, or eight, said it was great fun, but he would only have two children himself. Only the children who were one of four wanted families of the same size.

Since then I have noticed a similar trend in friends of mine. One who was a child of six was determined to stop at two, and did. But many who were one of four go on to have four themselves. It is a kind of magic number: enough people to have fun with, without going mad.

I have to say, though, that for many years we had four – both of us, true to form, being one of four ourselves. And I always knew, deep down, that it was not quite enough …

Perhaps the best answer is that you can never be too rich, or too thin, or have too many children.

Grandparents – and wider family

'Children need to have responsibility for others, to shield them from apathy and depression. If you just have responsibility for yourself it's easy to lose sight of your purpose. But if you need to keep going for someone else that won't happen. That's why it's important to have younger siblings. You need responsibility within the family.'

Bink

As I write, my father is shopping for lunch and my mother is doing maths with Alex; my brother is out sailing with Ben and Shaun and my niece's boyfriend, while my niece herself revises her chemistry; Serena lies on her bed reading a novel, and Rosie is sleeping in the garden, waiting for someone to pass and wake her up to give her a cuddle (which happens a lot, as she is the only baby here). This afternoon a bunch of us will swim and boogie-board before tea while Bink does Greek with my father, and tonight we are going to the theatre with cousins who have rented a house nearby.

We are by the seaside. My parents keep an alarmingly small terrace house in north Norfolk, within spitting distance of the beach, which my grandfather bought for exactly this purpose, and every August about eighteen members of the extended family squeeze into it somehow, sleeping all over the place, all higgledy-piggledy and luckily not usually all at once ... and this is what we call a holiday.

At the end of the month my parents will go back to Cambridge, where they live for the other eleven months of the year, and where they continue to work, in their mid-eighties, to pay for this wild extravagance every summer. And some bright spark among their contemporaries may ask them, as they have asked them before now, 'Don't you think you have earned the right to stop work, put your feet up, and pamper yourselves instead? A nice little Saga cruise to Turkey, for instance, just the two of you?'

My father will chuckle over this comment for months to come. A quiet, relaxing dry martini alone with my mother, in a deck chair overlooking sunset on the Bosphorus, before a four-course dinner and palm court music in the deck lounge and a spot of bridge with a bunch of other old crocks? No thank you. He prefers getting up at six to make me a cup of tea because I've got a BBC car coming at half past, taking a quick dip in the sea before any other demands are made on him, shopping for milk before breakfast because half a dozen teenagers drank it all the night before, helping someone with Latin A-level before shopping again for lunch, washing up all afternoon, shopping again, doing Greek GCSE with another, then taking several of them swimming before supper. There's no contest, really, is there?

Actually, no, there isn't. It is not the fashion, but I know my parents have made the right choice. And as they travel back home at the end of August, exhausted and broke and longing for a bit of peace and quiet, they know they wouldn't swap it for the world. Why? Because it is more satisfying to serve others than oneself. Because they are giving their children and grandchildren an incomparable heritage. Because the relationships will last for ever: there is no chance whatsoever of my parents having a lonely old age. (Though they might occasionally wish for one . . .) And because they love it and it keeps them young and they want to give their grandchildren what they were lucky enough to have themselves.

The extended family has been in demise for generations, and the losses are incalculable. We live in Fulham, which in living memory was a working-class area where daughters set up home within calling distance of their mothers. Not much chance of that now: five years ago, little two-bedroom 'cottages' in the street next to ours were selling for a half a million. The nearest that youngsters can hope to live to their parents is a good hour's drive away.

It is a great shame, because intergenerational intimacy benefits everyone. The children grow up with numerous advantages. Wisdom from those older than themselves. Tolerance towards those who are different. Even, if they are very lucky, a smattering of table manners that hark back to a gentler and more civilized age. Today, at lunch, one of my children (loyalty forbids that I should name which) made himself an enormous sandwich, oozing mayonnaise, olive oil, salad and meat from every aperture. We are used to the eating habits of today's teenagers, and hardly registered the sight of him attacking it much as his cave-dwelling predecessors might have taken on the challenge of a raw leg of antelope. His grandparents, however, were visibly shocked. We had to ask him to stop, take stock, wash his hands and consider why the strange invention of cutlery has stayed in vogue.

They may even learn from the example of self-discipline. I have noticed that anyone under twenty now considers it quite natural to get up at any time of day, honestly believing it can be impossible to rise before teatime. From time to time one can even see reports in the press arguing that there are biological reasons for teenagers to sleep around the clock. Such articles could only be written by journalists with short memories and an ignorance of history, since when I was a teenager we wouldn't have stayed in bed beyond breakfast-time unless we were seriously ill. A friend, visiting our house the other day, astonished our children by saying that he used to get exhausted at their age, and wished his mother had let him have a lie in, till eight or nine in the morning, say. I'm sure it does teenagers good to spend a few weeks with people who consider it normal to get up at seven o'clock and do a day's work even when they don't feel like it.

But the younger generation is not the only one to benefit. Just as young people gain maturity, manners and conversational skills from the grandparents, so the older generation gains insight, energy and fun. I would far rather be at a gathering where young and old are mixed together than one that is restricted to my own age group. It is much more interesting. When I am old as well as decrepit I shall much prefer being surrounded by riotous grandchildren and great-grandchildren than fellow senile members of the nursing home.

Extended families also benefit society as a whole. (Well, of course they do, if they benefit families, because society is only as strong as the families in it.) When I was at university I had a friend who was fortunate in living in a house large enough to accommodate various aunts and hangers-on as well as his immediate family. He had an uncle who disconcerted guests by standing a foot or so away from the wall and talking to it at great length, frequently during meal times. It was a sight I found oddly cheering. A family with fewer resources would have abandoned him to an institutional fate; but here, in the family home, he was happily part of the furniture, so to speak – though, admittedly, a fairly chatty part of the furniture. In the years since, when I have come across mental illness first hand, I have thought of Uncle Peter, living with his sister and her children, and smiled nostalgically. Accommodating such eccentricity enriches the lives of all who live with it.

But, you may say, much of this is easier said than done. We do not choose our children's grandparents. You may not have a family 'large' enough, in outlook, commitment or material assets. I'm aware that I am extremely fortunate, through no merit of my own, in the family I have inherited. But I also believe the spirit of the age teaches us to denigrate our parents instead of appreciating them, to blame them for every little fault instead of thanking them for all their good qualities. Nobody has a perfect upbringing, but most of us had a pretty good one, nonetheless. And we should all make the most of what we have.

First, we can include our parents and in-laws from the moment we have children. My mother-in-law came to stay with us for the births of our first two, and was a great boon. If she hadn't been there when Serena was born, there would have been no one to clear up after the dog, who got so excited he was sick all over the drawing room carpet. At Bink's birth, there would have been no one to finish Shaun's 2,000-piece jigsaw puzzle after he was called upstairs by the midwives. And because of her own experiences as a new mother, she knew she'd be far more use doing the shopping and washing up than cuddling the baby. Next, accept any offer you are given. After Serena's first Christmas, when she was eight months old and no longer breast-fed, my parents offered to have her for a week over the New Year. I can still remember the odd feeling we had as they drove off with her in the back of the car. She was crying, and I momentarily wondered whether we had done the right thing. But of course we had. Parents are not the only ones who have a stake in their children. She is my parents' granddaughter as well as our daughter: they had a right to her company, as well as some responsibility for her welfare. And that week we had to ourselves was one of the best Christmas holidays we've ever enjoyed.

Third, we must trust those who are helping with our children. When we were first married and living in a college flat, Shaun's tutor's wife rang me up in a fix and asked if I could baby-sit for her, as she had to nip out unexpectedly. I said I was very willing but had just sat down to lunch, so she told me to bring it with me. I turned up with my cheese sandwich and half-pint of lager, and the minute his mummy had left, her five-yearold asked me if he could taste my drink. I knew absolutely nothing about children, but I suspected this was not the thing, so I told him I doubted if he would like it. But he pleaded and pleaded, for 'just a tiny sip', till in the end I handed it over. He downed it in one, gave me back the glass, and said proudly, 'Mummy would *never* let me do that.'

Not sure whether he would pass out or throw up, I took his pulse at regular intervals and confessed to his mother in fear and trepidation as soon as she stepped through the door. I will never forget her response. 'If I trust you to look after my children,' she said, 'I trust you to do it your way.' I have frequently repeated this to myself when other people take responsibility for ours.

When children are with their grandparents, grandparents' rules apply. My father has what I consider extraordinary ideas about the constitution of a healthy diet. There I was, handing over children so frighteningly organic they could have been stamped by the Soil Association, knowing that the minute they were in his care they would be filled with so many E-numbers that, if they had died and been buried, they would have been preserved like mummies till Kingdom come. I was faced with a straightforward choice between my dietary faddishness and my children's relationship with their grandfather. You should see me now, the model of a non-interfering parent, biting it all back when he produces a tub of supermarket ice cream or margarine (it's hard to tell the difference) made from industrial-grade North Sea oil, and fairy cakes iced so fluorescent you could see in the dark with them. Their relationship with him is one cemented with refined preservatives.

Our parents are bound to have rules slightly different from ours. What time they go to bed, whether they are allowed to watch television, what they eat at table, is not going to be the same at Grandma's house as at home. This is one of the beauties of it. Our children learn to adapt. But this means we have to adapt first, and back up our parents or in-laws, whatever their rules may be.

There may be times, however, when the wider family simply doesn't work. And when this happens we must, however reluctantly, make our children our priority. A friend of mine believed passionately in the concept of the extended family. When her mother-in-law was widowed, Helen invited her to make her home with her husband and children. To begin with all went well, but as the months went by Helen's mother-in-law became more and more of a recluse despite the fact that she was perfectly fit and relatively young, till she seldom emerged from her room and had, to all intents and purposes, ceased to be a member of the family. Not only was this not doing her any good, but it was giving the children the clear message that family life was something to opt out of, as well as that their grandmother was not interested in them. Chiefly to help her mother-in-law, Helen gently suggested that she should make a habit of joining the family at teatime when the children came home from school, as it would be lovely for them to see more of her. Not only did she not take up the suggestion, she resented it so much that she told her friends Helen had only invited her to live with them so she could exploit her as a free babysitting service. In the end, she was having such a negative effect on family life that Helen and her husband had to ask her to leave. This was made the more difficult as the old lady had nowhere to live. Nevertheless, they made the decision that, being an adult, she would have to fend for herself – and she did.

We owe our parents the utmost respect, so this kind of thing is most regrettable. And if we still lived in a society that understood the ties and obligations of the extended family, such conflicts would be far less likely to arise. But when they do, our duty to our children takes precedence even over our duty to our parents. Our children are totally dependent on us for their welfare. Our parents are not: provided they are healthy, they are responsible for their behaviour, and can usually fend for themselves if necessary.

Happily, these conflicts of interest are unusual. So treat your parents well. After all, in this, as in everything, our children will follow our example. If we want to be revered in our old age, we should show our children how it is done.

The first of the Ten Commandments with a promise is that we should honour our father and mother, that it may go well with us and we will enjoy long life. It delivers its promise. When we honour our parents, our children honour us.

Not *Even* a Hint:
A Study Guide for Men

Joshua Harris
WITH
Brian Smith

Based on his bestselling book *Not Even a Hint*, Joshua Harris offers a companion study guide specifically designed to address the issues men face. Versatile in nature, this study guide can be used in one-on-one accountability or in a church group setting.

Multnomah Publishers
£4.50
PB / 1 5905.2253 2

JOSHUA
HARRIS

WITH BRIAN SMITH

A STUDY GUIDE FOR
MEN

not *even* a hint

Published by Multnomah Publishers, Inc.
PO Box 1720, Sisters, Oregon 97759

Introduction

This study guide is designed for men who are serious about helping each other grow in holiness. It's designed to spark open, honest, and godly discussion about male sexuality. Sex isn't just something to joke about in the locker room – it's a beautiful and sacred gift from God. We want to be both thankful for it and respectful of God's commands to be pure. This study guide will challenge you to apply the principles of *Not Even a Hint* in your daily lives in order to guide you to victory in the ongoing battle against lust.

Who Can Use It?

The *Not Even a Hint Study Guide* for Men is extremely versatile. It can be used in a group setting or individually. However, it is designed primarily for two or more men who want to work through the book together. Whether this is a group of three friends that meets weekly at a coffee shop or fifteen guys in a Sunday school class, the guide can be adapted to meet your needs.

There are different ways for a group to use it. One option is for each member to have his own copy of the study guide and work through the appropriate lesson on his own before each meeting, writing his answers and then coming to the meeting ready to share. (This is ideal, since it encourages each guy to think through answers more carefully.)

The second option is for only the leader to have a copy of the study guide. With this approach, group members read the appropriate chapter in *Not Even a Hint* before the meeting, and then the leader uses the study guide at the meeting to lead discussion. If you use this approach, make sure you encourage group members to do some of the self-examination exercises suggested throughout the book on their own time.

What's in Each Lesson?

There is one lesson for each of the ten chapters in *Not Even a Hint*. Each lesson contains the following elements to help you dig deeper into the message and apply its truth:

Easy Review

At the beginning of each lesson we've listed the *central issues*, or main points, of the corresponding chapter in *Not Even a Hint (NEAH)*. This summary is a great way to quickly refresh your memory about the essence of the chapter. We've also listed a few *key growth objectives* for you so you'll understand what we hope you will know, feel, and do after working through the lesson.

Questions

The first couple of questions in each lesson are meant to be *discussion starters*, to provide a nonthreatening way to get people talking. Have fun with them.

Most of the remaining questions are either *conceptual* questions, inviting you to deal with ideas or concepts in the book; or *application* questions, guiding you toward putting the concepts into practice in your life. (Many of the questions are preceded by a quote from *Not Even a Hint* to remind you of important principles and to help direct the focus of your discussion.)

Accountability Follow-Up

Near the end of each lesson are two *accountability follow-up* questions, usually relating to the main issues of the preceding lesson. Don't end the meeting until you've checked in on each other's progress in a truthful and caring manner.

Mediate and Memorize

We also list a key Scripture passage, which we encourage you to write out on a card and carry with you during the week. Only when you hide God's Word in your heart will His truth be readily available so that His Spirit can help you gain victory over lust. Ideas for meditating on and memorizing these passages are provided in *NEAH* (158) and in lesson 9 of this study guide.

Custom-Tailored Action Plan

If this study is to help you experience true freedom and victory over sexual temptation, you have to come away with a specific plan of action, and that plan must be tailored uniquely to you. There is no "one size fits all" solution for lust. Every guy's collection of battlefields, strengths, and weaknesses is unique to him.

Beginning with chapter 4 and continuing through chapter 10, you will be guided, step by step, through the formulation of a Custom-Tailored Action Plan using a simple worksheet on pages 68–71 of the study guide. Your plan is completely flexible – you can revise it whenever and however you wish. And it is designed so that you can easily photocopy it for accountability partners.

How to Lead a Group Discussion on Lust

Regardless of the size of the group, it's helpful to have one member serve as the leader. He's the one who is responsible to assign the appropriate chapter for the group to read before each meeting, to ask the questions, and to facilitate discussion. If no one else steps up to that role, we encourage you to simply start leading. You don't need a label ... just do the job, and the group will function more smoothly and effectively

Of course, the topic you're tackling is unique. In order to help each other feel safe about sharing honestly, we urge you to take these guidelines seriously:

1. *Promise and Maintain Confidentiality*

In the very first meeting, agree that nothing shared in the group will leave the group without the sharer's permission. (The rare and only exception is information you might need to divulge in order to protect a group member or someone else from harm. If you think this might be the case, seek a pastor's guidance.)

2. *Create an Atmosphere of Truthful Acceptance*

Each of us is capable of the darkest of sins, and each of us is fighting a hard battle. Group members should listen to one another with compassion and acceptance. This does not mean sacrificing truth, but rather listening with understanding and "speaking the truth in love" (Ephesians 4:15).

3. *Be an Example of Humble Honesty*

Whether you are the designated group leader or not, you can serve the group by stepping out and sharing honestly about your sin and your victories. As friendships and trust develop, you'll encourage others to overcome their fears about sharing by overcoming yours first.

More Tips for Leading a Group

1. *Strive for Application*

James 1:22 says, "Do not merely listen to the word, and so deceive yourselves. Do what it says." Remind the guys in your group that merely reading a book – even the Bible – and talking about it won't produce change. Real change occurs after we close the book and do something about it. As you progress through the study guide, take time during your meetings to have guys share what changes they've made.

2. *Start Small*

While application is important, no one can change in every area all at once. Encourage members of your group to begin by trying to apply just one point from each chapter.

3. Outlaw One-Word Answers

The questions in the *NEAH Study Guide for Men* are intended to provoke discussion and even debate. Ban yes and no answers. Encourage guys in your group to share from their heart, not just parrot the "right" answer from *Not Even a Hint*. Giving only expected or "acceptable" answers will not help them examine their own lives.

4. Listen to the Holy Spirit

This study guide exists to serve *you* – don't become a slave to it. If one question opens up a fruitful discussion, then go with it! Don't feel you have to work through all of the questions. Take opportunities for the group to pray spontaneously for someone who expresses a need. Let God's Spirit, not this book's format, guide you.

5. Encourage, Encourage, Encourage!

Point out to your friends when you see them growing in a certain area – no matter how small it is. The best way to motivate each other is to acknowledge where God is at work. Offer lots of encouragement.

6. Focus on God

In the midst of focusing on the challenge of lust, make sure that the group's primary motive is to please and honor God. Keep reminding each other of the gospel – Christ's death and resurrection has set us free from the rule of sin! We're forgiven! Begin and end your time with prayer. Enjoy the journey! Remember, only God's Spirit can work real change in our lives. May God use your study and interaction to bring about life-changing results.

LESSON 1

Not Even a Hint

Why Can't I Seem to Beat Lust?

Now that you've read chapter 1 of *Not Even a Hint*, we hope you realize that you're not alone. Almost everyone experiences frustration when dealing with lust. The enemy would like you to believe that you're isolated and unusual, but you're not. And you can find safety among carefully chosen brothers in Christ who are willing to honestly face their sin and together pursue holiness.

God offers real hope through the victory of Jesus Christ. Begin your study with a simple prayer expressing your trust in His death and resurrection. Thank Him for giving you the desire to change.

Central Issues

- Lust defined: craving sexually what God has forbidden.
- There are right and wrong *standards* for holiness, *power sources* for change and *motives* for fighting sin.
- We're not just against lust; we're *for* God's good plan for sex in marriage.

Key Growth Objectives

✔ To establish that lust is something we all face in some form.
✔ To understand why God's standard is "not even a hint" of impurity in our lives.
✔ To realize that killing lust leads to the joy and freedom of holiness.

1. Honestly, how realistic does the standard *not even a hint* seem to you with regard to sexual sin? Why did you choose this response?

1	2	3	4	5	6	7	8	9	10

Are you crazy?   We can do it!

2. Whether you think this is a realistic standard or not, rate how strongly you *desire* to have not even a hint of sexual sin in your life. Why?

1   2   3   4   5   6   7   8   9   10
Forget it!   I can't wait!

Lust Versus Sexuality

In *Not Even a Hint*, Josh writes, "I have a simple definition for lust: craving sexually what God has forbidden" *(NEAH* 18).

3. What is helpful to you in josh's definition? What would you change in the definition, if anything? Why?

4. Part of the challenge Christians face in a lust-filled world is remembering that neither sex nor sexuality is our enemy. Lust is our enemy and has hijacked sexuality. We need to keep reminding ourselves that our goal is to rescue our sexuality from lust so we can experience it the way God intended *(NEAH* 26).

Summarize from the following Scripture passages God's thinking about the differences between lust and pure sexuality (see also *NEAH* 25-28).
    Lust – Ephesians 5:3; Colossians 3:5; 1 Thessalonians 4:3-4

    Sexuality – Genesis 2:22-25; Proverbs 5:18-19; 1 Corinthians 7:2-5

5. God never calls us to sacrifice as an end in itself, but only *through* sacrifice on the way to great joy. On the other side of the seeming

loss and denial is always reward and pleasure so deep and so intense that it's almost impossible to call what you gave up a sacrifice at all (*NEAH* 27).

If this is true, then describe what is really happening ...

... *when you give in to lust*

... *when you resist lust.*

6 What is an example of you (or someone you know) passing up the instant pleasure offered by lust for a deeper, more lasting pleasure later? What sacrifice do you think God is calling you *through* for the sake of true joy and godly pleasure?

Our Efforts Versus God's Provision

7. At the beginning of chapter 1, Josh describes his futile efforts to live up to "the contract":

The year that followed was a very humbling lesson in how utterly incapable I was of being righteous in my own strength .... All my great ambitions, all my vows, all my self-efforts were revealed to be worthless (*NEAH* 18).

Describe a time when you tried to accomplish something good on your own when you actually needed outside help.

8. God's standard of *not even a hint* quickly brings me to the end of my own ability and effort. It reminds me that God's standard is so much higher than the standards I place for myself that only the victory of Christ's death and resurrection can provide the right power and the right motive needed to change me (*NEAH* 25).

Why was each element of God's plan better than Josh's original plan (see *NEAH* 22–25)?

	GOD'S PLAN	JOSH'S PLAN
Standard of holiness	*not even a hint*	*no masturbating for a year*
Power source for holiness	*the cross of Christ*	*his own willpower*
Motivation for holiness	*God's grace*	*to show God that he was good*

Forgiveness Versus Condemnation

In the preface, Josh writes, "I've learned that I can only fight lust in the confidence of my total forgiveness before God because of Jesus' death for me" (*NEAH* 10). If you have put your faith in Christ as your Savior, are you confident of your total forgiveness before God? Do you believe He loves and accepts you because of Jesus' sacrifice for you? Without this confidence, it will be difficult to be honest about lust in your life with other carefully selected Christian brothers.

9. Summarize the central point of each of these statements from God to you:
   1 Timothy 1:15–16

   Psalm 103:8–13

   1 Corinthians 10:13

   1 John 1:6–9

10. Honesty with others takes courage. Take a minute to talk with God the Father about any fear you have about discussing the topic of lust. Ask His Holy Spirit for courage and a deep hunger for holiness.

Accountability Follow-Up

Starting with lesson 2, this section will guide your group to review commitments or action points from preceding lessons in order to evaluate your progress and to encourage you toward greater obedience in God's strength. In this first lesson (especially if you're with a group of guys you don't know well), use the following questions to begin your journey

11. What is one question you would like us to ask you on a regular basis?

12. What is one way you want us to pray for you this week in keeping with this lesson? (Write down each other's requests and take a few minutes to pray for each other.)

Mediate and Memorize

> *But among you there must not be*
> *even a hint of sexual immorality,*
> *or of any kind of impurity, or of greed,*
> *because these are improper for God's holy people.*
> *EPHESIANS 5:3*

Detox Your Spiritual Life in 40 Days

Peter Greystone

Detox your Spiritual Life will help you renew your physical, emotional and, above all, your spiritual wellbeing. Peter Greystone's book is designed to help you do away with things that hold back your relationship with God. His day by day companion encourages you to break habits, let go of failures and put regrets behind you.

Canterbury Press
£8.99
PB / 1 8531 1606 8

DETOX
YOUR SPIRITUAL LIFE
IN 40 DAYS
PETER GREYSTONE

First Published in 2004 by the Canterbury Press, Norwich

Day 31

Be Different

'I acted differently because I honoured God.'

I've known those words almost all my life. Learning verses from the Bible figured strongly in my experience of church as a child. Most of the words I learnt have proved forgettable, but those seven have stayed with me. I think that sentence has had more impact on me than any other from the Bible. Remembering that verse at trivial or important moments has stopped me doing some things and prompted me to do others. It once flashed into my head just as I passed the concrete 'honesty box' of an unattended car park on the south coast without putting any money in. Unfortunately, it didn't stop me reversing into the pillar and denting my bumper when I attempted to put it right without the effort of getting out of the car!

For Nehemiah, who originally wrote the words, it was a matter of political integrity. Having been appointed to a powerful job in Jerusalem, he was in a position to accumulate a personal fortune through taxation. It was, after all, what every other leader did. However, he declined that opportunity because he saw his job as serving people, not benefiting from them. He set to work on a policy of relieving the poorest people in the surrounding area of debts that had reduced them to destitution. He could see no integrity in lining his own pockets while their misery increased. Of course, not many of us are in a position of political influence. We are not the people who set the standards of our society; we are those who are affected by them. Should we accept them as our own standards just because they are now the norm? Or should we draw attention to ourselves by insisting on alternatives? Those of us who are detoxing our ordinary, uneventful lives need to think about how to stand out in a crowd as people whose values are different, better and designed to please someone altogether more important.

> [Nehemiah wrote:]
> 'Earlier governors – those preceding me – placed a heavy burden on the people and took forty shekels of silver from them in addition to food and wine. Their assistants also lorded it over the people. But out of reverence for God I did not act like that. Instead, I devoted myself to the work.'
>
> *Nehemiah 5.15–16*

Paul wrote a letter to Timothy, a young man for whom he had a particular fondness as he trained him to lead the next generation of Christians. Paul's suggestion for a distinctive lifestyle was that Timothy should make it clear that his decisions were not driven by how much money he could earn from them. Five centuries had gone by since Nehemiah's time, but the problem was precisely the same. And let's be honest, the prevailing values of today's society are still driven by earning and owning in very much the same way. Paul challenged his protégé to have a different set of values in mind when he made his choices: 'righteousness, godliness, faith, love, endurance and gentleness'.

> Some people, eager for money, have wandered from the faith and pierced themselves with many griefs. But you, man of God, flee from all this, and pursue righteousness, godliness, faith, love, endurance and gentleness.
>
> *1 Timothy 6.10–11*

What do they mean in practice? First, they mean that a person of God is not deflected from his standards by peer pressure. When people are young it is often sexual ethics and the abuse of drugs that present the biggest challenge to acting differently. And when people are older the pressing issues are, well, sexual ethics and the abuse of drugs, actually! 'What will they think of me?' is a paralysing motivation when it comes to deciding what is right. 'How can I bring joy to God?' is a liberating alternative. That is what is meant by 'righteousness and godliness'.

Second, it means that a person of God is able to restrain himself or herself and keep to the law, even if everyone else is ignoring it. That is not very difficult if the law in question is murder or treason. But it is harder if the law concerns the age at which you can see a film or go into a pub. And it is harder still if you are surrounded by people who routinely pay less tax than they should, cut corners when it comes to fulfilling a business contract, or treat the M6 motorway like Le Mans. This is where Christians need to show the difference that can be made by 'faith and endurance'.

> The Church's service and mission in the world is absolutely dependent on its being different from the world; being in the world but not of the world.
>
> *Jim Wallis, founder of the Sojourners' Community, born 1948*

And third, the person of God can stand out by winning respect through humility, not by throwing his or her weight around. People are not impressed by fine words, but by straightforward actions. And that applies to friends, children, colleagues, members of a sports team, everyone! What does it mean to act differently when the conversation turns to gossip about a local scandal? What does it mean to act differently when a referee fails to notice that you have detox your spiritual life been fouled inches from the penalty area? These are the moments which give concrete meaning to 'love and gentleness'.

This chapter started with a politician creating a national taxation policy, and it ends with a thug of a defender aiming for your shins instead of the football. But that is the nature of God's call. He is at work to improve everything in life, from Parliament Square to Saturday afternoon in the park. And the difference each individual Christian makes, whether they are in a government office or face down in the mud, is his means of changing our world.

> Christians are no different from the rest of mankind. They do not live in cities of their own or have a different language or way of life ... but the way they live is marvellous and confounds all expectations ... They have children, but they don't try to get rid of them. They eat with all their neighbours, but they don't sleep with all their neighbours ... They obey the existing laws, but in their own lives they surpass the laws. They love all people, even though they are persecuted by all people ... They are poor, but they enrich other people's lives ... Their existence is on earth, but they are citizens of heaven.
>
> *Mathetes, author of a letter to Diognetus, circa 200*
>
> **Detox:** Look back on the opportunities you have had since you began this detox to stand out from the values that the rest of the world takes for granted. Think about your relationships, your finances, your work, your leisure, your moods. Is there anything you would do differently next time out of reverence for God?

Lord God, may the love I have for you make a difference to the way I behave. Not just once, but again and again and again and again. Amen.

Day 32

Explore Freedom

Duty used to feature prominently in the church in which I grew up. The church warden was head of the Lord's Day Observance Society, an organization campaigning to prevent the character of Sundays being changed by the legalization of shopping and work on that day. Today, of course, I can see virtue in keeping Sunday distinctive, but aged eight all I knew was that there was a newsagent opposite the church which, for 24 hours each week, turned into the repository of all the evil in London because it sold things on the Sabbath. I also knew that ice cream tasted its sin-flavoured best when you bought it furtively after a church service and ate it hiding behind the church hall, having decided who would be the lookout by drawing lots. So, not only Sabbath abuse, but gambling as well – oh happy days!

I have a different approach these days. I try to persuade children what a special day Sunday is by buying them ice creams twice the usual size.

The Sabbath was given by God so that on one precious day of the week some of us could be set free from having to do paid work. The point of a day of rest is that you find yourself saying, 'Day off! Praise the Lord!' And you can then improve it by doing the praising of the Lord together in the same building. The hope is that if your friends are there, the music is rip-roaring, and what the preacher says is interesting, it will be the highlight of the week. How miserable it would be if this thing that was given to set us free turned into a duty we all feel forced to go through for fear of angering God!

Miserable, yes, but easy to do! It was one of the difficulties the Pharisees got themselves into in Jesus' time. Fervently committed to obeying religious laws, they had allowed their lives to be imprisoned by a faith that was designed to free them. Aghast to see Jesus walking through cornfields picking ears of corn as a snack, they accused him and his disciples of working on the Sabbath. And technically they were – harvesting, grinding, winnowing! If buying ice cream on a Sunday counts as work, then rubbing and nibbling corn does too. I suspect, however, that the Pharisees' real objection was that Jesus and his disciples were enjoying themselves, blissful with God's freedom.

> One Sabbath Jesus was going through the cornfields, and as his disciples wlaked along, they began to pick some ears of cor. The Pharisees said to him, 'Look, why are they doing what is unlawful on the Sabbath?' … Then he said to them, 'The Sabbath was made for people, not people for the Sabbath.'
>
> *Mark 2.23–7*

And now I want to tell you the most important thing I know.

God loves you. He loves you completely and entirely. He will never love you more than he does at this moment. Even if you become a Christian tomorrow he will not love you more than he does today. He can't, because he loves you perfectly already. His love is absolute and has no qualifications attached to it at all.

But this liberating fact does not stop there. The truth is that not only will God never love you more, he will also never love you less. If you don't read your Bible this week he won't love you less. If you don't pray to him tomorrow detox your spiritual life he won't love you less. If you never go to church again he won't love you less. That is the freedom of worshipping a God who loves with no conditions, the God of grace.

When you realize this, an entirely different set of priorities takes over. You find yourself beguiled by this God who gives so much and asks so little. Captivated! Not captive to the duties, but captivated by the one we worship.

You hear God say, 'I love you completely,' and your heart is thrilled. And he says, 'Do you want to know more?' and of course you do because it's astounding. So he says, 'Well, all you need to know is available, so why don't you read about it?' And you shout out, 'Where, where, where?' and suddenly you're reading the Bible twice a day. Not as a duty but out of fascination!

> It is for freedom that Christ has set us free. Stand firm, then, and do not let yourselves be burdened again by a yoke of slavery.
>
> *Galatians 5.1*

You hear God say, 'I love you totally,' and your spirit is electrified. And he says, 'Is there anyone who you would like to tell?' and of course there is because it's fantastic. So he says, 'Well, there are opportunities to make it known, so why don't you take advantage of them?' And you cry, 'When, when, when?' and suddenly you're running a children's group, or leading a Bible study, or supporting mission. Not as a duty, but as a delight!

> There are two freedoms – the false, where a man is free to do what he likes; the true, where a man is free to do what he ought.
>
> *Charles Kingsley, novelist, 1819–75*

You hear God say, 'I love you perfectly,' and your soul is ablaze. And he says, 'Is there anything I can do to help?' and, of course, there is, because it would be ridiculous to waste that kind of help. So he says, 'Well, I'm listening any time you want to mention what's on your mind!' And you yell, 'How, how, how?' and suddenly you can't help yourself praying, almost every minute, for the needy world and your needy self. And you have walked out into freedom!

> God forces no one, for love cannot compel. God's service, therefore, is a thing of perfect freedom.
>
> *Hans Denk, Christian leader, 1490–1527*

What if this concept of unconditional love is too much to cope with? What if you feel that all you have to offer is a disciplined and dutiful collection of religious observances over which you labour week-in week-out? Well, strange as it seems, that is fine as well. You see, in heaven we will meet the disciples who, on occasion, tried so half-heartedly, but whose love shines out of the stories of the Bible. But we need to realize that in heaven we will also meet the Pharisees who, on occasion, tried so hard, but whose love was notably missing in that field of corn. Thank God that our salvation hasn't come as a result of the effort we put in, but as a gift of Jesus, who offered his life that we might be free.

And when you and I meet in heaven in the fullness of time, I would like to suggest that we head straight for whatever is the nearest equivalent to a cornfield that is available to us in the mysteries that lie ahead, and invite Jesus to the party.

> **Detox:** Make plans for next Sunday as a day to do something good, happily and open-heartedly. Choose something that can be done not because duty requires it, but just because the world is better when good people do good things!

Lord Jesus, lead me out into freedom – kindly and cautiously, thoughtfully and lovingly, joyfully and generously – as on that Sunday when life came leaping from the tomb. Amen.

Day 33

Risk Being Loved

There is a toy lamb that sits next to my bed. Its name is Larry and I have had it since the day I was born. It was a present from colleagues in the office in which my father worked at that time. It is so ragged that I am the only person who knows what species of animal it was once meant to be. It used to be covered with white, fluffy wool and it had a felt daisy in its mouth. However, every single tuft of wool has fallen out. It has been patched repeatedly. And I ate the daisy.

This is the one possession I would run into a burning house to rescue. I value it so highly because it provides an unbroken link back through every stage of my life to my birth. It has become a powerful symbol for me. You see, it has arrived at such a decrepit state because it has been loved so much!

My pitiful toy lamb speaks to me of the value of love far more realistically than any romantic film or Valentine's Day card. It reminds me that for some people love has meant years of unrelenting service, sometimes bringing rich rewards, but sometimes disappointment. For others it has meant devoted sacrifice, sometimes requited fondly, but sometimes thankless. Love is never wasted. It is only people who have loved until they are threadbare who begin to understand what it has cost God to love humankind with an unbroken devotion through every stage of its evolution from its birth.

In the New Testament, John tells us that anyone who has given or experienced love has begun to know God. Genuine love for another human is something that can only happen because of the existence of God. So is genuine love of a pet or a place or a piece of music. Even those who do not have a committed faith are not hopelessly adrift from God if they have known love, because every expression of love is an insight into the Lord. And he has proved it. Without a hint of market research to see whether there would be a worthwhile return on his investment, God sent his Son among men and women, giving himself to and for them in the most extreme way imaginable.

> Dear friends, let us love one another, for love comes from God. Everyone who loves has been born of God and knows God. Whoever does not love does not know God, because God is love. This is how God showed his love among us: He sent his one and only Son into the world that we might live through him. This is love: not that we loved God, but that he loved us.
>
> *1 John 4.7–10*

But now here is something unexpected to think about. It is easier to love than it is to be loved. Is that true? I think it is.

You can grit your teeth and force yourself to love someone. A stroppy teenager, a friendless neighbour, a senile relative, even a God who appears to have dealt with you cruelly – an effort of will can allow you to develop loving attitudes towards all of these. However, when you look down at a body that is past its prime and a spirit that has been bruised by the passing years, it is not always easy to accept that you are loved. It requires trust that the person expressing that love is telling the truth, has your needs and interests close to their heart, and will not let you down in the future. You cannot force yourself to accept any of those things; you can only abandon yourself to them in the hope that you will not be disappointed. It is hard enough to do that with a human into whose eyes you can look for signs of integrity; with an invisible God who refuses to be told what to do it can be even tougher. So come with me on a journey!

> Come with me from Lebanon, my bride,
> come with me from Lebanon.
> Descend from the crest of Amana,
> from the top of Senir, the summit of Hermon,
> from the lions' dens and the mountain haunts of the leopards.
> You have stolen my heart, my sister, my bride;
> you have stolen my heart with one glance of your eyes,
> with one jewel of your necklace.
> How delightful is your love!
>
> *Song of Songs 4.8–10*

Come to Edinburgh, which is my favourite city in the world. As you leave the city you reach a junction at which you can go either north or south. The road that goes north leads up into the craggy, bleak scenery of the Highlands. The road that goes south leads down towards the warm, green scenery of the Home Counties. I love those roads because both are spectacular in their own way.

> In the beginning God created humankind, not because he needed them,
> but so that he might have someone on whom to lavish his love.
>
> *Irenaeus, Bishop of Lyons, 130–202*

However, something in our experience makes us more at home in our Christianity with the north road. We expect our Christian journey to be one of dour duty and challenge. Lamentations! But the Bible tells us of a spiritual road that leads south as well. It is a road of detox your spiritual life contentment and generosity. It shows us God as a bridegroom devoted to the bride. It speaks to us with a language of love. A song of songs! 'Come with me my bride, come with me … You have stolen my heart … How delightful is your love! How pleasing!'

This is the language of God to his own people. It cuts through the guilt of the past; it cuts through the inadequacy of the present. Sometimes we are waiting to hear God communicate with us with the strict orders of a lord: 'You will do this because I am God and there is no other.' But it is possible that because of this we miss what he is actually saying to us, which is: 'Here is a day. It is full of beauty and potential because I made it. What would you like to do in it? Let's do that together!'

> Some day, after mastering the wind, the waves, the tides and gravity, we shall harness for God the energies of love. And then, for the second time in the history of the world, mankind will discover fire.
>
> *Pierre Teilhard de Chardin, scientist, 1881–1955*

Risk letting God love you. Grow old along with him, recognizing that the batters and bruises you are aware of, visible and invisible, have been acquired as part of a lifetime in which you have been deeply loved. Let go of the need to grind your way through an austere relationship with him, and attempt to hear him calling you into an embrace in which your aches can be tended to. 'Come with me my bride, come with me. How delightful!'

> **Detox:** Every time you see your name written down between now and the end of these 40 days, murmur to yourself, 'Someone loves that person.' Whenever you see it on a work document, letter or a rota, register that God knows your name and loves every wrinkled and imperfect inch of you. Each time, draw a little tick beside your name as a secret acknowledgement.

Dearest God, this is what I plan to do tomorrow and it would give me great joy if you were to come with me as my loving and faithful friend. Amen.

L is for Lifestyle

Ruth Valerio

So how can we live more responsibly? In this A-Z of lifestyle issues, Ruth Valerio highlights the main threats to people and our planet, God's beloved creation. She shows how, by making small changes to our everyday behavior, we can learn the secret of a life that is both fair and simple.

This book tells us how we can be faithful to God in the most mundane aspects of our everyday lives – about what it means to live as a Christian at the beginning of the twenty-first century.

IVP
£5.99
PB/1 8447 4025 0

L
is for
lifestyle

Christian living that
doesn't cost the earth

Ruth Valerio

U is for Unwanted Peoples

In this chapter we are going to meet four people: Kalim, Tamba, Amoru and Mandelena. Each one of them illustrates something of the situations faced by the world's most unwanted peoples: refugees.

Kalim came from a country ruled by a dictatorship. Ethnic conflicts and jealousies, provoked by the economic successes of the minority grouping, had led the majority group to use their political strength to gain dominance. Now the minority grouping was facing persecution and oppression. All the men were forced to do hard labour and family members were routinely murdered. One day Kalim saw one of his people being publicly beaten. Enraged by the injustice, he killed the perpetrator. When the dictator learned of this, he tried to kill Kalim. Kalim knew his only option was to flee, and he became a refugee in a nearby country.

Kalim is just one person among many facing similar difficulties. The refugee problem today is vast. Refugees are officially persons who are 'outside their country and cannot return owing to a well-founded fear of persecution because of their race, religion, nationality, political opinion or membership of a particular social group'. The latest figures from the Office of the United Nations High Commissioner for Refugees (UNHCR) estimates there to be 12 million refugees. Of these, Afghanistan is by far the largest country of origin, accounting for some 3.8 million refugees (a third of the refugee population). Asia hosts the largest overall population of refugees (5.8 million) while Africa hosts 3.3 million.

War and ethnic conflicts are two of the main factors that cause people to become refugees. The war in Kosovo brought this home forcibly to those of us living in the UK. Suddenly, refugees weren't people on the other side of the world. They looked like us, wore the same clothes as us and needed to be brought into our own country for help. The civil war that raged in Burundi, and culminated in the Rwandan genocide in 1994, caused over 500,000 refugees to camp along Tanzania's western border in the most awful conditions, lacking food, water, sanitation and proper shelter, and facing the rampant spread of diseases such as cholera. In Afghanistan in the mid-1990s, under the Mujahidin, there were 4.5 million Afghan refugees. Now there are still 3.5 million, mostly in Pakistan and Iran.

Tamba and his family were facing starvation. Throughout the region, the crops had failed and there was no food. In desperation, Tamba sent his sons to the neighbouring country, where, he had heard, there was plenty of food. Through an amazing series of events, his sons met one of the members of the Government, who personally gave them permission to bring the whole family into the country and granted them a special permit to stay there until the famine was over.

Families make up a large proportion of the refugee population. Indeed, around 45% of refugees are under the age of seventeen. Child refugees are extremely vulnerable. Tamba's sons, however, were exceptionally lucky. Liberia, for example, saw 60,000 people displaced in 2002 through cross-border conflict. Among these people are large numbers of children, who are at risk of family separation and are threatened by malnutrition and disease due to lack of access to food, water, sanitation and health services. Lack of income-earning opportunities forces many children into exploitative livelihoods such as joining fighting forces or prostitution, leaving them exposed to physical and sexual abuse.

Tamba and his family were forced to seek refuge elsewhere because of wide-scale crop failure. Incredibly, more people become refugees through environmental disasters than for any other reason; it is thought that there are at least 25 million environmental refugees today. Most of these are in Sub-Saharan Africa, the Indian subcontinent, China, Mexico and Central America, and it is estimated that numbers could double by 2010.

As a high-ranking army officer and the best friend of the son of the king, Amoru was able to enjoy all the luxuries of life. His situation fell apart, however, when his public popularity made him an enemy of the jealous king, who made three attempts at his life. Living in a country that gave him no access to the law, Amoru fled from the capital and became a fugitive in the surrounding hills.

Internally Displaced Persons (IDPs) leave their homes for the same reasons as refugees, but stay within their own country. There are currently an estimated 20–25 million IDPs and they are a subject of huge concern for the international community. Because they are still under the laws of the state from which they are fleeing they are especially vulnerable, 'falling between the cracks' of current humanitarian law and assistance. In a country in the throes of civil war, much of the basic services may have been destroyed; there may be no well-organized camps to receive IDPs, and fighting may make it difficult for aid organizations to provide relief. Thirteen million IDPs are children who have been forced to leave their homes because of armed conflict or violence. As a Save the Children report stated, 'Once displaced, many children spend at least six years away from their homes. Many live in fear, and are forced to move over and over again.'

Mandelena became a refugee ten years ago with her family. During those ten years she lost both her husband and two sons. Eventually she decided to return to the rural area in her homeland, accompanied only by her daughter-in-law, who insisted on coming with her, although she was from an ethnic grouping different from Mandelena's. On returning home, however, it was clear that the outlook was not good. Overwhelmed by poverty, Mandelena's daughter-in-law was forced to beg from the men in the fields. All alone, she laid herself open to sexual abuse.

Voluntarily returning home is generally seen as the best solution for displaced people, and the majority of refugees do indeed prefer to return home if able to do so safely. In 2001, 786,000 refugees went home. Conditions can be very hard, however, if basic infrastructures are still inadequate or ethnic tensions still simmer underneath.

Mandelena's story has a positive ending: she and her mother-in-law were able to return home and a relative still living in the area looked after them. The plight of the majority of women refugees, though, is not so good. Forty-eight per cent of refugees are female and they make up over half of the population in refugee camps. (40% of all people of concern to the UNHCR – including IDPs – live in camps.) Here they often face worse hardships than the men, rarely having a say in how a camp is run or where services such as water tanks or toilets are sited. While under the care of the UNHCR, three times as many boys as girls receive education.

All the people in our stories were able to find refuge or return home. As travel and communication improve, however, so the number of those seeking remote asylum is increasing. In response, countries are becoming increasingly unwilling to accept refugees. When an emergency situation leads to a massive influx of refugees, local people and communities can find their resources and environment stripped. This happened in the Karagwe district of Tanzania during the Rwandan crisis, when the local people's farms were taken over by huts for the refugees and their trees were destroyed for firewood. It is the poorer countries who bear the brunt of the global refugee problem, and the richer countries should recognize their responsibility to help.

Although the scale of the problem is peculiar to our time, refugees were known in the Bible. In fact, our four stories are all taken from biblical characters: Moses, Jacob and his sons, David, and Naomi and Ruth. We have already seen how the laws of the nation of Israel make particular reference to caring for those who are vulnerable, and this includes people from other countries – 'aliens'. Moses' story is especially instructive because it is through the events that he led that the foundation for Israel's laws of compassion was laid. As Deuteronomy 10:18–19 shows, Israel is to love those who are aliens because they once were aliens too, in Egypt. Because of God's great compassion for them, so they are to show compassion to others (see also Is. 58:7 and Ezek. 22:7).

A wonderful demonstration of this is seen in the early church. The Christian apologist Aristides gives this description:

> They walk in all humility and kindness, and falsehood is not found among them, and they love one another. They don't despise the widow and don't upset the orphan. He who has gives liberally to him who has not. If they see a stranger, they bring him under their roof and rejoice over him, as it were their own brother: for they call themselves brethren, not after the flesh, but after the spirit and in God ... And if there is among them a person who is poor and needy, and they have not an abundance of necessaries, they fast two or three days that they may supply the needy with their necessary food.

What an encouragement for us to live similarly!

Action point

• Sign up to receive the newsletters of some of the organizations involved in refugee issues: UNHCR or other overseas-development organizations that work with refugee communities abroad (e.g. Oxfam, Christian Aid, CAFOD, Save the Children, Church Mission Society, Médicins Sans Frontières). Allow your increased awareness to lead to other actions such as letter-writing or financial support.

Good contacts

Refugee Council: 3 Bondway, London SW8 1SJ; 020 7820 3145; <www.refugeecouncil.org.uk>. They also house *Student Action for Refugees* (STAR).

UNHCR (UK): 21st Floor, Millbank Tower, 21–24 Millbank, London SW1P 4QP; 020 7932 019; <u>www.ukforunhcr.org</u> >

Refugees Studies Centre: Queen Elizabeth House, University of Oxford, 21 St Giles, Oxford OX1 3LA; 01865 270722; <www.qeh.ox.ac.uk/rsc>

Growing Together.
A Guide for Couples Getting Married

Rev Andrew Body

So you've decided to get married ... the dress, flowers, reception and a million other things are organized. But have you looked further ahead to the day after the wedding, when suddenly there's nothing left to plan, and it's just the two of you again? *Growing Together* is a practical guide that will help you to develop a shared understanding of your future together through exploring your dreams and expectations of married life and by high-lighting some of the key issues that being married can raise.

Church House Publishing
£6.99
PB / 0 7151.4049 3

Growing together

a guide
for couples
getting married

Andrew Body

Published By Church House Publishing,
Church House, Great Smith Street, London, SW1P 3NZ

Commitment

> ... to have and to hold
> from this day forward;
> for better, for worse,
> for richer, for poorer,
> in sickness and in health,
> to love and to cherish,
> till death us do part.
>
> *(The Vows, The Marriage Service, p. 108)*

Martina Navratilova, the tennis player, once said 'Do you know the difference between involvement and commitment? Think of ham and eggs. The chicken is involved. The pig is committed.' That's a good image to run with. There are plenty of relationships that are 'egg', and don't develop into 'ham'. Real commitment means no barriers, no holds barred, no reservations. It's a strange thing in the wedding service that the example offered to a couple is not a great pair of lovers of the past, but the example of a bachelor – Jesus Christ. But his love for his friends was utterly without reservation. He could easily have said, when it became apparent what might happen to him 'I love you, but . . .' But his love went as far as it could possibly go. Inappropriate as it might be for a Jew, his love was 'ham' not 'egg'.

Some people living together outside marriage have that ideal kind of total commitment. But, for many, it is conditional commitment, a provisional arrangement, providing everything continues to be good for both of them. At least, that seems to be the evidence of the many couples who say that they see marriage as a further stage of their relationship, when they will be totally committed to a lifelong partnership.

There may be something about our time in history that makes such an absolute commitment hard. Young people don't join organizations like Scouts and Guides as they used to but, on the other hand, are often eager to commit to 'causes' like environmental groups. Organizations often say that they can get volunteers who are prepared to be on standby, but find it harder to get people to promise to help regularly as a matter of priority. People opt in and out of all sorts of things. In relationship terms, that may lead to 'playing the field'. People book for evening classes, and then drop out. Airlines have to overbook in order to ensure their planes are full, because they know some people who have booked will not turn up. To say words that mean total, unambiguous commitment is against the trend. Independence is a goal many are struggling to achieve and enjoy, and that can make it hard to commit to someone else.

> 'Most people don't have a conscious "shopping list" when they are looking for a partner.'

But what comes from commitment is a sense of well-being and security. 'My beloved is mine, and I am his' as it says in the wonderfully erotic Song of Solomon – a book in the Bible. In days past in the UK, the belonging was horribly unequal. The wife belonged to the husband, but not vice versa. Now, as a beginning to the marriage service says, 'In marriage husband and wife belong to one another.' Each is the most precious thing the other has. To know we come first, second and last in someone else's life is the most affirming thing that can happen to us. To love and be loved makes people blossom, like a flower opening.

Where are you coming from?

A television documentary traced the stories of some children who were bought the most amazing presents, and had extraordinary amounts of money spent on them. They were not particularly happy children. One of them, faced with a parent saying that she went out to work just so she could buy all these things, said that she would prefer just to have her mum's time and attention. We all want to be needed, not tolerated. We all want to be valued, not bought. Most parents do give themselves in huge measure to their children. But often children don't realize all that their parents give up for them until they are parents themselves.

It would be good to think through all the things that made you feel secure as a child, the things that made you feel loved, the things that made you feel that you belonged. By the same token, think of the things that made you feel less secure, and what effect that had on you.

People who come from homes where there has been little sense of commitment may find it harder to feel such security in adult life – but will almost certainly crave it deeply. Ron was such a young man. He had learned he could never rely on people. His parents were more concerned for their own interests than for anything they might do as a family. His father was a workaholic, and his mother busy with a whirl of social activities. He was left with a succession of babysitters. As he grew older, he realized they were simply paid to look after him, and had no interest in him as a person. In fact, he began to wonder if he was worth knowing. He didn't seem to matter very much to anyone.

Paula and Graham had lived together for over seven years before they decided to get married. The vicar asked why they wanted marriage after such a long time. Their reply was both warming and sad at the same time. 'It's taken us all this time to feel we could risk it. We have each seen both our parents divorced twice – six divorces in all. Marriage always seemed to spell gloom and disaster. It's only after being really happy for as long as this that we can dare put the label round our necks.'

Things to talk about and share

- What were the things the people who brought you up committed to?
  - You?
  - Work?
  - Money?
  - Pleasure?
- How did that show in practical ways?
- How much were you expected to 'see things through'?
- Did people around you in your childhood keep their promises?
- What makes you feel secure, or insecure?
- Have those things any connection with things that have happened to you?

In adult life we learn the hard way that we cannot trust everyone. In different ways, people sometimes let us down. They promise something but don't keep the promise. We think we can rely on them, but find that we were wrong. The more we are let down, the harder it is to trust someone else. That will be especially true of broken relationships that meant a lot to us. We bring those hurts into new relationships we make, in the hope of finding healing and new hope.

Where are you now?

Something remarkable has happened in your life. You probably wouldn't be reading this book unless you were on the verge of getting married. So someone has so deeply affected you that you feel able to say – 'Yes, this is the person I want to be with for the rest of my life.' No doubt you could analyse some of the reasons why they fit your bill – but most people don't have a conscious 'shopping list' when they are looking for a partner. In fact, most people are not consciously looking for a partner at all when they fall in love. It might be worth telling each other some of the reasons that you have confidence that this is the right thing to do. If you can't think of any, then maybe you have some serious thinking to do. One couple called off their wedding after they were asked why they had chosen each other. The message came – 'I couldn't think of any good reason last night to marry him, and I still can't, so we're calling it off.' People are generally not very good at telling people the positive things about why they value each other. In the old marriage service, when the ring was given, the man said 'with my body I thee worship'. Worship really means 'worth-ship'. That is why saying that you love each other matters so much. Taking stock of the things you value about each other simply adds to that. It is telling the other what he or she is worth to you.

Trust is part and parcel of commitment. It is easily lost, and only regained with great difficulty. So how much you trust each other is central. Brian and Joanna were talking about their financial arrangements. They didn't have a joint account because 'we could never trust each other enough' – not a very good omen for their marriage. If you can't trust someone with your money, can you trust them with your future? If people cannot trust each other, they are likely to be very possessive and suspicious. If people feel that is what is happening, they start to get anxious, and maybe even deceitful, in order not to feel trapped. Those are slippery slopes to be on. Jill's husband was intensely jealous, partly because he didn't think very highly of himself, knew that she was very pretty, and assumed that she would easily be enticed away by someone 'better'. She felt she had no freedom, because he demanded to know where she was all the time, and so began to find ways of escaping to have time with her female friends. Nothing she was doing could have been a cause of worry for him, but he was driving her away from him by the way he was treating her.

If you are already living together, think about what differences getting married may make. If you cannot imagine that it will make any difference to your excellent relationship, then why are you doing it? It seems an expensive way of achieving nothing. If, on the other hand, you think it will make a difference, what will that difference

Things to talk about and share

- What do you value about each other?
- How do your strengths and weaknesses complement each other?
- Would you ever want to 'check up' on each other? Why?
- Is it OK to have any secrets?
- What difference will getting married make to you?

be? Why does that matter to you, and what does it say about the way your relationship has already developed?

Where are you going?

The vows at the beginning of this chapter have their feet firmly on the ground. They talk about better and worse, richer and poorer, sickness and health. If you are a very unusual couple, you might stand there on your wedding day and say 'It's all going to be worse, poorer and sick.' But it is far more likely that you will be thinking it is all going to be better, richer and healthier! But the words say both. There is nothing dewy-eyed and romantic about them – they are tough words about real commitment.

Ted and Liz were a wonderful young couple. He was a fine sportsman. She was a bubbly personality who made everyone smile. But, six months into their wedding, she was taken seriously ill with a disease that amongst other things confined her to a wheelchair. Nothing in their marriage was like the dreams on their wedding day. Ted nursed her and cared for her for fifteen years. The week she died, he said 'I couldn't have had a happier marriage.' From the outside, anyone would have said that was nonsense. But he meant it. They were totally committed to each other, and they still had each other. That was enough for them.

Most people will have some ill health to cope with. Most people will have some poorer times, particularly if they have a family. There may be other things, like redundancies or family problems, that are the shadow side of those vows. But those words say that this is not a

Things to talk about and share

Have you had any health issues to face together yet?

- Can you imagine caring for your partner if they became dependent on you in some way?
- One of the prayers in the *Common Worship* marriage service says 'May they reach old age in the company of friends'.[1] How does that make you feel?
- Have you made a will? Will you be doing so when you get married?
- What inscription would you like on your gravestone?

'fair weather' relationship – it is an unconditional, come-what-may commitment to each other.

People spend fortunes trying to maintain their youth. There is nothing wrong in staying fit and healthy – far from it. But when the motivation is fear that, if I put on weight, or lose my hair, or in some other way become less superficially attractive, then my other half will lose interest in me, then that is a sign that commitment and trust are issues we need to face up to. The Beatles' song 'Will you still need me … when I am 64?' poses a real question.

The commitment is for life – 'till death us do part'. We hope that is a long time off. Share the confidence of William and Maureen, who, marrying when they were in their seventies and fifties respectively, promised a case of champagne to anyone who produced the invitation and the order of service at their silver wedding. But death is part of the reality of life. Talking about it, so that, for example, you know each other's wishes about burial or cremation, is healthy, not morbid. Making a will is a sensible and loving thing to do. If you have talked about your feelings about death, you are also ensuring that you are the best possible help to each other when either of you is bereaved as the years go by. People look to their partner more than to anyone else to be there for them at times like that, and can be dreadfully let down if their needs are not met.

Old age begins
And middle age ends
The day your descendants
Outnumber your friends.

(*Ogden Nash, 'Crossing the border'*)

Brave Enough to Follow

Stuart Briscoe

Simon Peter was an ordinary Galilean fisherman. Yet Jesus saw something in this bold
tradesman. In Peter, Christ was the opportunity
to build His church. What does he see in you?
The Master knew that Peter would do much
more with his life than just catch dinner for his
countrymen – he would courageously lead the
church and its efforts to share the gospel across
the globe. Looking closely at the metamorphosis of Peter, this book and Bible study from
Stuart Briscoe encourages us to discover our
specific place in the kingdom.

NavPress
£7.99
PB / 1 5768.3592 8

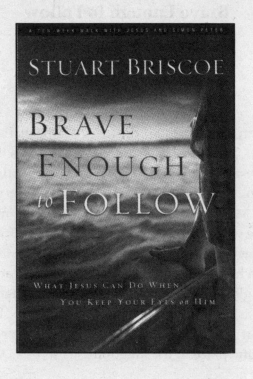

A TEN-WEEK WALK WITH JESUS AND SIMON PETER

STUART BRISCOE

BRAVE
ENOUGH
to FOLLOW

WHAT JESUS CAN DO WHEN
YOU KEEP YOUR EYES ON HIM

Copyright © 2004 by Stuart Briscoe.

Published by NavPress,
PO Box 35001, Colorado Springs, CO 80935

Unschooled, Ordinary Men

When they saw the courage of Peter and John and realized that they
were unschooled, ordinary men, they were astonished and they took
note that these men had been with Jesus.

ACTS 4:13

Near the Temple in Jerusalem, the Great Sanhedrin was in session. As
the high court of Israel, this group of formidable politicians was
responsible for judging the civic and religious issues of the day on
the basis of Jewish law. Simon Peter and John stood before a semi-
circle of seventy inquisitors, facing open hostility. The members of
the Sanhedrin were infuriated that Peter and John had performed a
spectacular miracle, healing a crippled man, and had been preaching
a powerful message to the crowds about Jesus rising from the dead.
These wretched followers of Jesus were becoming more and more credible.
Thousands were being persuaded. It was a major threat to the
Sanhedrin's power.

The interrogation began. Referring to the miraculous healing of
the cripple, members of the Sanhedrin asked imperiously, "By what
power or what name did you do this?" After a respectful acknow-
ledgment of the prestigious company before whom he was standing,
Peter made a comment dripping with irony. "If we are being called to
account today for an act of kindness ..." In other words, *if we are being
charged with the heinous crime of meeting a need, being generous and*

caring ... Then Peter went on to give a bold, uncompromising answer to their question. "It is by the name of Jesus Christ of Nazareth, whom you crucified but whom God raised from the dead." There it was – a direct indictment. Discretion might have required that Peter be more respectful. After all, these men could eliminate him at any moment. But Peter was in no mood for playing it safe. He wanted this distinguished body to know they were complicit in the murder of an innocent man. More than that – this man was none other than the Messiah.

The members of the Sanhedrin "couldn't take their eyes off them – Peter and John standing there so confident, so sure of themselves! Their fascination deepened when they realized these two were laymen with no training in Scripture or formal education" (Acts 4:13, MSG). No doubt these powerful men were taken aback that Peter and John completely flouted traditional Sanhedrin protocol, which demanded that persons brought before them should be dressed in mourning and appear humble in attitude. Peter was an unvarnished, straight-shooting rugged fisherman, unabashed and unashamed – and not exactly the picture of humility.

How could such a man – this nobody out of nowhere – take such a bold stance? Peter had deserted his Teacher at the time of his crucifixion – evidence of cowardice and an indictment on the credibility of Jesus himself. Yet, now Peter stood in the presence of the most powerful religious men in the land, and he was speaking with power, conviction, and a reckless disregard for his own well-being. The rulers, elders, and teachers of the law "were astonished."

It dawned on the members of the Sanhedrin, "these men had been with Jesus." That must have been the source of their transformation. John and Peter were desperately ordinary, but Jesus had made them capable of extraordinary feats. Yes, they had followed Jesus alright. And He had rubbed off on them, big time.

Simon Peter went on to become one of the greatest leaders the church has ever known, but if you had seen where he came from, you wouldn't have believed it possible. He was not known to be the most courageous of men. He was a humble fisherman, working with his hands, supporting his family, and enjoying the camaraderie of his family and good friends, fellow fisherman. His three years with Jesus would be marked by notable failures, particularly in the area of courage. Simply put, Peter may not have been brave enough to be the leader he was destined to become. But Jesus knew that Peter was brave enough to follow him – and that was all that mattered.

We often fall under the misconception that for God to do great work through us, we need to have "the makings" of greatness – a certain boldness, the guts to get up in front of people and take charge. But (as is often the case when we study God's way of doing things the reality is upside down from what we think it should be. We don't have to have the courage to lead; we just need to be brave enough to follow. When we follow him, Christ will make us into what He intends for us to be.

The history of great men in the Bible reveals that Simon Peter was just one in a long line of very unlikely leaders, chosen by God to play a pivotal role in bringing people to his kingdom. Abraham, Moses, David, Joseph – all were improbable choices for one reason or another. Some exhibited classic bravery as leaders; others did not. But they all had one major feature in common: They would commit to following the Lord their God. Soon, another unlikely disciple would join the scene – Saul of Tarsus, whose commitment to "following" transformed him into the great apostle Paul.

Why does Jesus choose to do his work through such seemingly unlikely people?

When the Sanhedrin responded to Peter's testimony by saying, "these men had been with Jesus," they were playing right into God's hand. By choosing to work through ordinary people – with obvious flaws and frailties – God ensures that when something powerful happens, *He alone will get the glory*. God's power always shines through, but it is especially apparent to others when a formerly gutless person appears suddenly bold. The Sanhedrin, who rejected Jesus, were unwittingly glorifying him by acknowledging him as the source of surprising, transforming power.

In fact, it seems the more powerless the leader, the more glory God receives. And He delights in this! Remember Gideon? A hesitant and fearful man, God nevertheless chose him to lead Israel in defeating the formidable Midianites, who dominated Israel at the time. Not only did God choose Gideon, He gave Gideon an army of only three hundred men to conquer the Midianite army of 32,000. Gideon seemed like the absolute wrong choice for the job – he was so fearful that he kept demanding miraculous proof that God was with him. But the key to understanding this choice is the fact that, once Gideon was clear *Who* was leading, he was able to muster the courage to obey. He never thought of himself as a leader. He simply had to follow. God made it clear that his decision to handle the Midianites in this manner was so that, when the Israelites were triumphant, He and He alone would get the glory.

Jeremiah 9:23 says, "Let not the wise man boast of his wisdom or the strong man boast of his strength or the rich man boast of his riches, but let him who boasts, boast about this: that he understands and knows me, that I am the LORD." In other words, if God always chose the obvious leaders to do his work, people would take all the glory for themselves. But if we are clearly weak and flawed, yet we have a part in establishing his kingdom, we cannot boast about ourselves but must instead boast that we know the Lord. God does great things through the not-so-brave among us, so the world can see that the glory is his and his alone. Paul reiterates this idea in I Corinthians 1:26–31, where he talks about how God chose the foolish, weak, and lowly among us to do his work, "so that no one may boast before him" (verse 29).

Right about now you may be wondering, *What does all this have to do with me?* Well you, my friend, just might have been thinking you'll never be significant in God's kingdom. I want you to know that all it takes for you to become everything that God intends for you is a willingness – yes, the bravery – to follow him. Jesus knows you. He has identified you in the lineup. He has called you to be part of his kingdom, and the role you will play, no matter how apparently small, is a crucial part of his vast plan for all of us.

Jesus knows your hidden potential. Gideon had an invisible potential to be a great warrior. Moses had the unknown potential to steer thousands of pilgrims across a barren desert. Simon Peter had an unseen potential for powerful evangelism. You may have been given a glimpse of your own potential, or you may be completely in the dark. Either way, Jesus knows your potential, and if you follow him, He will transform you – and you will glorify him.

But how does Jesus transform someone from ordinary to significant? How does God take that unseen potential He plants in all of us and develop it so that we reflect his image to the world?

Jesus transforms each of us, not when we summon up the courage to be leaders, but when we commit to following him. He invites us to become deeply acquainted with him. When we seek him, He gives us glimpses of himself and glimpses of our potential. He walks with us. He patiently draws out our courage. He encourages us, directs us, and challenges us. He asks questions and gives answers. He tests us and allows us to test him. Eventually our lives are transformed from mediocrity to maturity, and we become what He intended for us all along.

For three years Peter walked with Jesus, ate with him, and even climbed mountains with him. Peter's journey of transformation is well documented in the four Gospels. We are privy to the conversations, the flashes of triumph, and the moments of utter despair. We see Peter questioning Jesus, confronting him, praising him, and rejecting him. As I studied Peter's relationship with Jesus, I was amazed. Here, right in front of our eyes, is a blueprint for what Jesus can do when we keep our eyes on him. (Not to mention what happens in the moments we take our eyes *off* him! In the story of Peter's walk with Jesus, we see all the components of a life-changing journey of transformation.

This amazing thought led me to look even more closely at the steps Peter took to follow Jesus. In the midst of my study of the biblical text, it came to me that we might best understand Peter's metamorphosis – and by extension, our own – if I were to recreate his story in narrative form, telling it in an informal style, at times almost like a novel. Therefore you will note that this book interweaves the gospel story with touches of (I hope) sanctified imagination and a dash of humor. There are times when I'll speculate about the disciple's frame of mind or emotional response to a situation – things that aren't overtly stated in Scripture, but that we can legitimately surmise. By attempting to place ourselves in Peter's circumstances and imagining his motives, thoughts, and feelings, perhaps we'll be closer to our goal of comprehending what happens when a real-life person like Simon Peter commits to following the Master.

At the top of each chapter, I've listed the Scriptures from which I've drawn the subsequent material. You may want to read these verses in your Bible to orient yourself to the material being discussed, but it's not necessary to your understanding. Each chapter closes with a section that draws some connections between Peter's journey and our own (Brave Enough to Think About It), with some suggestions for discussion and action (Brave Enough for Action).

I will attempt to trace the ups and downs, the ins and outs of Peter's three eventful years with Jesus. We'll follow him and see how his experience reflects our own. From his mistakes we'll learn what not to do; from his triumphs we'll be challenged to identify his secrets of success and draw from the same resources made available to him. By God's grace we'll learn the lessons he learned. By applying what we learn from Peter and submitting to the journey ourselves, we will each become exactly the people God intends us to be. Most importantly, the reason for the journey – the reason it matters that we follow Christ – is that God will be glorified. Our very lives will become a testament to his greatness. People will look at us and realize, "this person has been with Jesus."

I've been enriched and changed through this journey – and I hope you will be, too.

It's All About Potential

JOHN 1:29-42
LUKE 4:31--5:11

Following one of his breathtaking performances, the world renowned pianist Ignace Paderewski was told by an admirer, "Maestro, you are a genius." He replied, "Genius? Perhaps. But before I was a genius, I was a drudge." He was referring to the many years spent in endless hours of practice, unnoticed and unheralded. He wanted to make clear that however much his talent appeared to be inborn, it nevertheless took a great deal of work to develop.

In our culture, we have the phenomenon of the "overnight sensation." Sports legends, movie stars, and popular music artists burst upon the scene out of nowhere. We are ignorant of the years they spent honing their skills, paying their dues, and waiting tables.

Before Peter strode center stage on the floor of the Sanhedrin chamber, he had spent his life in the relative obscurity of a Galilean fishing village. But it was his brief, life-transforming time in the company of the Master – paying his dues – that prepared him for that moment in the spotlight.

It all started one day in the deserts of Judea, close by the Jordan River. Peter, whose name at the time was Simon, was going about his business as a fisherman on the Sea of Galilee. His brother Andrew – his fishing partner – had apparently been missing in action for a few days. Suddenly, Andrew appeared and out of the blue told Simon, "We've found him! We've found the Messiah."

What? Simon might have wondered for a moment if his brother had spent a little too much time in the wine cellar. But I'm sure

Andrew went on to explain all that had happened in the previous few days. He had been following a mysterious prophet called John the Baptist, who was creating a stir down by the river. Born into a priestly family John had exchanged the prestigious life of a priest for the hazardous calling of a prophet. (It was hazardous because the people had a nasty habit of expressing disapproval by stoning the prophets) John had embraced a ministry of hard-hitting, challenging, prophetic preaching. His pulpit was a barren hillside, his sanctuary a desert wasteland. But his message was loud and clear: "The kingdom we've all been talking about is about to burst upon us. The Promised One we've heard about from our earliest days is about to appear. It's time to get ready – and that means a total change of heart. It's repentance time. Time to humble yourselves in public and confess that your lives need cleansing and forgiving. Time to decide whom you will serve."

This was radical preaching. Amazingly, the people flocked to hear John the Baptist even though he was rude and unkempt. People of social standing were not usually referred to as a "generation of vipers," but this is precisely what he called some of them.

An unknown carpenter named Jesus had joined the crowds and moved among them unrecognized. One day Jesus approached and requested baptism by John. At first declining, John finally agreed to baptize Jesus, and a remarkable thing happened. The Father's voice from heaven boomed out a powerful statement of approval of Jesus. There was a stirring in the heavens and the invisible Spirit of God assumed the form of a dove, resting intentionally upon Jesus, pointing out that Jesus was indeed none other than the Son of God.

Andrew and an unnamed friend were somewhere in the crowd, listening to John's preaching. They were there when John pointed to Jesus and proclaimed the stunning news, "This is the Lamb of God who takes away the sin of the world." Everybody within the sound of John's voice understood what this meant. The sacrificial system of the time required a lamb to be offered as a substitutionary sacrifice on the Day of Atonement. To be told that there was a man in their midst who would become a sacrificial substitute for the sin of the world – that was mind-boggling.

Andrew and his friend heard, and they badly wanted to believe. They promptly followed Jesus, who invited them to where He was staying. It was late afternoon, but they spent time together, and during those minutes or hours – who knows? – something profound happened. The men became convinced beyond a doubt that Jesus was indeed the Messiah, the Lamb who would take away their sin.

So Andrew rushed to tell his brother Simon. The news must have resonated with Simon, because the two brothers immediately took off looking for Jesus. They finally approached him, only to be stopped in their tracks. As Jesus looked at Simon He said, "You are Simon, son of John. You will be called Cephas." The Greek equivalent of Cephas is *Petros*, which in English becomes "Peter." And the meaning of all those names is "Rock." So without introduction or preamble, without ever having laid eyes on Simon before, Jesus got right down to business and said in effect, "I know who you are, and I know what you're going to become. You're going to be a rock."

Notice how Jesus phrased his declaration: "You *are* Simon ... you *will be* Cephas." Present tense, future tense. What is Jesus seeing in this man Simon? Potential. *You are one thing now, but you will be something else in the future*.

This encounter did not happen by accident. It was God at work, a divine appointment. It's important to recognize this because we need to be aware that God has his own perspective on our lives. He is looking at us, and He knows us in a way that no one else can know. Our friends and family and even our enemies have opinions about us, but the only accurate perception is God's. We need to be brought into the position where we're exposed to the divine perspective. Peter came face-to-face with the divine perspective on his life on the day that he met Jesus. But what exactly was it?

When Jesus lived in Palestine, names usually reflected the parents' hopes and aspirations for their children. When a new name was given, it usually spoke of an unmistakable change in character or direction. In Simon's case, when Jesus gave him a new name, it meant that Jesus had something special in mind for the fisherman. This man would become a rock in the plan of God for humanity.

It's interesting that we don't know how Simon reacted to his remarkable introduction to Jesus. He must have wondered what in the world this guy had in mind for him. But there is no doubt that when Jesus looked carefully at Simon, He saw right into the soul of the man and recognized something that others might never have noticed. He saw Simon's potential.

It takes a trained eye to see what others cannot see. It took a Michelangelo to look at a spoiled block of marble, on which others had worked to no avail, and "see" his famous statue, *David*. What others saw as a crude block of stone at worst, or an unmanageable project at best, Michelangelo envisioned as a figure of a young boy about to confront a giant. The fourteen-feet high masterpiece stands to this day in Florence, Italy, as a testimonial to the artist's skill and his eye for potential.

John tells us in his gospel that Jesus "did not need man's testimony about man, for he knew what was in a man" (John 2:25). But what did Jesus see in Simon that led him to rename him Peter – Rock? He saw exactly what Simon could become in his hands. In addition, He knew what it would take to get him from where he was to where he needed to be. There was a possibility, a potential for all manner of things to happen in Simon Peter's life. This is true of us all.

Let's think about the sheer potential wrapped up in any individual life. Look at an acorn. It's packed with potential. It is just a little nut, but if you put it in the right place, under the right circumstances, and hang around long enough, it can become an oak tree. We, even more than an acorn, are packed with potential. Of course, this potential can take different shapes and different forms. There are four key words that explain the way God views the potential in human beings: creation, fall, redemption, and glory.

My Story

Selwyn Hughes

This is an autobiography welcomed by all, inspirational and uplifting whilst being open and honest, this is an enthralling story of a life devoted to revival that traces Selwyn's story from his roots in Wales, through his conversion to his personal battle with cancer. A faith building read.

CWR
£9.99
PB/1 8534.5296 3

SELWYN
HUGHES

My Story

From Welsh mining village to worldwide ministry

4. The Most Important Decision of My Life

I have no hesitation in saying that the greatest and most momentous decision I have ever made in my life was the decision to become a follower of Jesus Christ. Prior to my conversion I had always felt, to some degree at least, that there was a longing within my heart to know God in the way my parents seemed to know Him, but I was afraid to pursue it in case I might be disappointed. Many times God had tapped at the window-pane of my soul. Like times just before bedtime when I would kneel to pray – something I had been taught as a child – and the feeling would come over me that I needed to take spiritual realities more seriously. Even in my most rebellious times, I would never slip under the blankets without saying a prayer. It was a simple and short prayer recited very quickly:

If I should die before I wake
I pray the Lord my soul to take. Amen.

Sometimes I would think to myself, 'What would happen if I died? Would my parents' faith be enough to save me?' I think, however, that the kind of person I was prior to my conversion needed more than tapping on the window-pane of my soul – the glass needed breaking! I needed God to confront me, wake me up, wrestle me to the ground, so to speak, pin me there and bring home to me as strongly as possible my need to open up my life to Jesus Christ.

Just before my sixteenth birthday, God began to move in my life in a very powerful way. It began one weeknight early in 1944, when I was making my way to the local dance hall. It was about 8pm and the route to the hall was past the local mission hall where they were holding their weekly prayer meeting. As I walked through the blacked-out streets I heard a familiar voice and was instantly stopped in my tracks. It was the voice of my father, who was obviously taking part in the prayer meeting. I stopped and listened as he prayed for me, pleading with God for my salvation.

I had heard my father pray many times at home and in church, but never with such passion as this. His voice took on a tone and power that penetrated deep into my heart. I was rooted to the spot. What should I do? Something inside me wanted to rush into the prayer meeting in response to this and say that I wanted to be saved. Or should I wait to see if this feeling would pass off? I waited – and it passed. I went to the dance that night but there seemed to be something odd about the whole place. The lights appeared less bright than usual; there was something missing in the music; the whole atmosphere of the place seemed as if it had been changed. God was calling me and I was beginning to see things from a new perspective.

The weeks that followed were dificult. The more I threw myself into the pleasures of the flesh, the less satisfying they were to my soul. I turned from one to the other – smoking, gambling, rugby, football – but for some reason they seemed not to thrill me as much as they once did.

For weeks I fought against the strivings of the Holy Spirit. I would lay awake at night and wonder what was happening to me. Things came to a head on a stormy Sunday night in February 1944. I went to church with my parents, but with so much rain pouring down, no one expected the guest preacher to turn up. The speaker booked for that occasion was a man who lived about six miles away and in order to get to us meant a tortuous bicycle ride over the mountain. As the service began I was, quite frankly, a little disappointed to see him walk in. It meant the service would be longer than usual, with my uncle not being the preacher. Now it meant we would be in church for two hours at least.

The back seat was always reserved for the young people. Seated next to me was a close childhood friend, Ronald Lewis. Ronald was a son of one of the elders of the church and though we were close he was not part of the gang I usually went around with. He was not a Christian, but there was no evidence of the rebellion in him that characterised my own life.

There was something that night about the whole service that was different. I found myself being strangely drawn to what the preacher was saying. There was nothing dynamic about him. He was an ordinary person, not much to look at. I had heard him a few times before, but now his words seemed to have some powerful conviction that reached deep into my soul. His face was irradiated with a strange light. His words seemed to be barbed, reaching deep into my soul. I especially remember these words: 'This is the night when God wants to draw you to Himself. Come to Jesus, who will save you from your sin, live in you and give you the power to be able to serve Him.' I had heard these or similar words many times from that pulpit, but that night they seemed to take hold of me with a power I had never known before.

'What is happening to me?' I thought to myself. The tears were coming into my eyes. I didn't cry often – especially in church. I felt the strong defences I had built against the Spirit were breaking down. My heart was crumbling. The preacher asked if there were any there who would walk to the front and commit themselves to Jesus Christ.

I was the first to move. The church was quite small and it took perhaps ten seconds to move from the back of the church to the front, but that night it seemed like a mile long. It was the most wonderful walk of my life. As I moved toward the front my pastor, who had been sitting on the platform with the preacher, quickly came down to greet me. The same arms that had held me and prayed the prayer of dedication so many years ago were thrown around me to embrace me.

I was conscious that others had come to the front also. My friend Ronald Lewis was there and so was his sister Mary, together with several other young men who had been sitting with me in the back seat. Altogether there were about ten of us who were converted that night. My uncle sat with me and read me these words from the Bible: 'Call to me, and I will answer you, and show you great and mighty things, which you do not know' (Jer. 33:3).

I sobbed out my heart as I knelt at the front seat of the church that evening and asked God to forgive my sins. I received the assurance that Christ was mine, that my sins were forgiven and I was saved. There was no doing the usual Sunday night thing afterwards – walking over the mountain to Rhymney and chatting up the girls. I went home, where my parents rejoiced with me and told me how glad they were for the step I had taken. That night I fell asleep wondering where it would all take me. I knew there were things I must break with – lying, cheating, stealing and so on. What would happen now? How was I going to tell my workmates and friends? I knew what they thought about Christians.

That morning, as I made my way to the railway station at about 6:30 to take the train to Dowlais, my mind was made up. The cigarettes would have to go. Nothing was said in our church about the evils of tobacco, yet I knew for me it was wrong. There were other habits I knew would have to go also – swearing, for example. I do not say this proudly but I have never used a swear word from the day of my conversion to this.

The train took about 20 minutes to puff its way up the steep incline to the steel town of Dowlais. In those minutes I made the discovery that when someone gives their life to Jesus Christ, He not only changes them but resides in them. 'To them gave He power to become the sons of God,' says the apostle John in the first chapter of his Gospel. The boys took out their cigarettes as usual, but I didn't. 'You're not smoking?' 'No,' I said. 'Last night I gave my life to Jesus

Christ and I don't think that is what I should now do.' There was an awkward silence. One of the young men tried to argue about religion but I sat and prayed that God would help me not to fail Him in any way. I proceeded to tell my friends just what had happened the night before, and as I gave my first stammering testimony to Jesus Christ I felt His presence and power wonderfully supporting me.

I needn't have worried about telling the men and boys in the engineering shop about my conversion. When I arrived some of the boys who had been on the train with me had gone ahead to tell everyone that I had become a Christian. When I opened the door of the engineering shop I found the place buzzing with excitement. One of the older men patted me on the back and said, 'Good morning, preacher. Are we going to have a sermon today?' It was all good-natured fun and I felt no animosity in what he said. Another man said, 'I'll give you a month.' Yet another commented, 'I'll give you a week!' I think I finally convinced them I had become a Christian when I said I would no longer be running the football pool. The baiting and teasing continued throughout the day, but though it was difficult for me to handle I did not feel their comments were malicious.

As the days passed and they saw I was serious, their respect for me grew, until eventually all came to accept the fact that I had become a Christian and I intended to run my life differently. The teasing stopped and there were times when some of the men would ask me to include them in my prayers as they struggled with various difficulties in their lives. In those early days of my conversion I remember ending all my prayer times with this phrase: 'Lord, You have made a world of difference to me; grant that I might make some difference to the world.'

My first weeks as a Christian were ones of joyous discoveries. Anyone who has not experienced the dramatic change of life and mind and the spiritual release that Christ brings to the repentant sinner can never understand the welling up of wonderful gratitude that is in the heart. The greatest news of all is that the blood of Jesus

Christ, God's Son, cleanses from all sin. I had heard good news. I walked the streets in fellowship with my unseen Friend. I knew now that Jesus Christ was alive, not because others had told me, but because He lived within my heart. The Bible, it seemed, was set to music. Carried on the crest of a boundless enthusiasm, I would burst spontaneously into song. I thirsted to know more of the Word of God and read my Bible at every opportunity. I was ready for every new discovery, every new challenge that would beckon to me on the Christian highway.

My appetite for spiritual things was so intense that the more I had of God and His Word the more I wanted. I was in church every night of the week. When there was nothing on in my own church I went to one in a nearby town or village. There was always something special on at weekends somewhere – a convention, a youth rally, a special speaker – so I was never at a loss to find food for the ever-increasing appetite of my soul.

A few weeks after my conversion I was baptised by total immersion, along with the others who had been converted on the same night as myself. The baptismal pool was outside the church building, which meant the public could see what was going on. The baptism was on a bitterly cold March day, but crowds sat on the mountainside opposite the church watching. Never shall I forget the thrill, before entering the baptismal pool, of telling everyone what Jesus Christ had done for me.

After baptism in water I was told about another baptism – the baptism of the Spirit. This was most puzzling to me as I thought I had already received the Holy Spirit at my conversion. My pastor explained that although that was so there was another operation of the Spirit for the impartation of power that I needed to seek God for.

Despite my puzzlement, I acted on my pastor's advice and attended a special service being held the following weekend 20 miles away in the town of Brynmawr for those wanting to be baptised in the Spirit. There, he told me, a young evangelist by the name of Handel Price would be speaking on this subject and praying for those who had not yet received this experience. On the Saturday evening I made my way to the small but crowded church. There were the usual preliminaries – chorus singing, reading of the Scriptures and so on – and then the speaker got up and announced his theme: 'Did you receive the Holy Spirit when you believed?' (Acts 19:2).

My heart began to throb within me as I listened to his powerful exposition of the text and its context. Since my conversion I had testified to different people that I had become a follower of Jesus Christ, but whenever I did so it was always with a little fear – fear that I might be ridiculed or rejected. I wanted to have done with this fear and enjoy the same kind of boldness that characterised the early disciples.

Halfway through his message, Handel Price said that later he would be praying for those who wanted to be baptised in the Spirit. I longed for him to finish his sermon, but he seemed to keep on and on and on. I could hold back no longer. The thirst in my soul was so great that I could not live a minute longer without the promised empowerment of the Holy Spirit. Throwing caution to the wind, I stood up and cried out, 'Please pray for me now! I want to be fled with the Spirit. I can't wait any longer!'

The preacher did not seem to be upset by me interrupting his sermon and said, 'Right, stay where you are, lift your hands to God and begin to praise the Lord.' I did as I was told and as I raised my hands and began to praise the Lord I felt a wave of supernatural power sweep into my soul. The English words I was using to praise Him merged into words that were unintelligible to me. My strongest memory of that moment was not just the feeling of spiritual exhilaration, but the sense that my personality was being endued with a new sense of boldness. I felt at that moment I could have stood in front of a whole stadium of rugby fans and preached to them about their need to put their faith in Christ!

Handel Price didn't finish his sermon. The service turned into one great prayer meeting where dozens of others received their 'personal

Pentecost' – a phrase used in those days to describe the experience of being baptised in the Spirit. I left the church that night with a spiritual boldness I had not known before and one that has never left me from that day to this.

The following morning, being a Sunday, I stepped out on to the street where I lived to head for church, when I realised that I had never told my neighbours about my Christian faith. The street on which I lived was called Martin Street, and consisted of about 40 terraced houses (20 on each side), built on a hill. My home, number 17, was at the top of the hill. As I stood there, considering how I could best tell my neighbours about my conversion, I found myself shouting the words of John 3:16: 'For God so loved the world that he gave his only begotten Son, that whosoever believeth in him should not perish, but have everlasting life' (KJV).

Several people appeared in their doorways, some in their pyjamas, wondering what all the shouting was about. Immediately I saw them I began to tell them the most wonderful thing that could ever happen to them would be to give their lives to Jesus Christ. This, I said, was certainly the most wonderful thing that had happened to me. They all seemed to be somewhat bemused by my action, but listened attentively as I spoke for about five minutes on the importance of putting one's faith in Christ. In a sense, that was my first sermon. I can't claim any converts from it, but years later, after I had moved away from the village, people who lived on that street would say to my mother, 'How is Selwyn these days? We still remember how he woke up the village that Sunday morning preaching to us about his conversion.'

Taming the Tiger

Tony Anthony

This Book documents the personal tragedy that turned a 'disciple of enlightenment' into a blood-thirsty, violent man. This is a fast paced and compelling account in Tony's deeply moving true story.

Authentic
£6.99
PB/1 8602.4481 5

TONY ANTHONY
WITH ANGELA LITTLE

TAMING THE

TIGER

FROM THE DEPTHS OF HELL TO THE
HEIGHTS OF GLORY

The remarkable true story of a Kung Fu
World Champion

First Published 2004 by Authentic Media, 9 Holdom Avenue,
Bletchley, Milton Keynes Bucks MK1 1QR

1

Shane D'Souza was barely recognisable. The guards scraped him off the cell floor and laid his mangled body on a dirty stretcher. He had been beaten, battered, cut, raped and ruined in every way. Pools of blood formed great purple patches on cold concrete.

The trail of mutilation snaked its way down the dark corridor as they carried him off to the hospital wing. The small gathering of men shuffled away. We all knew who was guilty of the assault on the young Sri Lankan. No one said a word. The authorities didn't care. There'd be one less con – *fylakismenos* they called us – on B-wing. Another would soon take his place. There'd be no inquiry, no punishment for the attacker. No justice for my friend.

It was just another day in Nicosia Central Prison. We were murderers, drug pushers and smugglers, gangsters, child abusers, thieves, rapists, terrorists and fraudsters: a miserable mixed bag of human depravity; the meanest of the mean and the downright unlucky, tossed together in a stinking hot-pot of a Cypriot jail.

There were many rules, but they weren't the ones laid down by the authorities. We each lived by a code of violence, necessary for self-preservation. You always had to watch your back. It was every man for himself and blood was often spilled for little more than recreation. Still, there was something of an alliance between me and Shane. When I saw what had happened, it triggered a dark and dangerous rage inside me.

Al Capone – or 'Alcaponey', as the Greeks called him – was a nasty piece of work. No one knew his real name. He was one of the mentally deranged, the criminally insane. The courts didn't bother with asylums; they just abandoned their madmen among the rest of us. They were a law unto themselves. Alcaponey was one of the worst. A barbaric Cypriot, he was a loner, who barely spoke his own language. Serving time for murder and multiple rape, he was a grade one psychopath. Whilst the rest of us occupied our time with drug use, petty theft (primarily cigarettes and chocolate, which were the main form of currency), and occasional arts and crafts, Alcaponey spent his days mutilating and raping other inmates. He was a lifer on a mission to make a living hell for the rest of us.

On the day Shane was brutalised, I vowed his vengeance would be mine. Alcaponey was a good foot taller than me. He pushed weights and his arms were as thick as my thighs, but I knew I could have him. I knew I could kill him with my bare hands and make him suffer for every blow, every stinking sordid deed, every drop of Shane's blood.

In the days ahead, a hushed anticipation hung over the jail. Everyone knew I was after Alcaponey. It wouldn't be pretty. I was just waiting for my moment. Almost two weeks passed and with each day I grew more angry and ambitious in the suffering I would cause him. It wasn't enough to kill him. I'd make him beg for mercy, before releasing him to his devils. I was a world class Kung Fu champion, with the skill to burst him open and break him into a million pieces. I could do it easily, with my bare hands, but these days I often carried a blade. Most men did. We broke them out from our razors and hid them under our tongues or some other place where they could not be easily detected. It wasn't as though the guards bothered much. Some of them took sadistic pleasure out of it. Others just turned a blind eye. What did they care if an inmate got cut up or raped with a blade to his throat?

Gammodi bastardos!

Suddenly, I was slammed against the wall as Alcaponey's screech echoed round the dark, desolate corridor. I was angry at myself for being caught off guard, but adrenaline raced through my veins. At last, my time with the demon had finally come.

The stench of his breath was sickening as he leaned the full weight of his huge body against me, pushing his nose to mine. A blade dug sharply at my neck, waiting to slice my jugular. Immediately, I grabbed his greasy face with my free left hand, my thumb over his eye socket, ready to puncture. We grappled with each other, as I quickly calculated my moves. I knew I would receive a life threatening cut, but that didn't matter. Nothing mattered any more. I might die, but I would kill him first.

I wanted his blood. I'd easily take his eye, before ripping off his ear with my teeth. Fury boiled within me, but suddenly there was something else. In the heat of those split seconds I was strangely aware of a much deeper battle raging. It had little to do with Alcaponey. This one was all mine. It was as though some kind of new consciousness was weakening the ingrained instincts that made me the combat fighter I was. As I fought to focus my attention on Alcaponey's ear, I had an image in my head from something I had read only that morning. A man unjustly arrested, his friend defending him, cutting off the ear of the servant of his accuser. Alcaponey's ear was just inches from my mouth.

'Come on Tony, just bite. You're fast, you can take it,' the voice of my instinct spoke.

'No, wait ... all who draw the sword, die by the sword ... ' Where did that come from?

'Come on boy, just do it! What are you waiting for?'

As the conflict raged within me, I felt Alcaponey's free hand grasping down at my groin. His evil grin bared broken, rotten teeth as my fingers dug into his face, stretching and tearing at the leathery skin. There was the voice again.

'Come on, are you going to let yourself be cut and raped like Shane?'

What was stopping me? I didn't know. I kept a tight grip on the brute, as his body locked me against the wall, but something was preventing me from making my next move. The two voices of my inner being battled in the time it took for a drop of sweat to roll down Alcaponey's face, but it was as though time was standing still. It was a debate that addressed a whole lifetime and challenged the very core of who I was, who I had become.

I knew which voice had to win. But what then? Could I allow myself to be mutilated, just like my friend? Or could I really trust this new consciousness, this new voice that seemed so determined, so sure? Suddenly, words came out of my mouth. They were calm, clear, authoritative. Alcaponey knew only Greek, but in the surrealism of the moment, I spoke English. As I said the words, I released my hold and waited.

In the next split second I felt the weight of shock run through Alcaponey's body. He shivered and goose bumps rose on his clammy skin. His murky eyes glared in terror and I braced myself for the assault. Suddenly, my body heaved as he loosened his grip. We stood, still inches apart, glaring at one another's faces. Then, in a moment, he turned and fled. He was like a man possessed, running with his hands shielding his head. His blood curdling scream bounced off the concrete walls as I watched him disappear into the darkness.

I put my hand to my neck and peeled the blade from my skin. It hadn't left a mark.

I was four years old when the stranger arrived. People didn't come to our house, so when the doorbell rang I stood excitedly at the top of the stairs. My father let him in and showed him through to the living room. The stranger was Chinese, like my mother. I crept down to take a peek through the half-open door. They were talking in such low voices I couldn't make out what they were saying. From my hiding place, I could see the stranger's face. It was mean looking.

'Come in Antonio.' Mum's voice startled me. Being careful not to look directly at the man, I pushed quickly passed him and tried to hide behind my father's legs. Mum reached out and pulled me to her. I didn't know what to do. I looked to Dad, but he just stared at the fireplace. He was blinking heavily, as though he had something stuck in his eye.

Suddenly, the stranger took me by the wrist. Flinching, I tried to pull away, but he held me tightly and Mum gave me that look, the one she used when I was to be quiet. She handed the stranger a small bag and, almost before I knew it, we were outside, walking down our garden path, leaving my parents behind.

I don't remember much about the journey. The stranger said nothing to me. I had no idea where he was taking me. When I found myself at the airport I began to tingle with a mixture of excitement and fear. This might be a fantastic adventure, but no, something was wrong, really wrong. The stranger still did not speak as we started to board a plane. As time passed, I grew more and more fearful. It seemed the flight was never going to end. Surely Mum and Dad would come soon? We'd go back to the house. Everything would be alright. Little did I know, I was on a plane bound for China.

At four years old I couldn't have understood the complexities of my parents' lives. What I did know, however, was my mother's hatred. Sitting on the plane, all I could do was think of her being angry with me. What had I done this time? I knew I had ruined my mother's life. She told me so. She was always angry.

Some time before the stranger came there was an incident I have never forgotten. We had moved from our little West End flat into a big house in Edgware, north-west London. To me it seemed huge and I remember squealing excitedly, running from one room to another. Mum and Dad bought a big new bed and I was bouncing on it, throwing myself face first into the soft new duvet. Suddenly Mum came storming in. 'Stop that immediately, you stupid child!' she yelled, dealing me a harsh slap across my legs. Moving over to the dressing table, she picked up the large hand mirror and started to look at herself, jutting out her chin, poking her lips and preening her eyelashes in the way she always did. I scrambled to quickly get off the bed but, in my haste, missed my footing and came bouncing down into the quilt once more. I couldn't help but let out a gasp of laughter.

Before I knew it, she was upon me. There was crashing around my head, an almighty cracking noise and my mother's voice, shrill, swearing and cursing at me. My head swam with sudden, intense pain.

'You idiot child, what did I tell you?' she was screaming in a frenzy. 'Now look at you!'

She marched out of the room slamming the door behind her. Somehow, I couldn't move. The frame of the mirror stuck tight over my shoulders and pointed razors of glass were cutting into my neck and face. There was blood too, and more came as I winced in agony, willing myself to pull a sharp edge away from my cheek.

I awoke with a start and realised we were getting off the plane. Where were we? I tried to rub my eyes, but the stranger still held my wrist. I wanted to cry. There was a lot of chatter, but I couldn't understand any of it. People were shouting, but their voices were high-pitched and peculiar. Fear and confusion swept over me. Who was this man? Where had he brought me? People scurried around with bags, trolleys and parcels, but it wasn't like the airport we had been in at the beginning of the journey. The air was thick with cigarette smoke and other strange smells. Overwhelmed with drowsiness, I began to cry, in big, breathless sobs. 'Sshh!' demanded the stranger, sharply tightening his grip so I felt his fingernails in my flesh. My wailing was quickly suppressed in pain and silent terror. He tugged again, this time pulling me out into the evening air. It was then I realised I was far, very far, from home.

Like a frightened rabbit, I scanned the scene, hoping to catch sight of my mother or father. The people wore strange clothes. There was a lot of shouting and dogs barking and a man with birds in a cage. We stopped. Before me stood a spindly man dressed in a silky black jacket with wide, loose sleeves and a high collar. Later, I learned this was my grandfather. At the time, there was no introduction. No smile. No welcome. I was hoisted roughly onto his horse-drawn cart and, at the click of his tongue, we pulled away into the night.

As we left the airport behind I could see strange shaped shadows of trees and animals moving around in the half-light. I was terrified and felt queasy with the stink that filled the air. (I was later to discover that it was the lily soap my grandfather used. It is very common among the Chinese, renowned for its antiseptic properties, but its odious perfume has always sickened my stomach.) It was to become the scent of my paranoia.

The journey seemed never-ending. When we finally came to a standstill it was pitch black. I could barely make out the shadowy surroundings, but I sensed there was a group of women standing at a gateway. Perhaps they were waiting for us. The women didn't like me. I felt that instantly. But what had I done wrong? My mind kept flashing back to my mother. Then, with looks of disdain and a crow-like cackle, the women were gone, all except one. She was, 'Jowmo', my grandmother.

Inside the house I shivered with cold. Still no one spoke to me. I wanted to ask where I was, but when I tried to speak I was met with a finger to the lips and a harsh 'Shush!' I was 4 years old and completely alone in a hostile, frightening world.

The house was very strange. I was shocked when suddenly a whole wall moved. The woman ushered me towards the bed in the corner. It looked nothing like my bed at home. Sticks of bamboo lay over a rickety frame. It creaked as I climbed onto it and pinched my skin when I moved. The thin muslin sheet barely covered me, but I tucked it round my shoulders, pulled my knees up to my chest and wept silently until sleep came. In the days and weeks ahead I quickly learned to stem my tears.

Each day began very early, around 4 or 5 o'clock. My grandfather (Lowsi, as I was instructed to call him, meaning 'master' or 'teacher') came into my room and beat me about the head with his bamboo stick to wake me. Soon I was rising before I heard his footsteps. I made sure I was up and ready to greet him. He hit me anyway. Lowsi's beatings were brutal. In the days and weeks ahead I got used to them, but they were always hard to bear. He used fresh bamboo cane, striking me over my ears, often until I bled. There was rarely any explanation or reason. He branded me *Lo han quilo,* meaning 'Little foreign devil'. It was his personal quest to 'beat the round-eye out of me'.

As my grandparents' only male grandchild, I might have been treated very differently. Boys in China are considered to bring good fortune and honour to a family and are often referred to as 'little emperors'. They are spoilt and doted upon by parents and, even more so, by grandparents. The problem was that my mother had married an outsider, an Italian, who was born and bred in England. She had brought shame on the family. It seemed I was to pay for the profanity. Each morning I dutifully followed Lowsi out to the courtyard where he began his morning exercises. For several hours I shivered in my thin muslin robe but I hardly dared take my eyes off him, for fear of being beaten again. Sometimes I stole a glance up to the roof and the tops of the walls. They were decorated with the most bizarre things: dragons, phoenix, flying horses, unicorns and a man riding a hen. At first I could only watch as Lowsi performed his strange movements. He made me stand very still and breathe deeply, in through my nose and out through my mouth. It was mind-numbingly tedious. As the weeks went by, and I began to pick up his language, he explained that his moves were 'Tai Chi', a discipline that is fundamental to the way of Kung Fu.

I quickly gathered that my grandfather was a Grand Master in the ancient martial art. He was revered by everyone in the village. That was why our house was grander than any of the others. I thought it looked a bit like the temple up on the hill.

Detail of my family tree is somewhat sparse in my mind, but I know that my grandfather originated from northern China. He fled down to Canton to escape the torturous atrocities of the Japanese invasion that extended into the 1940s. He was born into the Soo family, a direct descendant of Gong Soo, one of the so-called 'Venerable Five', who escaped the destruction of the original Shaolin temple under the Manchu dynasty in 1768. Gong Soo went into hiding and continued to practise Kung Fu. His knowledge passed down from generation to generation until my grandfather, Cheung Ling Soo.

As a Shaolin monk, my grandfather was proud of this 500-year-long heritage. Leaving the temple of his training, he began to develop his own styles and teach the ways of Kung Fu. He soon became a highly honoured Grand Master. Having no son of his own, however, meant the Soo lineage would be broken. I was his most unexpected and unlikely disciple. Perhaps it was for this reason that he would drive me to the harshest extremes of training. As part 'round eye', he knew I would have much to prove. In the years ahead, Lowsi would reveal to me the secrets and treasures of the ancient art. I would become a highly disciplined, truly enlightened disciple and an unbeatable combat warrior.

To become a true student of martial arts is to accept a whole code of living, unlike anything known in the western world. Its roots are derived from spiritual discipline and the practice of Taoism. According to martial arts lore, the father of Kung Fu was the Indian monk Bodhidharma. To the Chinese he is known as Ta Mo. Legend has it that he left his monastery in India to spread the teachings of the Buddha throughout China at the beginning of the sixth century. While wandering in the mountains of northern China, he stopped at a monastery called Shaolin. Shaolin means 'young tree', one that can survive strong winds and storms because it is flexible and can bend and sway in the wake of assault.

Ta Mo required that students be disciplined in the ways of meditation and the continual quest for enlightenment, but he found that the monks constantly fell asleep during meditation. He recognised that their bodies were weak and feeble, so he devised a series of exercises, explaining:

'Although the way of the Buddha is for the soul, the body and soul are inseparable. For this reason I shall give you a method by which you can develop your energy enough to attain to the presence of Buddha.'

These exercises were a series that served a form of moving meditation. They were also highly efficient fighting moves that helped the monks defend themselves from bandits when travelling between monasteries. Even so, Ta Mo's primary concern was not simply with developing physical strength, but with the cultivation of the intrinsic energy of 'Ch'i', perhaps most closely translated as 'breath', 'spirit' or 'life force'.

It is the development of Ch'i that lies at the heart of all the Taoist arts, including martial arts, philosophy and healing. Those early days in the courtyard, mastering my breathing through hours of practice, were to become the foundation of something extremely powerful.

One day Lowsi dressed me in orange robes and took me to the local Shaolin temple. The sky was a brilliant blue as we climbed the many steps to the entrance and a strange sweet smell hung in the air. 'Incense sticks and cherry blossom,' Lowsi said. 'We use them as a gift to pay our respects to Buddha.' Dutifully, I followed him as he lit some sticks on our behalf. 'Their therapeutic aroma will help calm your mind,' he explained. 'As you follow the path to enlightenment you will become like the smoke rising from the incense to the heavenlies.'

As my master led me over to a quiet area to begin our meditation, I couldn't help steal a glance at the monks who were combat training. 'They have bound their feet and lower legs with cords,' Lowsi said, noticing my interest. 'This is for strength and protection as they practise their footwork.' I watched in utter amazement at the speed and power of their kicks. 'They are learning the way of the crane, one of the traditional Shaolin systems of combat,' Lowsi explained. I concentrated hard to follow his story: 'One day a monk stumbled on a battle between an ape and a crane. It seemed that the ape would easily break the bird in two, however, the bird had far more stealth than the ape. It flapped its wings and darted in and out with its beak until, at last, the large beast was driven away. Notice the grace in their movements,' Lowsi instructed, 'the powerful long-range kick and the one leg stance. See how the hands are used like the cutting of the crane's beak.'

As my training progressed I, too, mastered the way of the crane and many other systems of Kung Fu. Chinese martial arts claim as many as 1,500 styles. The imitation of animals is the classical and oldest Shaolin Kung Fu exercise. My master taught me that the human, being weaker than the animal, relies on his intelligence in order to survive. Yet to truly imitate the movement and mind of a particular animal is to master the physical art of immobility and rapidity, observation and reaction, steady movement and instantaneous attack.

'Now concentrate!'

Immediately my attention was snapped away from the disciples.

'Focus your mind on this flame.' Lowsi drew my eyes to the burning candle he placed in front of me. 'Centre yourself on the inner flame and clear your mind. Now breathe.'

We spent hours in the temple, staring into the flame of a candle. I longed to close my eyes, but as they grew heavy the thwack of bamboo hit my face. Lowsi beat me at any point he thought I was losing concentration. The purpose of these hours of meditation was to get in touch with the Ch'i. I was taught that all things are products of cosmic negative and positive forces, the yin and yang, which can be harmonised in the study of Ch'i. In the human body the Ch'i is best understood as the flow of energy. It is the Ch'i that disciples of Tao believe governs muscular movement, the process of breathing, the regulation of the heartbeat and the functioning of the nervous system.

'When you can completely harmonise the Ch'i in both body and spirit, you will reach enlightenment and inner peace. You will discover seemingly supernatural power within yourself,' Lowsi taught me. 'Harnessing the Ch'i is essential in the art of Ku Fu,' he continued. 'It allows for fluidity.' Dipping his hand into a small vase of water he held it in the air until a small drop formed and lingered on the tip of his forefinger. 'A single drop of water. Alone, it is harmless, gentle and powerless. But what on earth can withstand the force of a tsunami? Its raging waves have power to destroy earth and overcome all in its path. Learn to control the Ch'i, boy. Tap into its universal energy and you, too, will have power many times your natural strength.'

In the years ahead Lowsi's instruction in the Ch'i became clearer to me. I understood it to be the 'god within', the root of my power. Harnessing my body's energy through the Ch'i, I could break bricks with my bare hands and perform much more amazing feats. It also gave me a heightened state of awareness, to the point where I could sense the movements of an opponent in the dark and withstand immense pain by redistributing it throughout my body.

Everything about my life in China was intertwined in Kung Fu training. As a novice, I was made to do the most menial and difficult work relating to the upkeep of both our home and the temple. All the time Lowsi was preparing my body to begin training in earnest. One of the first exercises he presented to me was plunging my hands into a bucket of sand. Hour after hour I did this under his watchful eye, until my hands were sore and bleeding. After a few weeks, my skin hardened until I no longer felt the pain. Lowsi introduced small stones into the bucket and the procedure began again. Every few days he added larger stones until I was pounding my hands, with great force, into sharp boulders without cutting or blistering.

One of my main chores was tending the animals. My grand-parents had paddy fields and we kept chickens, goats, cows and a horse. I was usually left alone to my work and I felt safe, away from Lowsi's harsh whippings. Among the animals I could momentarily set aside the pain of my training and the hatred I felt towards him.

Trips to the market with my grandmother were another welcome relief. I had to carry huge loads, but it was better than my master's merciless beatings. The market was noisy and colourful. People haggled and shouted to one another above the background rumble of the mah-jong houses. There were lots of live animals in cages: dogs, ducks, goats, rabbits, birds, reptiles and all sorts of strange fish on big wooden carts. I stuck close to my grandmother, afraid of being noticed by the 'reptile man'. He was very old and bent, with a wispy grey pointed beard, a thin moustache and a face that was creased like a dried up old prune. Long yellow nails stuck to his wizened fingers, and he used his sharply pointed thumb nail to cut up the throat of the terrapins he sold. On his stall were all manner of insects and snakes: live, dead, dried or skinned.

The medicine shop was another source of morbid fascination. Giant cobras were coiled in huge glass canisters and each shelf held row upon row of scary-looking jars filled with animal body parts, scorpions, beetles of all shapes and sizes, clusters of honey bees and snakes, all preserved in potent-smelling liquor.

Grandmother bartered for what seemed like ages with the herbalist. I marvelled at the huge chillies, brightly coloured powders and funny-looking roots that she bought to make ginseng and ginger teas. Back on the street there were delicious smells as people sat at the roadside, cooking in large woks. It was the 1970s and it seemed that much of Canton was under construction. Alongside the traditional shack-type stalls, giant western-style structures were being erected by barefoot or flip-flop clad Chinese, performing death defying feats on bamboo scaffolding.

We picked our way through mounds of rubble and pungent market waste, avoiding the constant pestering of people selling fortune-telling sticks. My attention was always caught by the calligraphers who set themselves up in the street with their brushes and inks. 'They use special xuan paper, made from bark and rice straw,' Jowmo explained. 'People hire the calligraphers to write letters for them and prepare special announcements.'

My grandmother could hardly be described as warm towards me, but she did seem to enjoy teaching me about the ways and traditions of our people. There are many festivals. New Year is the most important. The Chinese lunar year is based on the cycles of the moon and the calendar cycle is repeated every twelve years, with each year represented by an animal.

'Legend has it that the Lord Buddha summoned all the animals to come to him before he departed from earth,' Jowmo explained. 'But only twelve were prepared to come to bid him farewell. As a reward he promised to name a year after each one, in the order in which they arrived. The animals quarrelled over who should arrive first. Eventually, it turned into a contest. The first animal to reach the opposite bank of the river would be first in line and the rest of them would receive their years according to their finish. All twelve animals gathered at the river bank and jumped in. Unknown to the ox, the rat had jumped on his back and when the ox was about to jump ashore, ahead of the other animals, the rat jumped off his back and won the race, leaving the ox to come second. The others followed in the order of tiger, rabbit, dragon, snake, horse, sheep, monkey, rooster, dog and the pig, who was very slow and lazy, came last.'

Jowmo told me this story many times. She usually laughed out loud at the idea of the poor lazy pig. 'You were born in the year of the rooster,' she told me. 'The person born under the sign of the rooster is hard working and definite about their decisions. They are not afraid to speak their mind, but beware,' my grandmother cautioned, 'the rooster can be very boastful and overconfident. You will also be very brave,' she said, looking at me intently.

As New Year drew close, there was a great sense of excitement in the community. The twentieth day of the twelfth moon was set aside for the annual house cleaning. My grandmother referred to it as the 'sweeping of the grounds'. Every corner of the house had to be thoroughly cleaned. I helped her hang large scrolls of red paper on the walls and gateway. In beautiful black ink they pronounced poetic greetings and good wishes for the family. We decorated the house with flowers, tangerines, oranges and large pear-shaped grapefruits called pomelos. 'These will bring us good luck and wealth,' said my grandmother, as she carefully arranged a display of fruit. (In fact, this symbolism has developed through a language pun. The word for tangerine has the same sound as 'luck' in Chinese, and the word for orange has the same sound as 'wealth'.)

'When the house is clean we will prepare the feast and bid farewell to Zaowang, the kitchen god,' grandmother told me. 'Tradition says that Zaowang returns on the first day of the new year when all the merrymaking is over.' There was lots of work to be done. All food had to be prepared before New Year's Day. That way, sharp instruments, such as knives and scissors, could be put away to avoid cutting the 'luck' of the New Year.

On New Year's Eve the family gathered at our house. They travelled from all over China and I was curious to see my grandmother setting empty places at the table for family members who could not attend. 'This is to symbolise their presence at the

banquet, even though they cannot be with us,' she explained. I
wondered if there was a place for my mother, but I never asked.
Many of the guests treated me with the same disdain as my
grandfather, but at least there were some other children – my
cousins, all girls – to play with. There was also a large lady with a big
smiling face who winked at me mischievously. She was my
grandfather's sister, Li Mei, meaning 'plum blossom'. His other
sister, Li Wei, did little to live up to her name, 'beautiful rose'. To me,
she was far from beautiful. She looked at me through the same
shrew-like eyes as my grandfather. At midnight, following the
banquet, the other children and I were made to bow and pay our
respects to our grandparents and the other elders. I did as I was told,
but I still hated them.

When New Year's Day came we were given red 'lai-see'
envelopes. They contained good luck money. Everyone wore new
clothes and my grandfather wore a fine red silk suit, intricately
embroidered with an emblem of a dragon in gold thread.

I was quickly growing accustomed to my new life, but I soon
worked out that, among these people, I would always be an outsider.
In England, my mother had been proud of my oriental looks but, to
the Chinese, I was very much a 'foreign devil'. I was 6 years old
when I discovered that such prejudice, even in children, has no
mercy.

One day, on the way home from the market with my grandmother, we stopped to rest by the village pond. As Jowmo lay back in
the shade, I wandered around, casting stones into the water.
Suddenly a group of boys not much older than myself surrounded
me. 'Hey round eye, what are you doing here?' said one, spitting at
me. In shock, I tried to understand what I had done wrong and what
they were saying to me. 'He doesn't even speak our language,'
scoffed another boy, giving me a sharp slap in the mouth. 'Come on,
round eye, let's hear you say something.' I grappled for words,
horrified by the taste of blood in my mouth. Then came another blow
to my face. This time it was so hard that I lost my balance and went

flying backwards in the mud. At once, all the boys were upon me, beating, slapping, scratching and dragging me by my hair. Fighting for breath, I screamed out to my grandmother but she didn't come. They kept on and on, shouting as they struck me. The noise of their abuse rang in my head until I began spinning in blackness, beneath the sharp blows of their kicks and punches. Then silence. No pain. Nothing.

I awoke in hospital, some days later. Both arms and one of my legs were cased in plaster. As I moved, a stab of pain ran through my whole upper body.

One night, whilst still in hospital and barely in a state of consciousness, I was aware of Lowsi and another man standing by my bed. I could only catch a little of what they were saying, but I gathered that they knew the gang of boys who had set upon me.

'Children of the Triads, from Shanghai,' the stranger said, 'visiting the local family.'

'They did not know who this boy is then,' said Lowsi sternly.

'Quite obviously not.'

'Am I to understand they have been dealt with?'

'Oh yes, the family has dealt with them most severely and the elders wish to meet with you tomorrow to seek your forgiveness and pardon.'

In the coming years the Shanghai boys were careful to stay away from me. Being from Triad families (the notorious Chinese mafia) they, too, were taught the practice of Kung Fu, but everyone knew that they would never receive the same level of training as me. Had they realised I was the disciple of the highly revered Cheung Ling Soo, they would never have dishonoured my family in this way and would have approached me in respectful trepidation. Such incidents are not easily forgotten among the Chinese. Years later the boys still lived under the weight of their childhood error. One time, when I returned to the village as an adult, after a period of absence, I learned that one of the attackers believed I had come back to claim my revenge. He was so scared that he was preparing to move his family out of the area.

Following the attack I spent many weeks in hospital, but I was barely free from the plaster cast when my master had me back in the courtyard, doing the most rigorous of physical exercises. The pain was so great that tears stung my eyes. This, I knew, my master would not tolerate. Sure enough, as a single droplet escaped down my cheek I felt the thrash of the bamboo across my ears. Hatred boiled up inside me. I was 6 years old but every fibre of my body, every drop of my young blood screamed out in loathing.

That night I woke in a cold sweat. I could hear the croak of insects and knew it was long before morning. The house was still and peaceful, but haunted dreams brought the frenzy of my hatred to fever pitch. Tossing and turning on my bed, I winced in the heat of fresh wounds. The image of my grandfather and his wicked bamboo cane tortured my mind. It would never end. But how could I stand even one more day? There was only one thing I could do.

As I padded silently through to the kitchen I felt the whole house would hear my heartbeat. Lowsi kept some of his combat cleavers in a large chest. We cleaned and polished them every day, so I was very familiar with the feel of them. I chose one and held it up, turning it so it reflected light onto my face. The blade was razor sharp.

A shaft of moonlight broke through the bamboo shutters and I could see my grandfather's sleeping form. I stood at a distance, looking at him, anger and repulsion sweeping over me like waves. Suddenly, I was aware of the heaviness of my breathing. Ironic that I would draw on his teaching to calm myself for silent strike. 'Focus on the Ch'i, concentrate. Control your body through your mind.' With my breathing in check I moved stealthily towards the bed. He was motionless. I raised the cleaver above his heart.

The Road of Life

David Adam

In 13 years as Vicar, David Adam welcomed over one million adults and children to the Holy Island of Lindisfarne. All have something to teach us. As David Adam tells their stories, we catch glimpses of the inner searching and longing we often feel ourselves.

SPCK

£7.99

PB / 0 2810 5217 4

Other titles by the same Author

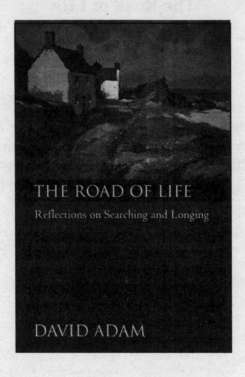

THE ROAD OF LIFE

Reflections on Searching and Longing

DAVID ADAM

Published in Great Britain in 2004 by SPCK, 36 Causton Street, London SW1P 4AU

Introduction

The invitation to become the vicar of Holy Island came as a surprise.
I was working on the North Yorkshire Moors, having three churches
and three railway stations in the parish. Denise, my wife, and I
thought, as we had completed twenty-three years in this one parish,
we would spend the rest of our lives there. We were reasonably
settled. Yet somewhere at the back of our minds there was something
else saying, 'Move on.'

In the latter part of 1989, the Bishop of Newcastle rang and said he
would like to offer me the parish of Holy Island. At first, the idea
filled us both with horror. Why move? But we decided we ought at
least to go and look at the parish and the vicarage. We knew the
Island, though not very well. 'How lucky to go to such a small
parish,' said a friend (the village covers less than a square mile and
there are only about 150 inhabitants). This friend was an inner-city
clergyman who actually had fewer people living in his parish! The
bishop told me of the small congregation who met regularly. He also
spoke of the Island being a special place, a place of the saints and also
one of outstanding natural beauty. We had our doubts and the idea of
such a saintly place was daunting. Fortunately, I knew that the
Islanders had a reputation of being very down to earth. We came. We
looked and we hesitated. We tried to escape the challenge, but it
would not let us go. Another friend said, 'It is just the sort of place
made for you. You can see God's hand at work.' I only wished that I

could see. I asked God to guide me but he gave me no clear directions! It took us three months to make up our minds, another three months to serve our notice and to get rid of twenty-three years of clutter. We arrived just after Easter 1990 to look after, to learn from and to share with 150 people: men, women and children.

We had our suspicions, but no one had mentioned the number of pilgrims to the Island. The pilgrims would come as individuals, in small groups or occasionally three or four thousand at a time. Nearly all these groups expected some input, or at least some guidance on how to cope logistically with 4,000 pilgrims at once. For example, I had to advise them on how long it took to walk the sands and how difficult it could be. They also had to know how long it would take 60-plus buses to leave the island with the threat of an incoming tide. Such large groups had to be told to inform the police of their coming, to bring a St John's Ambulance team with them and to bring their own portaloos! They needed to know how long it took to administer Communion to a large group and how many chalices, patens and assistants it would take. Such information helped to bring many groups down to earth! Then there were school groups, many unplanned, who thought they could just use the building. In a year we would deal with about 7,000 children. On one horrendous day – I should be able to say glorious, because the weather had stopped school groups doing other things – instead of the eighty to ninety we had booked in, we had over nine hundred and fifty children in three hours.

The vicarage would receive endless visitors looking for hope, healing, help or simply hospitality. Some booked, others arrived on the doorstep. You could not tell if someone was merely curious and fancied seeing into your house or whether they were suicidal. Each needed to be given time and attention and to be treated with discernment. The doorbell, the telephone and the church bell all demanded attention and often at the same time. There was the odd occasion when we had someone needing attention in each of our downstairs rooms and someone waiting across at the church. We averaged about three visitors a day for every day of the year, and that only counts the ones that took over a quarter of an hour of our time.

The rhythm of daily worship would ensure some balance in this hyperactive existence, though some might not think so since we had a minimum of three services a day, not counting any others for school groups or pilgrims. There were odd days when I was in church for over six hours. Fortunately we were able to build up a team of helpers. Still, there was little time to be proactive as we had too much to react to.

There was a great danger of not having time for each other, for ourselves or for the seekers who came to us. Yet this was a greatly rewarding life. We saw the Church alive, exciting and, often, in great numbers. So many people enriched us. As pilgrims shared their journey they often allowed us to share in their insights. We learnt from them new hymns, new modes of worship, deep and meaningful readings, and a great keenness of adventure in the faith. We learnt of humility, perseverance and tremendous courage. Sometimes we were given a material gift, such as when the group from Selkirk brought us a 'Selkirk Bannock' or when the pilgrims from Trondheim brought us St Olaf's head! Fortunately this latter gift was a small plaster cast and not the real thing.

Holy Island has been a place of pilgrimage for over 1,300 years. It is a small island off the Northumbrian coast and near the border with Scotland. The Island can be seen from the A1 when you travel north from Belford and also from the main railway line south of Berwick. As a tidal island the phases of the moon and the tides govern all movements. High tide is never at the same time two days in a row. The movements of residents, pilgrims, fishermen, the wading birds and the vicar are all controlled each day. Twice in every twenty-four hours the Island is cut off by the North Sea and no one can reach us by road.

Bede, who was an early authority on tides, calls the island a demi-isle and writes of it and its tides: 'As the tide ebbs and flows, this place is surrounded twice daily by waves of the sea like an island,

and twice, when the sands are dry it becomes again attached to the
mainland.'

Walter Scott, in his poem 'Marmion', writes more romantically of
tide and pilgrim:

> The tide did now its flood-mark gain,
> And girdled in the Saint's domain:
> For with the ebb and flow its style
> Varies from continent to isle;
> Dry shod o'er the sands, twice every day,
> The pilgrims to the shrine find their way;
> Twice every day, the waves efface
> Of staves and sandall'd feet the trace.
>
> *('Marmion' 2.8)*

No one can expect to cross to the Island just when they decide to.
Tide tables must be consulted to find out when the way is clear. It is
of no use to arrive just after the tide has closed the causeway or if you
need a quick exit at high tide. I had to instil this into the minds of
pilgrims and visitors and remind them it was the sea they were
dealing with. Occasionally I would offer a few extracts from the
parish register to those who took the North Sea lightly:

Jan. 8th 1584	old John Stapleton drowned.
Nov. 5th 1641	Samuel Waddell and his son drowned in the Low.
July 28th 1746	Rob. Brown, Clerk of Holy Island drowned.
April 8th 1801	William Macmillan drowned in passing the sands.
Dec. 15th 1802	Alexander Warwick died in crossing the sands.

I have to admit that there have been no deaths on crossing to the
Island since the 1950s, though many a car has been ruined by
seawater totally covering it.

It is a wonderful sight to see thousands of pilgrims singing as they
cross the sands. Large groups of pilgrims, often barefooted,

following a person carrying a cross, find this crossing to the Island very moving in itself. Every Good Friday, the Northern Cross Pilgrims meet to carry full size crosses over the sands. Some will have carried these crosses down from Scotland or across England from west to east. The same large crosses are decorated with flowers on Easter Day and brought into the church, which is not big enough to contain all the pilgrims.

The Pilgrims' Way has been used since the seventh century, when pilgrims came in great numbers to the shrine of St Cuthbert. Because of quicksand and the tortuous winding of the River Low, the Pilgrims' Way was clearly marked out. The monks placed cairns at regular intervals, some of which can still be seen. In the 1860s a series of posts were driven into the sand to be a clearer guide for pilgrims and travellers. Still too many people were losing their way. In 1954 a metalled road was provided for cars to cross the sands. It was only in 1965 that this road was completed, with a bridge over the River Low and a refuge box on stilts where anyone caught by the tide can climb into for safety. In 1987, to commemorate the 1,300th anniversary of Cuthbert's death, new poles were erected across the length of the Pilgrims' Way.

The journey to the Island is very like the pilgrimage of life. Sometimes the way is easy, level going and without hindrance. At other times we find our way blocked and we can do nothing about it but wait. No amount of jumping up and down or getting irate will change the situation, unless you are Moses or have the cloak of Elijah! There are times when we must move forward without delay or the opportunity will have gone and the road before us will be closed. Sometimes life is all at sea and then another time a road opens up suddenly before us. At all times we need to accept the wisdom, knowledge and guidance of those who have gone before us. We need to plan our journey and be aware of any hazards we may encounter. Without a doubt we are all travellers in this world, if not pilgrims. We are all on a journey along the road of life.

I believe we all need to find our own 'Holy Island', a place that is special and important to us. We should seek this place until we find it, though I do believe it can be of the heart and carried within us. It will be this quest and awareness that will distinguish a pilgrim from a traveller. Our pilgrim journey is not only measured in miles but takes us into the depths of our being and the mystery of creation. We are not just surface travellers; we are seeking to enter great deeps. We travel with and in God. Actually everyone does, but I am talking of awareness, no matter how tenuous it is. As pilgrims, we are seeking to extend our awareness and our love for God and for all of his creation. The road of life is a journey into love and into God and if we miss out on this we have lost our way.

This is a book about pilgrimage, about the great variety of pilgrims I have met and part of their story. Some pilgrims I have shared a few days with, some I have been with for only a few precious moments. When I write about them I tell only a little of what I see. I have always believed that each pilgrim, each encounter, each person, each creature is unique. No one is dull or unimportant. The closer you get to anyone, or in fact to anything, the richer and more mysterious you find them. The searching and story of any individual are unique to them; they have a long history and cannot be understood in a moment. Everyone must be treated with respect and dignity.

I want to look at pilgrims as mirrors of our own strengths and weaknesses. I want to see them as mirrors in which we recognize familiar reactions and expressions that we have, or have had, at certain stages in our journey through life. Yet at all times we must not forget they are living people, often with concerns of which we know nothing. I do not set them before you to be laughed at or pitied but rather that you may look at yourself more carefully. We are often angry with people who share the same tendencies and weaknesses that we have ourselves. We find it hard to forgive those that reflect our own weaknesses when we have difficulty in forgiving ourselves. Come with me and join these pilgrim people. Meet fellow travellers and seekers with similar passions, joys and fears. Learn from their mistakes and their delights. Know that the image they present to us is often our image and that we are all asked to be the image of God.

I want to capture moments, as a camera would capture a moment, for our own education and learning. Later, even a few minutes on, the person may be quite different. You must remember that the people I write about have all moved on and are not frozen into the posture in which I caught them. All are more wonderful, more mysterious and more complex than the snapshot I place before you. For some the very act of pilgrimage and the encounter on Holy Island was a turning point in their lives. For others it may have been just another experience to drop into the box of recollections. Yet, I believe that everyone who comes to the Island leaves something of themselves, and everyone takes away something of the Island with them.

In the same way I believe that the saints, such as Aidan, Cuthbert and Eadfrith, have left us a rich heritage of themselves as well as their works. It is this that makes the Island such a rich place and a good place for pilgrimage. We can walk where the saints have trod. We can pray where they have said their prayers. We can look upon scenery that is almost unchanged since the time of these holy people and let it inspire us too. We can journey down the road of life and be deeply aware of the past, or if we so choose we can walk the same landscape unseeing and unmoved. We may not be able to control where life will take us but we can choose how we react to it. Come and adventure with the pilgrims who sought deeper meanings to the road of life.

Come on pilgrimage.
Let us walk together the road of life.
We will go on well trodden paths,
and also open us new ways.
We will seek,
we will search,

we will rejoice,
and perhaps we will sing.

You cannot come as an onlooker,
that leaves you on the outside,
yet still influencing us,
as we influence you.
Come and share your experiences,
your sorrows and your joys.
If your prayer has gone dead,
your God is too small,
your vision too narrow,
Come journey into new depths,
let life be an adventure.

Come and participate,
come and discover –
we will go to strange places,
we may even meet dragons.
But we do not journey alone
we go together along the road
and our God goes with us.

Redeeming Love

Francine Rivers

Angel expects nothing from men but betrayal.
Sold into prostitution as a child, she survives by
keeping her hatred alive. Then she meets
Michael Hosea who obeys God's call to marry
Angel, and to love her unconditionally. But with
Angels unexpected softening come overwhelm-
ing feelings of unworthiness and fear. So Angel
runs ...

Monarch Books Publishers
PB/1 8524 4659 3

FRANCINE RIVERS

Redeeming Love

A NOVEL

Published in UK by Monarch Books in 2004 Mayfield House,
256 Banbury Road, Oxford OX2 7DH

Prologue

The prince of darkness is a gentleman.
SHAKESPEARE

New England 1835

Alex Stafford was just like Mama said. He was tall and dark, and Sarah had never seen anyone so beautiful. Even dressed in dusty riding clothes, his hair damp with perspiration, he was like the princes in the stories Mama read. Sarah's heart beat with wild joy and pride. None of the other fathers she saw at Mass compared to him.

He looked at her with his dark eyes, and her heart sang. She was wearing her best blue frock and white pinafore, and Mama had braided her hair with pink and blue ribbons. Did Papa like the way she looked? Mama said blue was his favorite color, but why didn't he smile? Was she fidgeting? Mama said to stand straight and still and act like a lady. She said he would like that. But he didn't look pleased at all.

"Isn't she beautiful, Alex?" Mama said. Her voice sounded strange … tight, like she was choking. "Isn't she the most beautiful little girl you've ever seen?"

Sarah watched Papa's dark eyes frown. He didn't look happy. He looked angry. Like mama looked sometimes when Sarah talked too much or asked too many questions.

"Just a few minutes," Mama said quickly. Too quickly. Was she afraid? But why? "That's all I'm asking, Alex. Please. It would mean so much to her."

Alex Stafford stared down at Sarah. His mouth was pressed tight, and he studied her silently. Sarah stood as still as she could. She'd stared at herself in the mirror so long this morning, she knew what he would see. She had her father's chin and nose, and her mother's blonde hair and fair skin. Her eyes were like her mother's, too, although they were even more blue. Sarah wanted Papa to think she was pretty, and she gazed up at him hopefully. But the look in his eyes was not a nice one.

"Did you pick blue on purpose, Mae?" Papa's words startled Sarah. They were cold and angry. "Because it brings out the color of her eyes?"

Sarah couldn't help it, she glanced at her mother – and her heart fell. Mama's face was filled with hurt.

Alex glanced toward the foyer. "Cleo!"

"She's not here," Mama said quietly, keeping her head high. "I gave her the day off."

Papa's eyes seemed to get even darker. "Did you? Well, that leaves you in a fix, doesn't it, darling?"

Mama stiffened, then bit her lip and glanced down at Sarah. What was wrong? Sarah wondered sadly. Wasn't Papa happy to see her? She had been so excited that she was actually going to be with him at last, even for a little while ...

"What would you have me do?" Mama's words were directed at Papa, so Sarah stayed silent, still hoping.

"Send her away. She knows how to find Cleo, I would imagine."

Pink spots appeared on Mama's cheeks. "Meaning what, Alex? That I entertain others in your absence?"

Sarah's smile fell in confusion. They spoke so coldly to one another. Neither looked at her. Had they forgotten she was there? What was wrong? Mama was distraught. Why was Papa so angry about Cleo not being home?

Chewing her lip, Sarah looked between them. Stepping closer, she tugged on her father's coat. "Papa ..."

"Don't call me that."

She blinked, frightened and confused by his manner. He was her papa. Mama said so. He even brought her presents every time he came. Mama gave them to her. Maybe he was angry that she had never thanked him. "I want to thank you for the presents you –"

"Hush, Sarah," her mother said quickly. "Not now, darling."

Papa flashed Mama a thunderous look. "Let her speak. It's what you wanted, isn't it? Why are you shushing her now, Mae?"

Mama stepped closer and put her hand on Sarah's shoulder. Sarah could feel Mama's fingers trembling, but Papa bent toward her now, smiling. "What presents?" he said.

He was so handsome, just like Mama said. She was proud to have a father like him.

"Tell me, little one."

"I always like the candies you bring me," Sarah said, feeling warm and proud beneath his attention. "They are very nice. But best of everything, I love the crystal swan."

She smiled again, glowing with joy that Papa listened to her so carefully. He even smiled, though Sarah wasn't sure she liked his smile. It was small and tight.

"Indeed," he said and straightened. He looked at Mama. "I'm so pleased to know how much my gifts mean."

Sarah looked up at her father, thrilled at his approval. "I put it on my windowsill. The sun shines through it and makes colors dance on the wall. Would you like to come and see?" She took his hand. When he jerked away, she blinked, hurt, not understanding.

Mama bit her lip and reached out a hand toward Papa, then stopped suddenly. She looked afraid again. Sarah looked from one parent to the other, struggling to understand. What had she done wrong? Wasn't Papa pleased that she liked his presents?

"So you pass on my gifts to the child," Papa said. "It's good to know what they mean to you."

Sarah bit her lip at the coldness in Papa's voice, but before she could speak, Mama touched her shoulder gently. "Darling, be a good girl and go outside and play now."

Sarah looked up, distressed. Had she done something wrong? "Can't I stay? I'll be very quiet." Mama couldn't seem to say more. Her eyes were moist and she looked at Papa.

Alex bent down to Sarah. "I want you to go outside and play," he said quietly. "I want to talk to your mother alone." He smiled and patted her cheek.

Sarah smiled, utterly enchanted. Papa had touched her; he wasn't angry at all. He loved her! Just as Mama said. "Can I come back when you're done talking?"

Papa straightened stiffly. "Your mother will come and get you when she's ready. Now, run along as you've been told."

"Yes, Papa." Sarah wanted to stay, but she wanted to please her father more. She went out of the parlor, skipping through the kitchen to the back door. She picked a few daisies that grew in the garden patch by the door and then headed for the rose trellis. She plucked the petals. "He loves me, he loves me not, he loves me, he loves me not ..." She hushed as she came around the corner. She didn't want to disturb Mama and Papa. She just wanted to be close to them.

Sarah dreamed contentedly. Maybe Papa would put her up on his shoulders. She wondered if he would take her for a ride on his big black horse. She would have to change her dress, of course. He wouldn't want her to soil it. She wished he had let her sit on his lap while he talked to Mama. She would have liked that very much, and she would have been no bother.

The parlor window was open, and she could hear voices. Mama loved the smell of roses to fill the parlor. Sarah wanted to sit and listen to her parents. That way she would know just when Papa wanted her to come back again. If she was very quiet, she wouldn't disturb them, and all Mama would have to do was lean out and call her name.

"What was I to do, Alex? You've never spent so much as a minute with her. What was I to tell her? That her father doesn't care? That he wishes she had never even been born?"

Sarah's lips parted. *Deny it, Papa! Deny it!*

"I brought that swan back from Europe for you, and you throw it away on a child who has no appreciation for its value. Did you give her the pearls as well? What about the music box? I suppose she got that, too!"

The daisies fluttered from Sarah's hand. She sat down on the ground, careless of her pretty dress. Her heart slowed from its wild, happy beat. Everything inside her seemed to spiral downward with each word.

"Alex, please. I didn't see any harm in it. It made it easier. She asked me this morning if she was old enough yet to meet you. She asks me every time she knows you're coming. How could I say no to her again? I didn't have the heart. She doesn't understand your neglect, and neither do I."

"You know how I feel about her."

"How can you say how you feel? You don't even know her. She's a beautiful child, Alex. She's quick and charming and she isn't afraid of anything. She's like you in so many ways. She's *someone*, Alex. You can't ignore her existence forever. She's your daughter ... . "

"I have enough children by my wife. Legitimate children. I told you I didn't want another."

"How can you say that? How can you not love your own flesh and blood?"

"I told you how I felt from the beginning, but you wouldn't listen. She should never have been born, Mae, but you insisted on having your own way"

"Do you think I wanted to get pregnant? Do you think I planned to have her?"

"I've often wondered. Especially when I arranged a way out of the situation for you and you refused. The doctor I sent you to would have taken care of the whole mess. He would've gotten rid – "

"I couldn't do it. How could you expect me to kill my unborn child? Don't you understand? It's a mortal sin."

"You've spent too much time in church," he said derisively. "Have you ever thought that you wouldn't have the problems you do now if you had gotten rid of her the way I told you. It would've been easy. But you ran out."

"I wanted her!" Mama said brokenly. "She was part of you, Alex, and part of me. I wanted her even if you didn't … . "

"Is that the real reason?"

"You're hurting me, Alex!"

Sarah flinched as something shattered. "Is that the real reason, Mae? Or did you have her because you thought bearing my child would give you a hold over me you otherwise lacked?"

"You can't believe that!" Mama was crying now. "You do, don't you? You're a fool, Alex. Oh, what have I done? I gave up everything for you! My family, my friends, my self-respect, everything I believed in, every hope I ever had … ."

"I bought you this cottage. I give you all the money you could possibly need."

Mama's voice rose strangely. "Do you know what it's like for me to walk down the street in this town? You come and go when and as you please. And they know who you are, and they know what I am. No one looks at me. No one speaks to me. Sarah feels it, too. She asked me about it once, and I told her we were different from other people. I didn't know what else to say" Her voice broke. "I'll probably go to hell for what I've become."

"I'm sick of your guilt and I'm sick of hearing about that child. She's ruining everything between us. Do you remember how happy we were? We never argued. I couldn't wait to come to you, to be with you."

"Don't – "

"And how much time do I have left with you today? Enough? You've used it up on her. I told you what would happen, didn't I? I wish she had never been born!"

Mama cried out a terrible name. There was a crash. Terrified, Sarah got up and ran. She raced through Mama's flowers and across the lawn and onto the pathway to the springhouse. She ran until she couldn't run anymore. Gasping, her sides burning, she dropped into the tall grass, her shoulders heaving with sobs, her face streaked with tears. She heard a horse galloping toward her. Scrambling for a better hiding place in the vines about the creek, she peered out and saw her father ride by on his great black horse. Ducking down, she huddled there, crying, and waited for Mama to come fetch her.

But Mama didn't come and she didn't call. After a while, Sarah wandered back to the springhouse and sat by the flowered vines and waited longer. By the time Mama came, Sarah had dried her tears and dusted off her pretty frock. She was still shaking from what she had heard.

Mama was very pale, her eyes dull and red-rimmed. There was a blue mark on the side of her face. She had tried to cover it with powder. She smiled, but it wasn't like her usual smile.

"Where have you been, darling? I've been looking and looking for you." Sarah knew she hadn't. She had been watching for her. Mama licked her lacy handkerchief and wiped a smudge from Sarah's cheek. "Your father was called away suddenly on business."

"Is he coming back?" Sarah was afraid. She never wanted to see him again. He had hurt Mama and made her cry.

"Maybe not for a long time. We'll have to just wait and see. He's a very busy and important man." Sarah said nothing, and her Mama lifted her and hugged her close. "It's all right, sweetheart. You know what we're going to do? We're going to go back to the cottage and change our dresses. Then we'll pack a picnic and go down to the creek. Would you like that?"

Sarah nodded and put her arms around Mama's neck. Her mouth trembled, and she tried not to cry. If she cried, Mama might guess she had been eavesdropping and then she would be angry too.

Mama held her tightly, her face buried in Sarah's hair. "We'll make it through this. You'll see, sweetheart. We will. *We will.*"

Alex didn't come back, and Mama grew thin and wan. She stayed in bed too late, and when she got up, she didn't want to go for long walks the way she used to. When she smiled, her eyes didn't light up. Cleo said she needed to eat more. Cleo said a lot of things, carelessly, with Sarah close enough to hear.

"He's still sending you money, Miss Mac. That's something."

"I don't care about the money" Mama's eyes filled up. "I've never cared about it."

"You'd care if you didn't have any."

Sarah tried to cheer Mama up by bringing her big bouquets of flowers. She found pretty stones and washed them, giving them to her as presents. Mama always smiled and thanked her, but there was no sparkle in her eyes. Sarah sang the songs Mama taught her, sad Irish ballads and a few Latin chants from mass.

"Mama, why don't you sing anymore?" Sarah asked, climbing up onto the bed with her and setting her doll in the rumpled covers. "You'll feel better if you sing."

Mama brushed her long blonde hair slowly. "I don't feel much like singing, darling. Mama has a lot on her mind right now."

Sarah felt a heaviness growing inside her. It was all her fault. All her fault. If she hadn't been born, Mama would be happy. "Will Alex come back, Mama?"

Mama looked at her, but Sarah didn't care. She wouldn't call him Papa anymore. He had hurt Mama and made her sad. Ever since he'd left, Mama had scarcely paid attention to her. Sarah had even heard Mama tell Cleo that love wasn't a blessing, it was a curse.

Sarah glanced at Mama's face, and her heart sank. She looked so sad. Her thoughts were far away again, and Sarah knew she was thinking of him. Mama wanted him to come back. Mama cried at night because he didn't. Mama pressed her face into her pillow at night, but Sarah still heard her sobs.

She chewed on her lip and lowered her head, playing distractedly with her doll. "What if I got sick and died, Mama?"

"You won't get sick," Mama said, glancing at her. She smiled. "You're far too young and healthy to die."

Sarah watched her mother brushing her hair. It was like sunshine flowing over her pale shoulders. Mama was so pretty. How could

Alex not love her? "But if I did, Mama, would he come back and stay with you?"

Mama went very still. She turned and stared at Sarah, and the horrified look in her eyes frightened her. She shouldn't have said that. Now Mama might guess she'd heard them fighting ... .

"Don't ever think that, Sarah."

"But – "

"No! Don't you ever ask such a question again. Do you understand?"

Mama had never raised her voice before; Sarah felt her chin quiver. "Yes, Mama."

"Never again," Mama said more gently. "Promise me. None of this has anything to do with you, Sarah." Mama reached out to pull her into her arms and stroke her tenderly. "I love you, Sarah. I love you so much. I love you more than anything or anyone in the whole wide world."

Except for him, Sarah thought. Except for Alex Stafford. What if he came back? What if he made Mama choose? What would Mama do then?

Afraid, Sarah clung to her mother and prayed he would stay away.

Jesus in Beijing

David Aikman

In *Jesus in Beijing,* David Aikman recounts the fascinating story of how Christianity began in China, even predating Francis Xavier and the Jesuits; the revival of an underground Christian Movement led by brave me and women risking death; and the current flowering of the Christian faith despite ongoing persecution.

Monarch
£8.99
PB / 1 8542.4687 9

Jesus Comes to Beijing

THE EIGHTEEN AMERICAN TOURISTS visiting China weren't expecting much from the evening's scheduled lecture. They were already exhausted from a day of touring in Beijing. But what the speaker had to say astonished them.

"One of the things we were asked to look into was what accounted for the success, in fact, the pre-eminence of the West all over the world," he said. "We studied everything we could from the historical, political, economic, and cultural perspective. At first, we thought it was because you had more powerful guns than we had. Then we thought it was because you had the best political system. Next we focused on your economic system. But in the past twenty years, we have realized that the heart of your culture is your religion: Christianity. That is why the West has been so powerful. The Christian moral foundation of social and cultural life was what made possible the emergence of capitalism and then the successful transition to democratic politics. We don't have any doubt about this."

This was not coming from some ultra-conservative from a think tank in Orange County, California, or from Jerry Falwell's Liberty University in Lynchburg, Virginia. This was a scholar from one of China's premier academic research institutes, the Chinese Academy of Social Sciences (CASS) in Beijing, in 2002. Though CASS has had a reputation since its inception for gently pushing the envelope of acceptable areas of research in China, it is hardly a viper's nest of liberal dissent.

We'll call the speaker Dr. Wu – an urbane academic in his late thirties who spoke excellent English, specialized in the study of religion, and was deeply knowledgeable about not just China but the history of the West in general and the U.S. in particular. During his presentation to the American visitors, he let them take notes and even record his voice, but he didn't want to be filmed or identified by name.

The Americans were not typical of the 12 million foreign tourists who flock to China every year. Although they made the requisite stops at the Great Wall, the Summer Palace, and a large Peking duck restaurant during their eight-day excursion, their tour was called "A Christian Heritage Tour of China." The group was made up of twelve middle-class professionals – most of them Christian ministers – almost all from California or Texas, and six of their wives, and they were in China to see what was still left of the historic Christian legacy in China.

Though China's tourism authorities were happy enough to indulge a quaint American taste for ecclesiastical archaeology, the tourists were more likely expecting to hear the official old Communist dogma about religion being the opium of the people and missionaries being tools of Western imperialism, not this enthusiastic reference to Christianity by a member of China's academic elite.

Had Christianity reached far deeper into Chinese culture and society than most people inside or outside China hitherto thought? My own answer is, definitely yes, as this book, based upon decades of interest in the topic and extensive reporting in China in the summer and fall of 2002, will show.

How Many Christians in China?

Just how many Christians are there in China? The answer is not a simple one.

As part of their tour, the Americans had visited several large churches that are allowed by the Communist government to operate formally, in both Beijing and China (beginning in the late 1970s). Some of these had been constructed decades earlier in the era of vigorous missionary activity in China. The visitors had been surprised to discover how packed these churches were, not just on Sundays, but even during mid-week worship or other teaching occasions.

The only Protestant Chinese organization that is permitted by the Communist Party to function openly is the China Christian Council (CCC), a sort of organizational umbrella for China's officially approved Protestant churches. The CCC was formed in the early 1980s to provide China's Protestant Christian church hierarchy just a little distance from the government organization established by the Communist Party in the 1950s to take control of Chinese Protestantism. This was the Three Self Patriotic Movement (TSPM), an administrative entity designed to ensure that all the activities of China's officially approved Protestant churches conformed to Beijing's political and social objectives. As we shall see, the relationship of the CCC and the Three Self from the beginning has been overlapping. The only Catholic organization permitted to function is the Catholic Patriotic Association (CPA).

The CCC routinely claims to have some 15 million baptized believers on its church rolls throughout China. The CPA says its churches have registered 6 million baptized Catholics.

But these figures are not considered credible even by China's own Public Security Bureau, the official police force, which in the past few years has indicated privately that there are at least 25 million Christians in China. Both Chinese within China and visiting outside observers generally believe that the numbers of Christians who attend churches not approved by the government – unofficial, so-called "house churches" – may exceed by a factor of three or four those under the various Chinese government-approved umbrellas.

In effect, the number of Christian believers in China, both Catholic and Protestant, may be closer to 80 million than the official combined Catholic-Protestant figure of 21 million. But, the reality is simply that no one knows for sure. All we do know is that Christianity has grown at a staggering speed since 1979, when China began to relax the fierce restrictions on religious activity that had been imposed during the Cultural Revolution in the 1960s.

Christians Everywhere

It was already clear in the 1980s that Christians were beginning to show up, though almost never identified as such, within the Chinese Communist Party. But during the 1990s it became clear that something else was happening too. I began to meet intellectuals, academics, social scientists, businessmen, artists and musicians, some of them party members, most of them not, who were unmistakably Christian believers, and who acknowledged this privately.

I began to meet increasing numbers of visitors to China, some of them ethnic Chinese, some of them Westerners, who had extraordinary tales of their own about visits with Christian contacts across China while visiting the country. I was unprepared for the dimensions of what I learned.

In 2000, I was in Guangzhou, to which several leaders of the Fangcheng fellowship, one of China's largest house church networks, traveled in order to update me on their views of the latest condition of Christianity in China. By then, it had long since become clear to me that the progress of Christianity in China was not something that belonged just in the annual newsletter of some church missionary group in America's Bible Belt.

From the grassroots of the peasantry to high within China's establishment, the country was being seeded with believing Christians. In numerical terms they were still a small minority, perhaps 7 to 8 percent of the country's 1.2 billion population. But they were being noticed, and they kept turning up in the most unexpected places.

Consulate officers

I learned, for example, that at least three of the six Chinese consulates in the United States have Christian believers among their officers. The embassy in Tokyo has at least one. It is very probable that Christians are among the officers of Chinese embassies all over Europe, Asia, Africa, and Latin America. I discovered, that there are deputy provincial governors, judges, and lawyers in China who are Christians, and that legal experts were working hard behind the scenes to try to implement laws of religious freedom and the larger concept of the rule of law-not just for Christians to be able to worship without harassment, but for followers of all faiths.

Entrepreneurs

There are Christian entrepreneurs at every level of Chinese society, including some of the richest men in the country. Zhang Jian, thirty-eight, is the founder and CEO of Broad air conditioners, founder and president of the Hair Air-Conditioning Company, and the first Chinese to own his own helicopter. Jian has also been a Christian for more than a year now and is eager to link up with other Christian businessmen around the country.

Actors, singers, and more

There are Christian actors, singers, and conductors in China, and these have been able to acknowledge their faith with much greater openness than those in other professions. For the second year in a row, in December 2002, Beijing's Forbidden City Concert Hall resonated to the solos and choruses of Handel's *Messiah*, performed in Chinese by the choir of the National Symphony Orchestra and the China Film Symphony Orchestra, under the baton of Su Wenxing, an openly professing Chinese Christian. Perhaps even more remarkable than the performance itself was the report in the official English-language newspaper, *China Daily*, on the event, and on Su himself. "Many great composers such as Bach and Handel were loyal

Christians," the paper quoted Su, who also goes by the Christian name of Timothy, as saying. "Since I became a Christian [in 1996], I have had a new understanding of them and interpret them much better." The paper, noting Su's youthful age of thirty, quoted a renowned Chinese conductor describing Su as "one of the best conductors in the country for oratorio and religious songs."

There are Christians in journalism at both the national and the local levels, but it is harder for them to indicate their beliefs to colleagues and outsiders because, in an authoritarian regime, journalism is always considered primarily a government propaganda tool to control and influence thought.

There are Christian-run homes for old people, Christian-run orphanages and hospitals, and Christian private schools the length and breadth of China.

The Communist Party and the People's Liberation Army

I heard from many Chinese Christians that there are Christian officers and enlisted men in the People's Liberation Army. I have not been able personally to meet any, and for obvious reasons I would not reveal their identity if I had.

Chinese officials have acknowledged several times that there are Christians within the Communist Party, though we do not know how high up they go, any more than we know how high up Christians can be found in China's government apparatus. I have certainly met a few.

What we do know is that several of the sons and daughters of current or past Chinese leaders have become Christian and been baptized. Li Peng, a former premier whose last post before retirement in the spring of 2003 was chairman of the National People's Congress, has a daughter who studied in Japan and was baptized a Christian there. Wang Guangmei, widow of Mao's primary political target during the Cultural Revolution, Liu Shaoqi, has three daughters, all of whom have been baptized as Christians.

Students and scholars.

In fact, perhaps half of all of China's students and scholars studying in the U.S., estimated to number as many as 150,000, according to statistics from the Ministry of Education, attended church at least once during their time in the United States. Many, of course, become Christians and get baptized while they are here.

Zhang Boli, a former student dissident who was on the police list of the twenty-one most-wanted student leaders of the 1989 Tiananmen Square protests, became a Christian while on the run in his own country before escaping in 1991. Now a pastor of two Chinese churches in the Washington, D.C., area, he estimates that as many as 20 percent of all Chinese at universities outside of China may by now have become Christian.

Political dissidents

Zhang Boli notes that he is one of at least two Christian clergy from the original twenty-one most-wanted student protest, leaders, both now in the U.S. The other is Xiong Yan, who had been part of the Tiananmen hunger strike team and one of the student representatives who met, futilely, with leaders like Ll Peng himself in an effort to defuse the tensions shortly before the June 4, 1989, crackdown. Xiong is now preparing to be a chaplain for the U.S. Army.

Two other Tiananmen protest leaders are also Christian. One of them, Wu Er Kaixi, currently lives in Taiwan with his Taiwanese wife. Originally of Uighur ethnic minority background in Xinjiang province, Wu was baptized in Taiwan by Zhang Bolli in 2002. The other is Han Dongfang, the founder of the Beijing Autonomous Workers' Federation. Han actually walked into a police station in July 1989 to protest his inclusion on the most-wanted lists, convinced that he had done nothing wrong during the student protests. He was promptly arrested and was thrown into a cell in the infectious diseases ward of a prison, where he contracted tuberculosis and nearly died in prison. Released and permitted to go to the U.S. in

1992 on medical grounds, he was converted in an overseas Chinese church in New Jersey in 1993. He now resides in Hong Kong, broadcasting to China about Chinese labor problems for Radio Free Asia.

Some other Christian dissidents include Wang Xizhe, who was imprisoned for helping pen a "big-character" protest poster in Guangzhou in 1974 and subsequently spent seventeen years in prison in China. He was baptized as a Christian in California in 2001. Two other prominent dissidents who became Christian while in exile are Dr. Wang Bingzhang and Dr. Yang Jianli; both were arrested within the past two years and are currently serving prison terms.

The Impact of a Christianized China

Clearly, Christianity is filtering into multiple aspects of Chinese society. But what does this mean? During three months of reporting the situation of Christianity in China in 2002, I was startled to discover other aspects of the Christian growth that are of profound importance to how the world responds to Islamic-origin terrorism in the wake of the events of September 11, 2001.

One journal of Chinese Protestant house church Christians, printed clandestinely, admitted that some Chinese had applauded the terrorist attacks on American civilians, but pointed out – quite accurately – that a number of Chinese (along with citizens from more than seventy other nations) had died in the New York World Trade Center attacks. Therefore, the magazine pointed out, President George W. Bush's decision to claim war against the terrorists was to maintain justice, and so was Biblical in nature.

The vast majority of China's Protestant house church Christians, it turns out, are deeply pro-American and determined to evangelize the Muslim world, something Americans generally have been too frightened to do with much boldness. Among Chinese Christians themselves is the belief – indeed some Chinese Christians refer to it as a divine calling – for Christian believers from China to bring the Gospel to the Muslim nations of the world.

"Muslims prefer Chinese to Americans. They don't like Americans very much," one Chinese Christian said boldly. He outlined several reasons why Chinese Christians can succeed where Westerners have failed. "The Chinese government supports [Middle Eastern] terrorism [he didn't mean literally, only in the sense of supporting the anti-American objectives of some political groups in the Middle East] so the Muslim nations support China. Besides, we have a lot of experience of persecution. As Chinese missionaries, wherever we go, when we arrive in a place we always see what the escape route will be."

This Chinese Christian articulated the view that Chinese believers would play a major role in the circumnavigation of the teachings of Jesus back to the Middle East. "We have the view that Chinese missionaries will be part of the mainstream on the highway back to Jerusalem. The Muslim religion is the biggest obstacle on the road back to Jerusalem," he said.

A Christianized China is poised to change the face not just of Christendom worldwide, but potentially of the world of Islam.

An Opportune Time for Christianity

Economic Growth and the "Open Door"

China has never been as intellectually and philosophically open to the outside world as it is today. Deng Xiaoping, who came to power in 1978, opened China up both to its own latent internal creative energies and to the outside world with his famous "open door" policy. To unleash the considerable energy and creative talents of China's entrepreneurs and workers, the regime took a conscious decision to loosen many of the clamps that had been fastened in place on Chinese social and civil life for decades.

For example, until the 1980s, every Chinese was at the mercy of his or her work unit, the *danwei*, a control system that determined residence location, job description, often even whether marriage was permissible or not. As the demand for flexible labor deployment grew, the *danwei* system, though still in place in much of the country, began to break down.

As China came to require a much deeper knowledge than hitherto allowed of the outside world in order to compete economically in the global marketplace, it became possible for ordinary Chinese to have contact with foreigners, then to travel overseas, and more recently, to have access to foreign-source information – including much information about China – through the Internet. Though the Chinese Communist Party still blocks key Internet sites, and occasionally resorts to blocking search engines like Google, overall, China's authorities have permitted their people unprecedented freedom of intellectual investigation and social activity at the *private* level for most of the past decade.

An inquisitive Chinese in China today would have no difficulty finding out the name of the prime minister of Montenegro, the total size of the U.S. defense budget, or for that matter, what the Christian theological issues at stake were in the fourth-century dispute between Arius and Athanasius. A Chinese interested in religion can attend, without fear of the consequences, any officially approved Protestant or Catholic church, can purchase books that explain, even sympathetically, the nature of Christian belief, can buy a Bible (but only at a TSPM or CPA church, not in any ordinary bookstore), and can openly question a pastor or priest about the differences between, say, Premillennialist Dispensational eschatology and that of the Protestant Reformed tradition.

Foreign capital, technological expertise, and management skills flowed into the country. From 1979 until the late 1990s, China's GDP grew at an annual rate of 9.5 percent, in some years reaching into the superheated zone of 14 percent. Things have slowed down somewhat since then, but not by much. Annual growth rate for the period 1996–2000 has been about 8.3 percent, and it appears to have slowed down by only about one percentage point in the two years since then.

Yet, the headlong growth of the economy has brought along plenty of downsides, including company collapses, stock market volatility, and dangerously widening income gaps between China's rich coastal cities and the impoverished inland provinces. The migration from countryside to city has led to a "floating population" of millions of illegal squatters in Beijing and other major cities and has depressed industrial wages in many parts of the country. Working conditions in many of China's urban factories may well be worse today than at any time in China's Communist history. Corruption in China is broadly acknowledged, and regularly deplored, at the very highest level of political leadership. Virtually every American business executive who has had anything to do with China can rattle off personal encounters with corruption. Beyond the occasional high-profile arrests and executions, little is done to fix the problems.

"In China you can do anything you like if you have money. The only thing you can't do is what you can't think up to do," said a Chinese who lives in the United States but visits his home country several times each year. One of his good friends, a senior judge in an inland province, told him that, for 30,000–50,000 yuan (approximately $3,750–6,250), even a man on death row could buy his freedom. Furthermore, if the sentence were commuted to fifteen years in prison, not even that would have to be served. Many Chinese, the judge told this Chinese, will actually do the prison time for you if you pay them, say, $30 a month.

China's Communist regime still ruthlessly represses people for any explicit display of political protest, as practitioners of the Falungong meditation practice discovered to their painful cost during 1998–2001. At the local level, sadistic provincial officials also can, and do, take the law into their own hands for arbitrary purposes. Christians who choose to meet together without formal authorization or registration of their organization can be, and have been, right up through 2003, arrested, beaten, and tortured without compunction by local officials of the Public Security Bureau.

But compared with the blanket of desolate socialist totalitarian-
ism that smothered the creative springs of China's culture and
thought-life from the late 1950s until about 1978, today's civic freedom is a heady breath of intellectual liberty.

These factors – economic growth, increasing access to information, added civic freedoms, and the need for a consciousness to combat the social ills of prosperity – combine to create an opportune
atmosphere for the growth of Christianity in China both as a movement and as an ideology.

Filling an Ideological Vacuum

It is significant that Christianity is emerging in China at a time when
there is a massive ideological vacuum left in society by the
nationwide collapse of belief in Marxism-Leninism.

Mao's catastrophic Cultural Revolution had "cured" almost all
Chinese of any belief in the veracity of Communist theory. It is hard
to find anyone in China today who truly believes in the theoretical
truth of China's official political ideology, ponderously called
"Marxism-Leninism, Mao Zedong thought." Marxism was tried in
the extreme form during Mao's nearly two decades of utopian
economic and social tinkering (1958–1976) and it was found to be
irremediably destructive.

The Communist Party has managed to maintain power for more
than a decade after the Tiananmen Square demonstrations in 1989,
despite predictions that it would probably fade from power quite
soon, for two reasons: sheer inertia and the fear among most
ordinary Chinese of *luan*, or chaos, that destructive anarchic
condition that many foreigners thought was China's natural
condition in the past two centuries. Fewer than four years after the
1989 crackdown, in 1993, I spoke to Chinese intellectuals at several of
the nation's universities. The consensus was uniform: democracy,
yes, but please not next week. They did not want to see any political
change come *quickly* to China.

When Deng launched his "open door" movement of internal reforms and access to China of foreign capital and expertise, Chinese quickly grasped that, from an economic point of view, capitalism was now becoming the system of choice to make China strong. With straight-faced chicanery, the regime called the new system "socialism with Chinese characteristics."

This phrase obscured a more important point: what way of looking at life in general should Chinese now adopt? Marxism-Leninism itself was a dead letter. Confucianism, the ethical and moral system that China's ruling dynasties and ordinary people had sought to emulate for millennia, was certainly admired for its emphasis on family cohesion and mutual responsibility. But most Chinese considered it an unwieldy philosophy, incapable of the social change, capitalistic creativity, and entrepreneurial success needed in the newly globalized world of economic competition.

Many Chinese wondered: is capitalism just a way of doing business, or did it come with concrete ethical and philosophical foundations? Many Chinese sociologists note that, in the coastal city of Wenzhou, in Zhejiang province, south of Shanghai, Christianity in the 1980s seemed to surge proportionately to the success of Wenzhou retailers in making money. In fact, a decade ago, some Chinese, thinking about capitalism, Christianity, and Wenzhou, were making the intellectual connection between religion and the rise of capitalism, the central thesis of R. H. Tawney in his influential book with the same name, *Religion and the Rise of Capitalism.*

Perhaps, some Chinese began to think, Christianity itself, which had been such a powerful, if not fully understood, ingredient in the global pre-eminence of Western civilization, may be a worldview, even a metaphysic, that could guide China's pathway into the twenty-first century. Perhaps it could even provide a lens for Chinese to understand their own history with greater insight than ever before.

A New Worldview for the Chinese?

By the early 1990s, a new kind of Chinese had come into existence at Chinese universities and research institutions: "cultural Christians." Many reject the name, as we shall see later, and prefer to use the ponderous phrase "Chinese scholars interested in Christianity." But the phenomenon was real enough: highly educated Chinese who were not satisfied that either the Marxist interpretation of religion or the standard Western Darwinian understanding of life adequately explained the human condition in general and the Chinese condition in particular.

Nor was it among just Western-trained academics or Shanghai yuppies that these ideas began to be discussed. Early in 2002, China's then president and Communist Party leader, Jiang Zeming, attended a dinner party in the private home of another senior Chinese political figure in the heart of Beijing. The conversation turned to the party's upcoming sixteenth congress, a momentous, once-every-five-years gathering then scheduled for the late autumn of 2002 (the Congress eventually met November 7–15, 2002).

The company was relaxed, the mood ebullient. "Comrade Jiang," a guest asked, "if, before leaving office, you could make one decree that you knew would be obeyed in China, what would it be?" Jiang put on a broad smile and looked around the room. "I would make Christianity the official religion of China," he replied. Jiang, of course, formally relinquished the reins of power at the sixteenth party congress to his successor as party general secretary, Hu Jintao, and even if he wanted to implement that wish, is no longer in a position to do so. But even if he were being merely playful with his fellow guests, his whimsical comment was telling.

In 1949, the world's most populous nation adopted the materialist philosophy of a nineteenth-century German and a twentieth-century Russian in its search for wealth and power after a century of foreign encroachments on its government and culture. That philosophy turned out to be bankrupt and China is almost self-consciously casting around for something to replace it. Christianity has not yet been embraced as that replacement by the Chinese people, but today it is in a very good position to do so.

Foreigners, and especially foreign Christians, have for centuries yearned for China to change in a direction they considered desirable for both Chinese and themselves. Often, their hopes and aspirations have been illusory or just plain naive. But China, whether it becomes Christian or goes in another direction, is changing right before our eyes. It is the Christian component of that change, and the remarkable potential that it contains, that this book is about.

More

Simon Ponsonby

This Book invites us to swim 'in the deep end' of Gods love. With a preachers art and a pastors heart, he gives us a readable, moving and direct book. You will finish it with a fresh sense that with God, there is always more to discover, more to enjoy, more to come.

Kingsway
£7.99
PB / 1 8429.1209 7

SIMON PONSONBY

MORE

How you can have
more of the Spirit when you already
have everything in Christ

A remarkably gifted new author
– MICHAEL GREEN

First Published by KINGSWAY COMMUNICATIONS
Lottbridge Drove, Eastbourne, BN23 6NT

1. Longing for the Deep

Many Christians are unaware that there is a deep end. They have become so used to living in the shallows that they think this is the norm. Perhaps this is not all they expected when they first found themselves in the pond, but they are generally content to paddle until they get to the big pond in the sky. Occasionally they hear rumours that there is a deep end, they meet the odd person who claims to have come from the deep end, one or two of their fellow shallow-enders have even left them and said they are off to the deep, and every now and again they wonder, 'So, how do I get to this deep end?' That great statesman of the church, Billy Graham, once wrote,

> Everywhere I go I find that God's people lack something. They are hungry for something. Their Christian experience is not all that they expected and they often have recurring defeat in their lives. Christians today are hungry for spiritual fulfilment. The most desperate need of the nation today is that men and women who profess Jesus be filled with the Holy Spirit.[1]

Billy Graham's global itinerant ministry perhaps gave him a better insight into the condition of the church than any other twentieth-century Christian leader. First, he rightly identifies

---

[1]Billy Graham, *The Holy Spirit*, Word, 1988.

the desperation in the lives of many Christians. Secondly, he suggests that a failing church has implications for influencing the nation. Thirdly, he offers a resolution – immersion in the Holy Spirit.

Many Christians are like the Pope in Robert Browning's poem 'The Ring and the Book', crying, 'Is this little all that was to be? Is this thing Salvation?' He expected so much more. Johann Christoph Blumhardt was responsible for steering an extraordinary awakening in his little village of Mottlingen, Germany, in the late nineteenth century. Accompanied by signs and wonders, this renewal sent shock waves throughout the country, and many thousands travelled to the village specifically to meet God, confess their sins and find personal spiritual renewal. The key to Blumhardt's authority and influence stemmed from his discontent with the status quo of his and the church's spirituality, and his persistent prayer for and pursuit of the deep end which he knew to be a reality from his study of God's word. Listen to him on his knees, beseeching God for more:

> I long for another outpouring of the Holy Spirit, another Pentecost. That must come if things are to change in Christianity, for it simply cannot continue in such a wretched state. The gifts and powers of the early Christian time – Oh how I long for their return. And I believe the saviour is just waiting for us to ask for them ... When I look at what we have, I cannot help sighing ... Oh Lord Jesus is that the promised Spirit for which you hung on a tree? Where is the Spirit that penetrates nation after nation as swiftly as at the time of the apostles and places them at Jesus' feet?[2]

This prayer, this pursuit, this rediscovered power, brought deliverance to the captives, salvation to the lost and renewed hope and joy to the believers. It also shook the nation, prophetically challenging the inexorable advance of a bloodless, Bible-less, God-less Liberal Protestant theology. As with Billy Graham in the

---

[2] F. Zuendel, *The Awakening*, Plough Publishers, 1999.

following century, Blumhardt incisively recognised that the church was asleep, wretched, lukewarm, blind and poor, living below her birthright, failing herself and her Master and the lost world, because she had failed to avail herself of all that the Holy Spirit would, could and should bring.

The Reformed theologian Karl Barth, in his farewell speech on retirement as professor at Basel, declared of the church's theological endeavours, 'Everything is in order but everything is also in the greatest of disorder. The mill is turning, but it is empty as it turns. All the sails are hoisted, but no wind fills them to drive the ship. The fountain adorned with many spouts is there, but no water comes.'[3]

It is my intention throughout this book to deduce from Scripture and the church's testimony the reality of an essential, personal, tangible, repeatable Pentecost. We are searching for that place of encounter, depth, intimacy with God, that place of power to serve, of character to conform us to Christ, from which we may live, move and have our being in the fullness of God's Holy Spirit.

One of the great expositors of the church, Dr Martyn Lloyd-Jones, once thundered at those Christians who claim to have it all, who claim that there is nothing more of God to receive and experience, 'Got it all? I simply ask in the name of God, why then are you as you are? If you have got it all, why are you so unlike the New Testament Christians? Got it all? Got it all at your conversion? Well where is it, I ask?'[4] His point is incisive: if we have what the first Christians had, why do we not do what they did? We must conclude that either God gave them more than he has given us, or we have failed to avail ourselves of what he has given us.

Lloyd-Jones was thinking particularly of what he and others call 'baptism in the Spirit'. He believed that this was a specific experience, often following conversion, which was repeatable,

---

[3]Despite owning many of Barth's works and spending years studying him, the only place I can locate this quote is in Hans Wolf, *Joel and Amos*, Hermenia Commentary Series, Fortress Press, 1977, p. 267.
[4]Sermon on 'Baptism in the Spirit', 25th May 1961.

definite, tangible and manifested in some particular, sensorily perceptible manner. It issues in changed countenance, bold speech and specific gifting. It produces deep assurance – beyond mere assent to truth at conversion – that we are children of God and ultimately directs attention away from the recipient to Christ.[5] The strident Calvinist John Piper, in a sermon series on Acts,[6] has similarly spoken of baptism in the Spirit as 'an overwhelming experience of the greatness of God, spilling over in courageous passionate praise and worship'.

While I hesitate to use the term 'baptism in the Spirit',[7] I cannot question the reality of the experience, both scripturally and in the life of the church. Suffice it to say at this point that my main hesitation with this teaching is that it is too often reduced to a once-only experience, subsequent to conversion – although Lloyd-Jones believed it was repeatable. I believe it may happen concurrently with conversion (see Acts 19:6f.; 10:44f.) or subsequent to conversion (see Acts 2; 8:4f.; 9:17). It may be an overwhelming event or a progressively deepening encounter. At the swimming pool my son Nathanael jumps into the deep end, while I prefer to lower myself in more slowly. The net result is the same, however: we know we are in the water and not on the edge. I simply do not believe it is a once-only 'second blessing'. It is, rather, a constantly repeatable,

---

[5]See a very helpful discussion of this whole issue and a summary of Lloyd-Jones' thought in the significant book by Stuart Piggin, *Firestorm of the Lord*, Paternoster Press, 2000, p. 98. Lloyd-Jones' own writings on this are most notably found in *Joy Unspeakable*, Kingsway, 1984, p. 91f.

[6]Sermon entitled 'Tongues of Fire and the Fullness of God', 14th October 1990, www.tx3.net/~justice/finmood/piperfire.htm

[7]This is a contentious term and concept which we shall be exploring throughout the book, notably in Chapter 6. Let me simply say here that I believe the term is the wrong one: baptism in the Spirit, mentioned in all the Gospels and twice in Acts, is shown in 1 Corinthians 12:13 to be conversion to Christ and incorporation into his church. I personally prefer to call the ongoing experience of the Spirit 'the fullness of the Spirit' (see Eph. 3:19; 5:18). Whatever the term, the ongoing experience is the right and necessary one which we may know and must seek.

deepening experience of God's Spirit, who brings a greater revelation of the person and work of Christ, a blazing love for Christ, a greater and more effective empowering witness to Christ, and a transforming conformity to the character of Christ.

Recently I have been gripped by a worship song by Tim Hughes, 'Consuming Fire', which has captured the hearts of many in articulating their yearning for more of God. Beginning with the line, 'There must be more than this: O Breath of God, come breathe within,' this prayer in song invokes the Holy Spirit to come and establish in us a greater sense of God's presence, a greater anointing of power, a greater deliverance from bondage and a greater release in worship. This theme should always be a prayerful song on the church's heart and lips. Tim Hughes' contemporary song has a long pedigree. One of the most ancient and beloved hymns, *'Veni Creator Spiritus'*, comes from the ninth century and was written by Archbishop Maurus, a devout monk and noted theologian who knew the need in the church for an ongoing Pentecost:

> Come, Creator Spirit,
> Visit the minds of those who are yours.
> Fill with heavenly grace
> The hearts that you have made.[8]

This prayer in song continues by asking for a visitation and extension of the work of the Spirit, inflaming our devotion, transforming our characters, equipping our service with gifts and power, enlightening our minds, filling our hearts with love, delivering us from darkness, directing our paths and entering us into intimate union with God. The authority of the hymn is seen by its unique usage across a millennium and as the only Roman hymn adopted by

[8]Translation by Raniero Cantalamessa in his outstanding book, *Come Creator Spirit*, The Liturgical Press, 2003, p. 5. The whole book is a remarkable commentary on this ancient hymn. For an alternative translation, see Jürgen Moltmann, *The Spirit of Life*, SCM, 1992, p. 311.

all Protestant denominations. But it is possible to sing such songs, for centuries even, without intention, expectation or appropriation – and I fear that, for too long, the church has done just that. We must learn to sing these songs, not out of tradition, but in travail, longing for and begging God to visit us.

There have been many church luminaries who knew they did not have it all and who longed for a closer, fuller walk with their Lord. Marked by holy discontent, their search was not in vain. Their experience of more of God was made evident in personal delight, strengthening to the church, salvation to the lost and glory to God. We can point to John Wesley who, after years of fruitless gospel ministry and personal moral defeat, had his heart 'strangely warmed' by God's anointing at Aldersgate in May 1738.[9] Immediately he sensed he had moved from the faith of a slave to the faith of a son, and with this new-found anointing he subsequently shook the nations with apostolic authority. In 1721 Jonathan Edwards entered a season of experiences of God, beholding the loveliness and beauty of Christ. Given a deep revelation of the majesty and meekness of Christ, he was 'swallowed up in God'. These experiences set the trajectory for his whole life and issued in the precipitation of the New England Awakening and his massive production of some of the most significant and respected theological works in the church. D.L. Moody, already an established and effective minister in Chicago, recalled the street in New York where, in 1871, following a time of deep crying out for more of God's Spirit, he had such an encounter with God that he was never the same again: 'One day – oh what a day – God revealed himself to me.' His subsequent evangelistic ministry in America and the United Kingdom, particularly London and Cambridge, was marked by many significant conversions. The most effective evangelist in the twentieth-century church, Billy Graham, drew the attention of the lady who would become his wife when both were students at

---

[9]See John Capon, *John and Charles Wesley*, Hodder and Stoughton, 1988, pp. 71f.; 99f.

Wheaton College. She said, 'There was a seriousness about him; there was a depth ... he was a man who knew God; he was a man who had a purpose, a dedication in his life; he knew where he was going. He wanted to please God more than any man I'd ever known.'[10] Such consecration, devotion and passion for God brought a rent heaven over this man's life and ministry. One man's pursuit of God can influence the nations for God. For all these men this would not be the end of their search for more of God, but they would never settle for less.

One could argue that in each case this was a special anointing, for a special person, at a special time. Perhaps – but it could equally be argued that it was the anointing which made these ordinary men extraordinary. That said, what these notable persons experienced was what hundreds of anonymous folk also equally experienced along with the famous apostles at Pentecost (Acts 2). It was what, besides the named Cornelius, all anonymously experienced when the Spirit came to his household (Acts 10). It was the same for the nameless converts at Samaria (Acts 8) and for the nameless converts at Ephesus (Acts 19). Thus, while the experience may make some exceptional in God's purposes, the actual experience is not exceptional.

While these particular experiences by these particular men were of particular remembrance, a study of the lives of such men shows that experiences like these were not always unique for them and that these men continued occasionally to encounter similar experiences. If I may be frank, I remember well the first time I kissed Tiffany, on the eve of our engagement, but it was not to be the last time! If it had been the only time, I would have been the most delighted of men, and it would have been memorable – but, praise God, it was not unique, just the memorable start of even greater things to come. So I believe in the baptisms of the Spirit, the fillings with the Spirit, the anointings of the Spirit, the ever increasing, ever deepening immersion into God. Bishop David Pytches famously said, 'Yes, I

[10]John Pollock, *Billy Graham*, Hodder and Stoughton, 1966, p. 46.

believe in the second blessing – it comes after the first and before the third.'

It is this ongoing experience of God that is the longing of so many Christians, the need of the nations, and the gift of God through Christ by his Spirit. But unless we are, like the psalmist (Ps. 42:1f.), consumed by desire for the streams of the living God, the chances are we will never know how these waters satiate and we will live our Christian life parched and cracked and trying in the flesh to hang on in there until we reach heaven. Unless we are filled by the living waters of the Holy Spirit, which Jesus promised would flow *out*, not in (Jn 7:38), we will never be the blessing God intended us to be. We will never water and transform the dead and barren deserts around us into life, as we see with the river that flowed from the temple, turning the salty seawater fresh (Ezek. 47:8).

I was recently invited to Spain, to minister at a pioneering church-planting ministry among the drug addict community. In fifteen years, missionaries Elliot and Mary Tepper have developed the largest evangelical church in Spain, named Betel, made up almost exclusively of heroin addicts converted to and delivered by Christ. While I was there, I was invited, along with Elliot, to attend a national Catholic charismatic meeting. I tell you, I had some quick repenting to do of my critical attitudes and certain Reformed theological a priori prejudices. The Lord was there with the thousands who had gathered from all over Europe to meet him. There were four outstanding features: the glorious, Christcentred worship; the palpable sense of God's presence which had me weeping most of the day; the powerful and lengthy expository preaching that would have impressed Spurgeon; and the hunger of these Catholics for more of God, as they queued up outside to be prayed for by myself and my missionary friend. I cannot express how challenged I was by seeing nuns on their knees in front of me,

---

[11] A French Catholic monk told me that the Catholic churches in the parishes have been suffocated to death by the institutionalised secularism of France. However,

seeking the laying on of hands, seeking more of God.[11] The senior bishop who had preached from Colossians for an hour like Savonarola humbly asked us to remember him in our prayers.

A sincere singing of the Spirit's song, seeking more of God, has marked some within the Roman Catholic Church since the latter part of the twentieth century.[12] The Spirit blows where he wills. Pope John XXIII, a prophetic, pneumatic figure, believing he was directed by the Holy Spirit, called a general council of the whole Church of Rome which issued in Vatican II, where he sought to see the whole of the Church's life and doctrine renewed by the Spirit and made holy. Pope John famously prayed what became the essential theme of the council: 'Renew your wonders in our time, as though by a new Pentecost.' Here Rome caught the wind of the Spirit, and in doctrine and practice, as Jaroslav Pelikan commented, largely caught up with the Reformation, from which some Liberal Protestants have subsequently sadly slipped. Pope John's successor, Pope Paul VI, carried on this theme, insisting repeatedly, 'The church and the world need more than ever that the miracle of Pentecost should continue in history.' Their prayers, joining the longing of many sincere Catholics, appear to have been heard. God has been renewing the dry and cracked wineskins of Catholicism. Unbiased observation shows that, wherever the new wind of the Spirit has blown through Catholicism, she has sought to realign herself with evangelical norms – in terms of both Scripture and evangelism.

---

he said there are several communities throughout France which are beacons of gospel light and life, and he emphasised that these are the evangelical charismatic communities.

[12]Is Rome turning out to be like the son who said 'no' but then acted 'yes' to the Father (Mt. 21:28f.)? The evangelical world has for a long time, not without justification, felt that the Roman Church had followed a wrong trajectory in terms of authority and spirituality. Despite our concerns, God's grace appears to be visiting and reforming this historic Church. See 'Prayers for Pentecost by Popes', in Kilian McDonnell (ed.), *Towards a New Pentecost for a New Evangelisation*, Malines Document 1, The Liturgical Press, 1993, p. 62.

Out of the Comfort Zone

R.T. Kendall

Many Christians are today sitting happily in the middle of their personal comfort zones, and feel God has confirmed their right to be there. But is this the God of the Bible? This is a book of huge significance for the church today, designed to inspire, encourage and challenge us to seek God's greater anointing. Chapters include 'For the Love of Money', 'Chances are you are a Pharisee if...', 'The Seeker-Sensitive God?' and 'Whatever Happened to Hell?'.

Hodder & Stoughton
£7.99
PB / 0 3408.6293 9

Also by the same Author

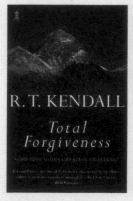
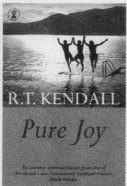

1. When God Plays Hard to Get

'If I were hungry I would not tell you.'

Psalm 50:12

It seems to me that the modern Church has drifted so far from the biblical revelation of the true God that any resemblance between him and the popular God of today's generation is quite remote. I think we are in a Romans 1 situation,

> Although they claimed to be wise, they become fools and exchanged the glory of the immortal God for images made to look like mortal man and birds and animals and reptiles. (Rom. 1:22–23)

It is a case in which the God of the Bible is either too holy or too terrible for us; so we have come up with a God that we are comfortable with, at home with, so that we can feel sufficiently religious without having to identify with the ancient God of Israel and the earliest Church.

When I was in seminary I was required to read a book about God 'in an age of atheism'. In this book the author managed to concoct a God whereby one need not be regarded as an atheist after all, even though the God of the Bible was rejected. The theologian Paul Tillich (1886–1965) even suggested that an atheist might be a believer when faith was defined as 'ultimate concern'.

But if you think my own book is an attack on liberalism in the modern Church you would be wrong. I fear that those who deny the historic truths of Holy Scripture are beyond the pale and I seek not very hard to reach them. It is those closer to home that worry me, those who seem to want to hold on to the Bible up to a point but none the less distance themselves from disturbing things we all know are contained in Holy Scripture.

As I said in the Introduction, Ludwig Feuerbach opined that God was nothing more than man's projection upon the backdrop of the universe; that people want to believe in something, especially a God who will take care of them in time of trouble and then give them a home in heaven when they die. Such people mentally project such a God and claim he really does exist. Such a God does not exist of course, says Feuerbach, but he exists in their minds and gives comfort.

It is my view that many Christians do this. They know full well there are things in the Bible they don't want to believe but they are not prepared to throw out everything in the Bible so they fancy a God who approves of their own comfort zone. This God is happy with Christians who reject Bible – denying liberal theology while at the same time approving of their unease with the total revelation of God as revealed in the Old and New Testament. In fact some of these people would go so far as to claim they believe in the whole of the Bible 'from Genesis to maps' – while ensuring that they are at ease in their folk religion. They have been baptised and (in some cases) confirmed; they are (almost certainly) approved of by their church leader; they attend church in varying degrees of regularity and feel quite right indeed in themselves.

What does God himself think of this? Is he so neglected by the masses that he is simply thrilled to have anybody – anywhere – whatever their level of conviction, to give him any attention at all? Is he so hard up or starved for recognition that he will make any measure of concession to any person who makes any effort at all to acknowledge him? Will he therefore show his approval toward any kind of profession of faith because some tipping of the hat toward him is better than nothing?

The nice God of today's religious people might do just that. But not the God of the Bible. Unless he chooses for a while to withhold his real feelings and intentions from us, which is the basis of this chapter.

One reason I abandoned 'Your God is Too Nice' as a title is because I didn't want to make the reader feel guilty or for you to think I feel qualified to judge you. I write out of experience of over fifty years of preaching, most of which have been as a pastor.

If God is too nice, what does this mean? It may mean that he mainly exists in your mind, as we saw when I referred to the German philosopher Feuerbach. Perhaps even you have been worshipping a God you can be comfortable with but who is not the God of the Bible at all. And yet it could mean that the true God has decided to be nice to you for the moment and let you remain in your comfort zone – undisturbed. You might want to say that this isn't being very nice at all if he will eventually show that he was unhappy with me. Yes. But what if he tried for a while but you wouldn't listen? So he let you carry on as if nothing happened. What if he simply decided to be 'nice' to you by letting you remain in your comfort zone and seek a person elsewhere who would indeed listen to him?

Rodney Howard-Browne told me that the Lord put it to him, 'If you don't do what I tell you I will find someone who will.' Jesus said to the church at Ephesus, 'If you do not repent, I will come to you and remove your lampstand from its place' (Rev. 2:5). This is what happens when a church goes astray or soft and God raises up movements to carry on with what ought to have been the Church's own mandate.

Arthur Blessitt, the man who has carried a cross around the world, said that as a student in university he prayed in his dormitory room, 'God, give me a work nobody else will do.'

Someone asked Arthur, 'Why does God speak to you but not to me?'

Arthur replied to the lady, 'Did you ever feel an impulse to speak to someone about Jesus that you didn't know?'

She replied, 'As a matter of fact I have.'

Arthur then said to her, 'Start obeying that voice and it will become clearer and clearer.'

One of the most stunning lines I have come across is in Psalm 50:12: 'If I were hungry I would not tell you.' One evening when our children were sitting on the floor in front of me watching television, not being too interested in what they were watching, I found myself reading that verse. I began to feel very uneasy. I thought to myself, 'I wish the Lord would tell me if he were hungry.' I began to wonder, what if God wanted me to spend more time with him than I had been giving him, would he tell me? I kept reading it, 'If I were hungry I would not tell you.' I couldn't shake it off. I read it again. And again. I began to get the definite feeling that by saying this God was telling me after all he needed and wanted me.

The context of this verse in Psalm 50 is that, though the world is his and although he has cattle on a thousand hills, God is hungry for me. Though he has countless angels – millions and billions – not to mention other people all over the world worshipping him and spending time with him, he wanted me. I seized the moment, for some reason. I decided to fast the next day. I sought his face as I had not done before. The curious thing was, God was hinting the very opposite of what he was saying in Psalm 50:12.

The unveiling of that verse was part of a process that led me to one of the most unusual teachings I have ever come across in Scripture. I have racked my brain many times over what to call it and I still struggle with the best term or phrase for it. I used to call it 'the divine tease'. This was the phrase I used in our School of Theology at Westminster Chapel. This phrase could be defined as God's somewhat playful but deadly serious set-up to let us find out what is in our hearts. It is when he says or does the very opposite of what he intends for us to perceive. But I have since decided to refer to this startling and profound truth as *when God plays hard to get*. For he does! You may say, 'That's not fair.' Perhaps. I still struggle with Jeremiah's words, 'O LORD, you deceived me, and I was deceived' (Jer. 20:7). I don't claim to know all that that means. The theme of this chapter is therefore but the tip of the iceberg of a teaching most extraordinary.

Perhaps the best introduction to this truth is when Jesus was walking with two people – who were kept from recognising who he really was – on the way to Emmaus. It was the same day on which he had been raised from the dead. They came to this village and, when it was time to say good-bye, Jesus 'acted as if he were going further'. This was not his intention at all. He fully intended to stay with them a while longer. He had more to show them. But he did not tell them that and they certainly did not know that. He 'acted' as if he were going further – and he played the role so well that they clearly were going to be upset if he did leave them. The truth is, Jesus wanted them to do exactly as they did – to plead with him to stay on with them. They did not know they were persuading him to do precisely what he planned for them; 'They urged him strongly, "Stay with us, for it is nearly evening; the day is almost over." So [Jesus] went in to stay with them' (Luke 24:29).

When God plays hard to get, then, he often means the very opposite of what he says. And yet it is only because God wants us to plead with him when he appears not to care whether we do or not.

This aspect of God's unusual ways of dealing with us is often in operation when our circumstances suggest it is okay this time to put not God but other things first for the day. If I am so busy, and God knows this, he surely does not expect me to spend time alone with him in praying and reading my Bible. If I am in debt and can't pay my bills he surely does not expect me to return my tithes to him. If there are important people who want to see me he surely would want me to put these people ahead of spending time with ordinary souls. If I did not sleep well last night he understands this and surely would not expect me to try to have my usual quiet time.

Listen to these words from Martin Luther's journal: 'I have a very busy day today. I must spend not two hours, but three, in prayer.' The suggestion might well come to most of us that, given the situation, we need not spend as much time in prayer; but to Luther it meant he must spend more time than ever – to receive divine help to get more done! The movers and shakers and the great saints in church history recognised when God plays hard to get – even if they did not call it that.

Why does God do it? To see what is in our hearts. It is not for him. He already knows. It is for us. It lets us see the truth about ourselves. The truth of this 'side' of God, if I may put it that way, brings out the truth of what we *want*; it brings our true feelings to the surface. The two people on the road to Emmaus had been captivated by Jesus' teaching although they did not have a clue at first it was Jesus. When our hearts burn within us it is a wonderful, wonderful sign that God is at work and wants us to seek his face. The burning heart is there not to mock us but to prod us on to seek his face.

And what do you suppose motivated them then and would do it now for us? You might say, 'If Jesus were there playing hard to get, I would have urged him to stay too – like those two men. They had Jesus himself interpreting Scripture for them. And if he did that with me, I too would plead with him to stay around.' Quite. But they didn't even know it was Jesus. The truth and the application of it is what set their hearts on fire.

It is a strong hint to us that when the truth of the Word of God has this kind of effect on us (Charles Spurgeon used to say to preachers 'When a text gets a hold of you, chances are you have got a hold of it') it is because God himself is at work to draw us closer to him than ever. It is his way of subtly beckoning to us – 'Seek my face.'

Therefore on that night when I kept reading the words, 'If I were hungry I would not tell you', I was gripped and did not know why. It turned out that God was telling me he was yearning for me to spend more time with him. It was a demonstration of God playing hard to get. He does this sort of thing with us. This is one of the reasons he hides his face from us, as he did with Hezekiah: 'God left him to test him and to know everything that was in his heart' (2 Chron. 32:31).

Another time Jesus did this sort of thing was when the disciples were rowing against the wind and waves on the Sea of Galilee. Jesus had gone up into a mountain to pray – and watched the disciples struggling. I have often been fascinated how Jesus did not go at once to help them; he just watched them. Would it not have been nice had Jesus left his place on the mountain at once and turned up on the sea to help them? Or could he not have interceded for them – to ask the Father to stop the wind? But he only watched them.

He does that with all of us. He sees us in our struggle and anxieties – and does not step in. There these disciples were, 'straining at the oars', with Jesus doing nothing to rescue them! He waited until four o'clock in the morning before he showed up. Then when he did so, walking on the water, he was 'about to pass by them' – as if he wasn't even going to identify himself, and they too were kept from recognising him; they thought he was a ghost. But he intervened and said, 'It is I. Don't be afraid' (Mark 6:47–51; cf. Matt. 14:22–27). God is never too late, never too early; he's always just on time.

Jesus did this with the Syro-Phoenician woman. She was not Jewish but Greek, but still approached Jesus and begged him to drive a demon out of her daughter. Jesus treated her with an almost callous coldness. 'First let the children eat all they want,' he told her, 'for it is not right to take the children's bread and toss it to their dogs.' That was enough to put most people off! If the Lord did that with many of us we would walk away in disgust and sarcastically say, 'Thanks a lot – sorry to be such a nuisance to you' – and never know what might have been our lot had we persisted as this woman did. Instead of being offended, acknowledging what would be an insult by today's reckoning and going away in a huff, she reasoned with him: 'Yes, Lord, but even the dogs under the table eat the children's crumbs.' She knew her place and realised Jesus owed her nothing. Then Jesus told you, 'For such a reply, you may go; the demon has left your daughter' (Mark 7:24–30).

There is a widespread feeling among people today that God owes us something, that if we do something that is good or righteous, God should stand to attention and salute us. Our self-righteousness creeps in and we say to ourselves, 'Most people don't even go to church at all. This puts me in a special class; therefore God should be very happy that I am doing this good deed.' This good deed might be anything from attending church, tithing or spending extra time in prayer. We think God should reward those of us who we assume are a cut above most people.

My wife Louise was miraculously healed in 1995 when Rodney and Adonica Howard-Browne laid hands on her and prayed for her. They invited her to come to Lakeland, Florida, to attend the camp meeting there. She agreed to go. On the first night when she walked in, nothing went right. Thousands were there, strange people were doing what seemed to her as very weird things, the people around her were rude where she was sitting. She got up and moved to another area. She wanted to go back to her hotel, pack her bags and get on the next plane to England. But she stayed. She phoned me two days later to say of the camp meeting, 'It is the nearest you get to heaven without dying; it is the greatest experience of my life' (a word I promised myself I would not take too personally). Louise was never to be the same again; those days in Lakeland were more precious than gold. But she had every reason at first to reject everything.

You might think that God would be nice and immediately acknowledge those who sincerely seek his face with a tangible sign on a silver platter. I would have thought he might be nice to Martin Luther the night before he stood before the authorities at Worms, Germany, in the sixteenth century. After all, Luther was standing alone for the gospel – the truth of God's own Word. But Luther walked back and forth in his cell the night before the trial. 'O God, are you dead?' he cried out. No angelic visitation. No congratulations. No sense of God. Only silence. But the next day he uttered those words that changed history: 'Here I stand. I can do no other. God help me. Amen.'

'For my thoughts are not your thoughts, neither are your ways my ways,' declares the LORD. 'As the heavens are higher than the earth, so are my ways higher than your ways and my thoughts than your thoughts.' (Isa. 55:8–9)

God wants us to accept his ways and affirm him as he is, not the way we may want him to be. It is out of our comfort zone where we can learn his ways.

Moses was possibly the greatest leader of men and women in world history. He was a brilliant military strategist. He understood people and their feelings. He had an extremely high degree of patience. He did not take rejection personally. He knew what it was to be loved by his people as well as being hated and rejected. Things were so bad on one occasion that God stepped in and made a deal with Moses. It was a proposition that most leaders I know would have taken with both hands. It was something like this: 'Moses, these people who are supposed to be following you are a sorry lot. I am tired of them as I know you are. Here is what I am going to do: I will destroy them, wipe them off the face of the earth and start all over again with you as the leader.' That is essentially what God said; read it in Exodus 32:9–10 (cf. Num. 14:11–12).

Moses wasted no time in replying to the offer. 'No! It will dishonour your great Name if you do this.'

Then the Egyptians will hear about it! ...They have already heard that you, O LORD, are with these people and that you, O LORD, have been seen face to face, that your cloud stays over them, and that you go before them in a pillar of cloud by day and a pillar of fire by night. If you put these people to death all at one time, the nations who have heard this report about you will say, 'The LORD was not able to bring these people into the land he promised them on oath; so he slaughtered them in the desert.' (Num. 14:13–16)

Moses then reminded the Lord that he was 'slow to anger, abounding in love' and interceded for the people to be forgiven. Had not Moses

been knowledgeable in God's ways – or cared more about his own ego
– he would have said 'Yes – kill these unworthy people, Lord.' The
psalmist picked up on this event and said, 'So he said he would
destroy them – had not Moses, his chosen one, stood in the breach
before him to keep his wrath from destroying them' (Ps. 106:23).

It was God playing hard to get. God wanted Moses to respond
exactly as he did. But had Moses taken the Lord's words seriously
when God said, 'Let's start all over again and I will make a new
nation', it would have been because Moses did not know the Lord
very well. Moses had developed such a love for the glory of God that
his personal feelings and ego were subservient to that honour. Moses
did not value his own reputation and esteem; he cared about the way
the world thought about the Lord. God also let Moses see for himself
that he was getting to know the Lord's very ways. There are not
many leaders like Moses. This was the key to his greatness.

God played hard to get in the case of King Saul. But Saul failed to
see it and lost the privilege of passing on the kingship to his family.
Here is what happened. The prophet Samuel had agreed to be
present at a critical time but was overdue for some reason and kept
Saul waiting. Nobody knew what was really going on. It was a
divine set-up to see what Saul would do. Would the new king
honour the word of God? Would he stick to the ways of God as
revealed in Scripture or would he presume he was an exception to
the revelation of God? Had Saul done what was right he would have
said, 'Let us not be hasty. We will wait for Samuel before there is any
administering of the burnt offerings because he is the only one the
Lord would approve of for this.' If only.

How many of us have done this? In church and during a time of
inspiration we may sing 'Have thine own way, Lord' or some
devotional hymn by which we pledge to get closer to him. We tell
him we want more anointing, that we want to please him in all our
ways. Some will go forward at the end of a service and promise the
Lord all sorts of things and assume that God applauds such
devotion. It is not that he is unimpressed with us at a time like this;
he is more interested in how we are in real life a few days later rather

than our emotional response at church – however sincere we may have been. God tests our earnestness days or months later – to see how we will react when the divine set-up occurs. We may feel this is not very nice for God to do. But does he not have a right to test our promises?

King Saul's downfall came about because he put himself above the revealed word of God in a time of testing, when the people were quaking with fear because of the Philistines. Samuel set a time at which he would turn up to offer the burnt offerings. When Samuel did not show up as scheduled Saul took it upon himself to offer the burnt offering. The Mosaic Law laid down specific instructions that only a priest – no one else – is authorised to present the burnt offerings (Num. 3:10). But King Saul did it anyway. He explained to Samuel that he felt 'compelled' to do it since Samuel had turned up too late (1 Sam. 13:11–12).

Saul's claim that he felt compelled to do what he did smacks of the behaviour of some people today who fancy that their feelings are an objective basis on which to operate when it comes to the things of God. Some go so far as to say, 'The Lord told me to do this' even though it was blatantly contrary to his own word! To quote Rob Parsons, Christian men who leave their wives often say such things as: 'Darling, we were so young when we got married – we didn't really know what we were doing'; 'In the long run this will be better for you'; 'This will also turn out to be better for the kids'; or 'I've prayed about this – this is fine with God.'

Joseph played hard to get with his eleven brothers when he was prime minister of Egypt. Twenty-two years before they had sold him to the Ishmaelites, never expecting to see him again. It was an awful, cowardly thing to do. The time came when these brothers had to go to Egypt to buy food but did not know it was their brother Joseph they had to face. He had totally forgiven them in his heart and then did something that could be easily misunderstood. When he sent his brothers on their way he secretly put his cup in Benjamin's bag and shortly had Benjamin arrested for stealing his cup! On the surface this seems like a cruel joke. But it was anything but that.

It was a set-up to see whether the brothers had changed in twenty-two years, to find out if they would do to their brother Benjamin (who had replaced Joseph as his father's favourite son) what they had done to Joseph. They had a perfect opportunity to get rid of Benjamin. When Benjamin was found to have Joseph's cup in his bag the brothers could have said, 'Sorry, Benjamin, you are in trouble and you brought this on yourself – you will have to pay for this and remain in Egypt for your crime.' That was what they could have done but they did not do that. They all 'tore their clothes', stood by Benjamin, accompanied him to the prime minister's quarters and pleaded for mercy.

It was a set-up and they passed with flying colours. They had indeed changed. They were not the same jealous brothers who had wanted to get rid of Joseph. Joseph wept when they pleaded for Benjamin's innocence and then revealed to them that he totally forgave them for what they had done twenty-two years before.

Elijah was carrying out this same tactic – playing hard to get – when he kept putting off Elisha. Elisha wanted a double portion of Elijah's anointing – a bold wish. On the day it was known that Elijah would be taken away Elisha doggedly stayed at Elijah's side. Elijah would say to him, 'Stay here; the Lord has sent me to Bethel', but Elisha replied, 'As surely as the Lord lives and as you live, I will not leave you.' Elijah did it again, 'Stay here, Elisha; the Lord has sent me to Jericho.' But Elisha followed Elijah to Jericho. A third time Elijah tried to put Elisha off, 'Stay here; the Lord has sent me to the Jordan.' But Elisha never left his side and was rewarded for his commitment not to let Elijah out of his sight; he received the double portion of Elijah's spirit (2 Kgs. 2:1–15).

For over ten years I have added a petition to my daily prayer list: that I will recognise the exact moment when God is playing hard to get and never miss God's intentions for me. This teaching has profoundly affected my life and outlook and I predict it will have the same effect on you too.

Come Thirsty

Max Lucado

We were not meant to live with dehydrated hearts... come and learn how to quench your soul. Are you a dry sponge? Edgy and rigid? Ineffective? Would you like to be softened up some? Would you like to be more useful in the hands of the One who made you? Then come to the well, says Max Lucado.

Thomas Nelson
£8.99
PB / 0 8499.9130 7

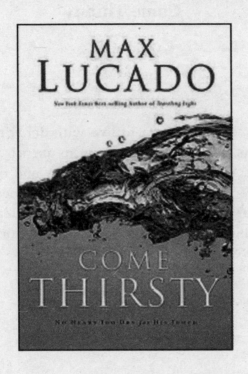

MAX
LUCADO

New York Times Best-selling Author of Traveling Light

COME
THIRSTY

No Heart Too Dry for His Touch

Published in Nashville, Tennessee by Thomas Nelson, Inc.

Foreword

We all know what it is like to be thirsty – both physically and spiritually. That longing to quench your dry mouth can be powerful. But a dry heart – that's unbearable. You need refreshment, and you need it now. If your heart has become a little crusty, if your spirit is dry, if your heart is parched, you've come to the right place. In the pages of this book, Max leads us to the *w-e-l-l* that God provides for us. And, just as importantly, Max shows us how to receive from God all that He longs to give us.

It is often difficult for us to receive. But Max helps us grasp that, more than anything, God wants us to receive, to come thirsty and drink deeply from the living water available to each of us.

I have learned so much from Max Lucado. For years his books have been a consistent source of inspiration to me. And his friendship is something that I will always treasure. I have had the privilege of being ministered to one-on-one by Max, and I have had the wonderful opportunity to watch as he ministers – just as effectively – to an arena of fifteen thousand people.

Acknowledgements

They prodded, applauded, extolled, and cajoled. These friends made the book a book. And to them I offer great gratitude.

Jim Barker – the God – seeking golf professional. You sowed these seeds while trying to fix my swing. At least the seeds bore fruit.

Liz Heaney and Karen Hill – If dentists had your skill, we'd have wider smiles and less pain. Great editing!

Carol Bartley – You did it again. We applaud your patient addiction to detail and precision.

Thanks to Hank Hanegraaff for generously giving your time and your insights.

David Moberg and W Publishing – You make me feel like a middle-schooler playing on an NBA squad!

The Oak Hills leadership and church family – celebrating our greatest year yet!

Susan Perry – Look up the word servant in the dictionary and see your picture. For your gracious service, thank you.

Jennifer McKinney – We appreciate your service almost as much as your smile.

Margaret Mechinus – Your skill at organization matches my proclivity toward chaos. Thanks for ensuring that at least my bookshelves make sense.

Charles Prince – true sage and dear friend. Thanks for the research.

Steve Halliday – Thanks to you, readers once again have another great discussion guide.

Andrew Cooley and the UpWords staff – a home – run-hitting team!

Steve and Cheryl Green – Denalyn and I regard you as permanent partners and dearest friends.

Michael W Smith – Here's to many great moments together, and we're just getting started.

Jenna, Andrea, and Sara – The galaxy is missing three stars. Thanks to you, the whole world is brighter, especially mine.

My wife, Denalyn – Who would give a Renoir to a hillbilly? The Hope diamond to a pawnshop? Entrust a Lamborghini to a ten-year-old? I guess God would. For he gave you to me. And I'm still amazed.

And God – For your endless aquifer of grace, I thank you.

If you are thirsty, come!
If you want life-giving water,
come and take it.
It's free!
– *Rev. 22:17* CEV

Each of us is now a part of his resurrection body,
refreshed and sustained at one fountain –
his Spirit – where we all come to drink.
– *1 Cor. 12:13* MSG

Meagan

Bentley Bishop stepped out of the elevator into a buzz of activity, all directed at him. The first voice was the urgent one of Eric, his producer.

"Mr. Bishop, I've been trying to reach you for the last two hours." Eric simmered with nervous energy. He stood a couple of inches over five feet in a wrinkled suit, loose tie, and the same scuffed loafers he'd worn for the last year. Though he was barely thirty, his hairline had retreated halfway and appeared on pace to soon evacuate the dome. His fashion turned no heads. But his media savvy did.

Eric read society like a radar screen. Departing fads, incoming trends, who teens followed, what executives ate – Eric knew the culture. As a result, he knew talk shows. He knew the hot topics, the best guests, and Bentley Bishop knew his show was in good hands with Eric. Even if he was prone to panic.

"I never carry a phone on the golf course, Eric. You know that."

"Didn't the pro shop tell you I'd called?"

"They did." By now the makeup artist was tying a bib around Bishop's neck. "Did I get some sun today, honey?" he asked, sizing her up with a head-to-toe look. She was young enough to be his daughter, but his glance wasn't paternal. "Then again, the red face may be your fault, Meagan. Seeing you always makes me blush."

Bishop's flirting repulsed everyone but Bishop. The production crew had seen him do the same with a dozen other girls. The two receptionists cut their eyes at each other. He used to sweet-talk them. Now he toyed with the "sweet thing in the tight jeans," or so they had heard him describe her.

Eric would fire Meagan in a heartbeat, but didn't have the authority. Meagan would leave in half a heartbeat, but needed the money.

"Mr. Bishop." Eric scowled, looking at his watch. "We've got a problem."

From down the hall came the announcement. "Fifteen minutes to air."

"Oops." Bishop winked, untying the makeup bib. "Looks like we'll have to finish this later, babe."

Meagan powdered his cheek one final time and forced a smile.

"Dr. Allsup canceled," Eric inserted as the two headed for the studio.

"What?"

"Weather. He called from O'Hare."

"The Midwest is having weather problems?"

"Apparently Chicago is."

The two stopped in the middle of the hallway, and for the first time, Bishop gave Eric his full attention. He loomed over his producer by a full foot, his mane of thick white hair making him look even taller. Everyone in America, it seemed, recognized that square jaw and those caterpillar eyebrows. Twenty years of nightly interviews had elevated him to billboard status.

"What's our topic?" he asked.

"Surviving stress."

"Appropriate. Did you phone some fill-ins?"

"I did."

"Dr. Varner?"

"Sick."

"Dr. Chambers?"

"Out of town."

"What about those two guys we had last month who wrote that breathing book?"

"*Breathe Right, Live Right.* One has a cold. The other didn't call back."

"Then we're stuck with the rabbi."

"He's out too."

"Rabbi Cohen? He's never out. He's been subbing for ten years."

"Fifteen. His sister died and he's in Topeka."

"So where does that leave us? Doing a remote? I don't like remotes." By now Bishop's voice was beginning to boom and Eric's face to redden. The ninth-floor hallway of the Burbank Plaza Building was silent – busy, but silent. No one envied Eric.

"No remote, Mr. Bishop. The system is down."

"What?"

"Lightning from last night's storm."

"Did we have a storm last night?" Bishop asked everyone in hearing distance.

Eric shrugged. "I had us hooked up with the president's physician, then discovered the technical problems. No outside feeds."

The smile had long since vanished from Bishop's face. "No guests. No feeds. Why didn't you call me?"

Eric knew better than to answer honestly.

"Studio audience?"

"Packed. They came to see Dr. Allsup."

"So what do we do?" Bishop demanded.

"Ten minutes!" came a voice. '

"We have a guest," Eric explained, slowly turning toward the studio door. "He's already in makeup."

"Where did you find him?"

"I think he found us." By now they were walking fast. "He sent me an e-mail an hour ago."

"How did he get your e-mail address?"

"I don't know. Nor do I know how he found out about our situation, but he did." Eric pulled a piece of paper from his jacket side pocket. "He told me he's sorry about Varner, Chambers, the Chicago weather, and last night's lightning. But he didn't like the breathing book anyway. And, knowing our plight, he volunteered to do the show."

"That's crazy." Eric opened the door. Bishop entered, never losing eye contact with Eric. "You let him in?"

"Actually, he sort of let himself in. But I called around. He's causing quite a stir, mainly in smaller markets. Teaches ethics at a junior college near Birmingham. Some religious leaders are concerned, but the rank and file like him. He lectures at colleges, popular on the banquet circuit. Talks a lot about finding peace in your soul."

By now Bishop was stepping toward the set. "I could use some peace. Hope this guy's good. What's his name?"

"Jesse. Jesse Carpenter."

"Never heard of him. Let's give him fifteen minutes. For the last half of the program, rerun the highlight show."

"But we did that last week."

"People forget. Go to makeup and check on this Carpenter fellow."

Meagan could see both her face and Jesse's in the mirror. She would later describe him as nice looking but not heart stopping. He wore a brown, elbow-patched corduroy coat, khaki slacks, and an acceptable but forgettable tie. A straight part separated his hair on the side, giving it a just-cut look. Meagan tied the apron around his neck and began with polite chitchat. His smile required no coaxing.

"First time on the show?"

"Yes."

"First time to the West Coast?"

"You might say that."

Meagan dabbed base powder on his cheeks, then stopped. He was staring at her. "Is this required?" he asked. He wasn't enjoying the drill

"Keeps the glare down," she explained.

As she powdered, Jesse closed his eyes, then opened them and looked at her, saying nothing.

Meagan wondered about him. When men stared at her, she knew what they wanted. He's probably the same. She stepped behind the chair and sprayed his hair. He closed his eyes again. She looked at herself, curious what he might think of her – tattooed rose on her neck, jet-black hair and fingernails. T-shirt tied tight in the back, leaving her stomach exposed. A far cry from her role as a majorette in the high-school band. Her older brother, who managed the family pharmacy in Missouri, was always calling and asking, "You're not getting a tattoo, are you? And keep those rings out of your nose." She didn't listen.

She really didn't care what he thought. After all, she was twenty-one. Can't a girl have a life? '

"Architecture?"

The one-word question caught Meagan off guard. "What?"

Jesse had opened his eyes, and with them he gestured to her open backpack that sat on the counter. A copy of *Architectural Digest* leaned out.

"Call it a secret interest," she explained. "Who knows, some-day …"

"Have any other secrets?"

Meagan sighed. Of all the come-ons. "None that you need to hear about." She shrugged.

Men never ceased to amaze her. Her mother's warning was right: no matter how nice they look, first the line, then the hook. For a couple of minutes neither spoke. Meagan liked it that way. She found safety in silence. Jesse, however, wasn't finished.

"Bishop asks a lot of you."

Meagan cocked her head. "Is that a question?"

"No, just the truth."

"He's all right." Meagan sidestepped the topic, intentionally avoiding Jesse's eyes as she dusted his forehead one last time.

Jesse's tone was solemn. "Meagan, don't let your heart get hard. You were not made to be this edgy, this crusty."

She dropped her hands to her side and looked at Jesse, at first offended, then curious.

"What do you know about me?"

"I know you are a better person than this. I also know it's not too late to make a change. This street you're traveling? The houses look nice, but the road goes nowhere."

She started to object, but his eyes caught hers. "I can help, Meagan. I really can."

"I don't need your help" were the words she started to say, but didn't. He smiled softly, reassuringly. More silence followed. Not awkward. Just silence. Meagan felt a smile forming in reply, but then ....

"Five minutes!" shouted a studio voice. Meagan looked up to see Eric's face.

⌒⌒

Meagan never watched the *Bentley Bishop Show*. The first couple of days she had tried but quickly grew weary of his piano-key smile and disc-jockey voice. So she lost interest. She tried chatting with other staff members, but they knew how she got and kept her job. Show veterans formed a tight club, and girls like Meagan needn't apply for membership. "You'd think I was a leper," she'd mumbled after her final attempt at conversation.

Meagan followed her daily ritual of cleaning her counter, pulling out her magazine, and sitting in the makeup chair. But on this day, as she lifted the remote to turn off the makeup-room monitor, she saw Jesse walk out on stage.

People offered polite applause. She watched Jesse greet the host, take his seat, and nod at the crowd. Bishop turned his attention to the index cards resting on the table, each bearing an Eric-prepared question. He gave them a shuffle and set things in motion.

"Tell us about yourself, Mr. Carpenter. I understand you teach at a community college."

"Night courses mainly."

"In Alabama?"

"Yessir. Sawgrass, Alabama."

"Do people in Sawgrass know the meaning of stress?"

Jesse nodded.

Bishop continued: "This is a tough, tough world, Jesse. Brutally competitive, highly demanding. Tell us, how do we handle the stress?"

The teacher sat up a bit straighter, made a tent with his hands, and began to speak. "Stress signals a deeper need, a longing. We long to fit in, to make a difference. Acceptance, significance these matter to us. So we do what it takes; we go into debt to buy the house, we stretch the credit card to buy the clothes ... and life on the treadmill begins."

"Treadmill?"

"Right, we spend a lot of energy going nowhere. At the end of the day, or the end of a life, we haven't moved one step. We're stuck."

"What do we do about it?"

"What we *typically* do doesn't work. We take vacations. We take pills. We take our chances in Vegas. We take advantage of younger women ..." Jesse looked straight at Bishop as he spoke. But if Bishop connected the dots, he didn't show it.

Meagan did, and for the first time in a long time, she smiled.

"Doesn't work, Mr. Bishop. Back home we call it 'sipping out of the swamp.' There's stuff in that water we were never made to drink." This time Jesse turned toward the camera.

For a moment Meagan felt as if he were speaking to her, just to her. In self-defense, she muted the sound and watched him speak.

His minutes on the show totaled no more than seven. She later heard that Bishop and Eric were pleased, even interested in asking him to return.

She hoped they would.

∽

Jesse spotted Meagan through the window of a café, squeezing lemon into her glass of water. For a couple of minutes he watched. The restaurant had a retro look, a throwback to diner days with soda counters and silver-rimmed tables. Two men in an adjacent booth said something to her; she ignored them. A server offered her a menu; she declined it. A car screeched to a stop and honked at a jaywalking pedestrian; she looked up. That's when Meagan saw him.

Jesse smiled. She didn't. But neither did she turn away. She watched him cross the narrow street, enter the cafe, and walk toward her booth. He asked if he could join her, and she nodded. As he signaled the server, Meagan noticed Jesse looked tired.

He said little as he waited on his coffee. She spoke even less, at first. But once she began, her whole story tumbled out. Dropped by a boyfriend in Missouri. Fed up with her family. Someone told her she could make fast money in commercials. Escaped to the West Coast. Audition after audition. Rejection after rejection. Finally cosmetics school. "I never even finished," she confessed. "I heard about the opening at Bentley Bishop's. Went for an interview and …" – she looked away – "after doing what he wanted, he hired me. And now" – a tear bubbled – "I'm here. I pay the rent and don't go hungry. Twenty-one years old and surviving L.A. Sounds like the chorus of a country-western song. But I'm okay. At least that's what I tell myself."

Jesse's sandwich arrived. He offered her half, but she declined. After a couple of bites, he wiped his mouth with a napkin.

"Meagan, I know you. I've watched you stain pillows with tears and walk streets because you couldn't sleep. I know you. And I know you hate who you are becoming."

"So" – Meagan touched the corner of her eye with the back of a knuckle – " if you're such a psychic, tell me: where's God in all this? I've been looking for him a long, long time." With a sudden increase in volume, she began listing misdeeds on her fingers. "I ran out on my folks. I sleep with my boss. I've spent more time on a barstool than a church pew. I'm tired, tired of it all." She bit her lip and looked away.

Jesse inclined the same direction and caught her attention. She looked up to see him beaming, energetic, as though he were an algebra professor and she was struggling with two plus two.

"Where is God in all this?" He repeated her question. "Nearer than you've ever dreamed." He took her glass and held it. "Meagan, everyone who drinks this water will get thirsty again. But I offer a different drink. Anyone who drinks the water I give will never thirst. Not ever."

Again, silence.

With a finger Meagan bounced the ice cubes in the glass. Finally she asked, "Never?"

"Not ever."

She looked away, then looked back, and, with every ounce of honesty she owned, asked, "Tell me, Jesse. Who in the world are you?"

Her new friend leaned forward in response and replied, "I thought you'd never ask."

ONE

The Dehydrated Heart

You're acquainted with physical thirst. Your body, according to some estimates, is 80 percent fluid. That means a man my size lugs around 160 pounds of water. Apart from brains, bones, and a few organs, we're walking water balloons.

We need to be. Stop drinking and see what happens. Coherent thoughts vanish, skin grows clammy, and vital organs wrinkle. Your eyes need fluid to cry; your mouth needs moisture to swallow; your glands need sweat to keep your body cool; your cells need blood to carry them; your joints need fluid to lubricate them. Your body needs water the same way a tire needs air.

In fact, your Maker wired you with thirst – a "low-fluid indicator." Let your fluid level grow low, and watch the signals flare. Dry mouth. Thick tongue. Achy head. Weak knees. Deprive your body of necessary fluid, and your body will tell you.

Deprive your soul of spiritual water, and your soul will tell you. Dehydrated hearts send desperate messages. Snarling tempers. Waves of worry. Growling mastodons of guilt and fear. You think

God wants you to live with these? Hopelessness. Sleeplessness. Loneliness. Resentment. Irritability. Insecurity. These are warnings. Symptoms of a dryness deep within.

Perhaps you've never seen them as such. You've thought they, like speed bumps, are a necessary part of the journey. Anxiety, you assume, runs in your genes like eye color. Some people have bad ankles; others, high cholesterol or receding hairlines. And you? You fret.

And moodiness? Everyone has gloomy days, sad Saturdays. Aren't such emotions inevitable? Absolutely. But unquenchable? No way. View the pains of your heart, not as struggles to endure, but as an inner thirst to slake – proof that something within you is starting to shrivel.

Treat your soul as you treat your thirst. Take a gulp. Imbibe moisture. Flood your heart with a good swallow of water.

Where do you find water for the soul? Jesus gave an answer one October day in Jerusalem. People had packed the streets for the annual reenactment of the rock-giving-water miracle of Moses. In honor of their nomadic ancestors, they slept in tents. In tribute to the desert stream, they poured out water. Each morning a priest filled a golden pitcher with water from the Gihon spring and carried it down a people-lined path to the temple. Announced by trumpets, the priest encircled the altar with a libation of liquid. He did this every day, once a day, for seven days. Then on the last day, the great day, the priest gave the altar a Jericho loop – seven circles – dousing it with seven vessels of water. It may have been at this very moment that the rustic rabbi from the northlands commanded the people's attention. "On the last day, that great day of the feast, Jesus stood and cried out, saying, 'If anyone thirsts, let him come to Me and drink. He who believes in Me, as the Scripture has said, out of his heart will flow rivers of living water'" (John 7:37–38 NKJV).

Finely frocked priests turned. Surprised people looked. Wide-eyed children and toothless grandparents paused. They knew this man. Some had heard him preach in the Hebrew hills; others, in the city streets. Two and a half years had passed since he'd emerged from the Jordan waters. The crowd had seen this carpenter before.

But had they seen him this intense? He "stood and shouted" (NLT). The traditional rabbinic teaching posture was sitting and speaking. But Jesus stood up and shouted out. The blind man

Come Thirsty

shouted, appealing for sight (Mark 10:46–47); the sinking Peter shouted, begging for help (Matt. 14:29–30); and the demon-possessed man shouted, pleading for mercy (Mark 5:2–7). John uses the same Greek verb to portray the volume of Jesus's voice. Forget a kind clearing of the throat. God was pounding his gavel on heaven's bench. Christ demanded attention.

He shouted because his time was short. The sand in the neck of his hourglass was down to measurable grains. In six months he'd be dragging a cross through these streets. And the people? The people thirsted. They needed water, not for their throats, but for their hearts. So Jesus invited: *Are your insides starting to shrivel? Drink me.*

What H_2O can do for your body, Jesus can do for your heart. Lubricate it. Aquify it. Soften what is crusty, flush what is rusty. How?

Like water, Jesus goes where we can't. Throw a person against a wall, his body thuds and drops. Splash water against a wall, and the liquid conforms and spreads. Its molecular makeup grants water great flexibility: one moment separating and seeping into a crack, another collecting and thundering over the Victoria Falls. Water goes where we cannot.

So does Jesus. He is a spirit and, although he forever has a body, he is not bound by a body. In fact, John parenthetically explains, "(When he said 'living water,' he was speaking of the Spirit, who would be given to everyone believing in him …)" (John 7:39). The Spirit of Jesus threads down the throat of your soul, flushing fears, dislodging regrets. He does for your soul what water does for your body. And, thankfully, we don't have to give him directions.

We give none to water, do we? Before swallowing, do you look at the liquid and say, "Ten drops of you go to my spleen. I need fifty on cardiovascular detail. The rest of you head north to my scalp. It's really itchy today." Water somehow knows where to go.

Jesus knows the same. Your directions are not needed, but your permission is. Like water, Jesus won't come in unless swallowed. That is, we must willingly surrender to his lordship. You can stand waist deep in the Colorado River and still die of thirst. Until you scoop and swallow, the water does your system no good. Until you gulp Christ, the same is true.

Don't you need a drink? Don't you long to flush out the fear, anxiety, and guilt? You can. Note the audience of his invitation. "If anyone thirsts, let him come to Me and drink" (v. 37 NKJV, emphasis mine). Are you anyone? If so, then step up to the well. You qualify for his water.

All ages are welcome. Both genders invited. No race excluded. Scoundrels. Scamps. Rascals and rubes. All welcome. You don't have to be rich to drink, religious to drink, successful to drink; you simply need to follow the instructions on what – or better, *who* – to drink. Him. In order for Jesus to do what water does, you must let him penetrate your heart. Deep, deep inside.

Internalize him. Ingest him. Welcome him into the inner workings of your life. Let Christ be the water of your soul.

How is this done? Begin by heeding your thirst. Don't dismiss your loneliness. Don't deny your anger. Your restless spirit, churning stomach, the sense of dread that turns your armpits into swamplands-these are signal flares exploding in the sky. *We could use a little moisture down here!* Don't let your heart shrink into a raisin. For the sake of those who need your love, hydrate your soul! Heed your thirst.

And drink good water. You don't gulp dirt or swallow rocks. Do you drink plastic or paper or pepper? Mercy no! When it comes to thirst of the body, we've learned how to reach for the right stuff. Do the same for your heart. Not everything you put to your lips will help your thirst. The arms of forbidden love may satisfy for a time, but only for a time. Eighty-hour workweeks grant a sense of fulfillment, but never remove the thirst.

Take special concern with the bottle labeled "religion." Jesus did. Note the setting in which he speaks. He isn't talking to prostitutes or troublemakers, penitentiary inmates or reform school students. No, he addresses churchgoers at a religious convention. This day is an ecclesiastical highlight; like the Vatican on Easter Sunday. You half expect the pope to appear in the next verse. Religious symbols are laid out like a yard sale: the temple, the altar, trumpets, and robes. He could have pointed to any item as a source of drink. But he doesn't. These are mere symbols.

He points to himself, the one to whom the symbols point and in whom they are fulfilled. Religion pacifies, but never satisfies. Church activities might hide a thirst, but only Christ quenches it. Drink *him*.

And drink often. Jesus employs a verb that suggests repeated swallows. Literally, "Let him come to the and drink and keep drinking." One bottle won't satisfy your thirst. Regular sips satisfy thirsty throats. Ceaseless communion satisfies thirsty souls.

Toward this end, I give you this tool: a prayer for the thirsty heart. Carry it just as a cyclist carries a water bottle. The prayer outlines four essential fluids for soul hydration: God's work, God's energy, his lordship, and his love. You'll find the prayer easy to remember. Just think of the word *W E-L-L.*

> Lord, I come thirsty. I come to drink, to receive. I receive your *work* on the cross and in your resurrection. My sins are pardoned, and my death is defeated. I receive your *energy*. Empowered by your Holy Spirit, I can do all things through Christ, who gives me strength. I receive your *lordship*. I belong to you. Nothing comes to me that hasn't passed through you. And I receive your *love*. Nothing can separate me from your love.

Don't you need regular sips from God's reservoir? I do. I've offered this prayer in countless situations: stressful meetings, dull days, long drives, demanding trips, character-testing decisions. Many times a day I step to the underground spring of God and receive anew his work for my sin and death, the energy of his Spirit, his lordship, and his love.

Drink with me from his bottomless well. You don't have to live with a dehydrated heart.

Receive Christ's *work* on the cross,
  the *energy* of his Spirit,
    his *lordship* over your life,
      his unending,
        unfailing *love*.

Drink deeply and often. And out of you will flow rivers of living water.

Jesus and People Like Us

Nick Baines

An exceptional and insightful reflection into the nature of a God who loves so deeply that He will risk anything for his world and His people.

Saint Andrew Press
£8.99
PB/0 7152.0820 9

'A fascinating portrayal of what it means to
walk with Jesus and participate in the grace
that leads us home.'
Rev. Selwyn Hughes, Founder and Life
President of Crusade for World Revival

Jesus
and people like us

THE TRANSFORMING POWER OF GRACE

Nick Baines

Published by Saint Andrew Press, 121 George Street,
Edinburgh, EH2 4YN

1. Facing Jesus

In one of the most powerful visual experiences of the early twenty-first century, the audience is invited to set out with Frodo Baggins and his friends from the settled tranquillity of the hobbits' Shire to journey to Mordor, the place of destiny and judgement. If the dangerous and eventful progress of the hobbits, elves, wizards and other assorted creatures was not enough, nine hours of film was more than some people could take. Frodo's regular temptations to give up the trip were mirrored by the audience's temptation to take refuge in popcorn or abandon the cinema to the people who would regard as sacrilege any criticism of Peter Jackson's *Lord of the Rings* trilogy. In this sense, the progress of the characters in the films reflects in some ways the experiences of those who found themselves enthralled by the films' narrative or simply bored by the idea of the rings in the first place.

There comes a point in any journey where the traveller knows that the point of no return has been reached. It might simply be that one has gone so far that there is no point in turning back now. Or it could be that there are strong psychological reasons why this particular journey must be completed, regardless of how far one has already gone. Indeed, that particular point can be reached even before the journey itself has begun. But it could also be, however, that one reaches a point both psychologically and physically at which a new view opens up before the eyes, and one is drawn towards the unknown future. Anyone who has walked in the Lake District of England knows this experience only too well: you tread the rocky path, looking at your feet and the way ahead, hearing your pulse throbbing in your ears as you trudge onwards and upwards until you turn the corner that reveals the valley and vista ahead of you while still allowing you to look behind and see whence you have come. And, setting your face towards the goal ahead, you feel the weakness of the knees as you begin to head downhill, your head up and eyes scanning the landscape before you. You know you are going to get there and it is just a matter of time; so you might as well enjoy the journey towards the inevitable destination.

What is true of the walker is also true of the traveller through life. There are times when the going is tough, or maybe just routine and unspectacular. But there sometimes comes a point when the future opens up and its possibilities or inevitabilities beckon. You still have the choice of going forward, staying put to savour the experience, or turning your back and returning. The problem, however, is that you can never go back exactly to where you began; the experiences that have brought you thus far mean that the world has changed: you have glimpsed new possibilities and have turned them down. Those who press on will do so with a mixture of motives: fatalism, recklessness, trepidation, adventure, joy or dread. The point is simply this: staying where you are for ever is not an option. You have to choose, and your choice will determine your future (or lack of it).

The pilgrim people of God

The people of God have always been called to travel. They have been invited or commanded to leave some things and places behind them and journey into the unknown – always travelling light and uncertain of their ultimate destination. Both metaphorically and really, this has always been the experience of those whom God has called his own – as a brief and selective excursion through the biblical narrative will demonstrate.

Adam and Eve

In the creation narratives of Genesis, human beings are called to leave the familiar social and family structures and cleave to another person. Adam is told that the responsibility for naming the animals is his – that God expects him to take responsibility and live with the consequences of his choices. After their encounter with the seduction of power, Adam and Eve are told to leave the Garden of Eden and enter a new world in which God will still care for them, but for which they will have to work and suffer. Their children also face choices which determine their own leavings (Abel of his life and Cain of the security of his previously known world and network of relationships).

Noah

Noah was just a good man with a good family and a vivid imagination. By heeding the prompting of God, he left behind his reputation (for sanity, among other things) and built a large boat in the middle of the desert. It is easy to read over this narrative with the benefit of hindsight and to miss the point that Noah had no hindsight and that his foresight was apparently off-beam. However, when the flood came and he was vindicated, there is no hint of 'I-told-you-so' self-righteousness; after all, he was leaving behind the world he knew and seeing his neighbours lose their lives. Noah did not leave his world and its routines behind in order simply to slip directly into a new world; rather, there was a very long period of nothingness and empty, fruitless waiting, with apparently no guarantees of a future. The journey probably looked different from within the ark to how it does from a cursory reading of the text.

Abram and Sarai

The narrative having opened up to the peoples of the world, Genesis 12 brings the focus back down to one man, one who will be the father of the nations although for most of his long life he has been completely ignorant of this calling. Abram is invited by God to leave

Ur of the Chaldeans and go with his family 'to the land that I will show you'. He could have declined. An old man with an elderly wife, he could have suggested God would be better off with a younger man whose wife was still fertile. After all, both reason and experience would have been on his side, given that God's promise involved the childless couple in populating the world. The absurdity of this particular calling was not lost on Abram the retired, or on Sarai his barren wife, who laughed with derision when she was told what the future might hold. But they went anyway – and the rest is, as they say, history.

Moses

The people of Israel had been in captivity in Egypt for 400 years, and the oppression was getting heavier and harder to bear. All oppression is born of fear, and the

Pharaoh was no exception to this. It appears from the Old Testament narrative that there was no light at the end of this tunnel. But then a weak-willed murderer, compromised by a complicated ethnic identity and a bizarre and bewildering upbringing, is invited by God to confront the Emperor and threaten him with vengeance – not once, but seven times. All the excuses in the world (fear, pessimism, a more proficient brother, a stammer) won't let him shake off the calling that is his alone. To cut a long (and well-known) story short, Moses reluctantly does what he is told to do and leads his people to a liberation of sorts. But all this looked remote when Moses first came across a burning bush in the desert and thought that worship would simply involve removing his footwear and paying homage. In fact, a messy business involving blood, angels and deep waters opens the door to a scarcely believable new future in which freedom and new ways of living become possible.

The desert

However, the Bible does not encourage fantasy or illusion. This people is led out of captivity – not into a utopian theme-park of perpetual entertainment and eternal privilege, but into a desert where their mettle would be tested. It is not enough to be free from oppression; the future depends on the will to exercise freedom with responsibility for shaping the world as it ought to become. The liberated people of Israel want to leave responsibility behind with their oppressors, but the God who has created them, liberated them and called them will not be fobbed off with sentimentality. So, it is into the desert that they go, led by God himself, and it is here, deprived of the imagined and illusory fruits of liberation, that they are faced with the inescapable questions of what sort of a people they are to be, what sort of a world they are prepared to shape, and at what cost this will come.

As the Asian theologian Kosuke Koyama has put it, they took forty years to learn one lesson: that you can't live by bread alone, but you need the word that proceeds from God himself if you are to be truly free and truly human. Simply to see freedom as a lack of oppression envisages a future and a world as full of opportunity as a vacuum is full of air. So the people of Israel journey through the desert, grumbling and mumbling, romanticising the past – yes, even the recent cruelly oppressive past – and seeking gods who will lead them on an easier path. The result is that many of them do not see the end of the people's journey to freedom in the land of promise, but die en route. Even Moses, the great hero of the story, dies having just glimpsed the goal of all his struggles, travels and travails. The journey followed by the individuals was an end in itself, not simply a means to an end which alone and of itself justified the journey in the first place.

Exile

It is perhaps not surprising that the journey of God's people continued to be bumpy. Called to be God's people for the sake of the world, these people saw their vocation instead as privilege. The warnings of the prophets (who saw reality more lucidly than ordinary mortals) were clear: recover the true nature of your calling as God's people, or the desert will once again be the place where your values and character undergo painful re-examination. Twice in 200 years, in the eighth century BC and the sixth century BC, the people lose their land, the guarantee of their identity and calling as God's people, and wonder if they have also lost their future. Indeed, how can they sing the songs of this Lord (creator, sustainer, sovereign ruler) in a strange land of exile where he appears to have been defeated, diminished and exposed as a fraud? The journey away from the security (psychological, political, national, economic) of 'home' is the means of their re-discovery of their true identity and vocation – to be the people of God, in the world but not of it, called to show God to this world which is God's, and to expend themselves in the fulfilling of this role. The eventual return of a remnant of this people does not permit them to indulge in the nostalgic recovery of past comforts. Rather, it forces them to remember who they truly are and to venture into a new future in the light of their past experience. They are not exactly successful.

Jesus

This calling of Israel is supremely fulfilled in Jesus, the builder from Nazareth in Galilee. Even in the womb of his young mother, he is on his travels as she and her husband ride to Bethlehem for the census. His birth leads to exile in the land that, for his people, characterises oppression and bondage: Egypt. Already, say the gospel-writers, the world and our expectations are being turned on their head: how can Egypt of all places ever be seen as a place of refuge? The world is not all it seems to be, and present reality does not represent all there is to be said on the matter. The answer will come with horror and surprise and will demand that we see differently and look through a different lens – one that ultimately will appear to be cross-shaped.

At the age of twelve, Jesus journeys to the metropolis, Jerusalem, where he engages in debate with the religious (and, therefore, political) teachers of his day. He more than holds his own, but returns to obscurity to continue his growth into adulthood. His calling is developing, and he has to wait until the time is right before he can go public. Indeed, his calling involved his growing up, his childhood and adolescence, his learning and questioning, his relationships and choices, his business and artistic life; it is ludicrous to suggest, as many do, that his calling was simply to die on a cross and be raised from the dead as if all that went before in his life was irrelevant to what and who the man became.

Clearly, the gospel-writers were not just filling in time when they carefully constructed their particular narratives. They put together the story of Jesus and his friends, fully aware of the implications of the structure they hung it on: the structures of the gospels are saying something to those who have the eyes to see and the ears to hear and who refuse to read the books in bite-sized fragments but, rather, see the narrative as a carefully worked whole. They constantly drop clues that intrigue and entice the reader to ask questions and read on.

When he eventually begins his public ministry, Jesus is first baptised in the Jordan by John the wild man of the desert. Emerging from the waters, a remarkable thing happens: Jesus sees and hears God's approval and affirmation and knows his life is about to change radically and irrevocably. But, instead of having a farewell party from his old life and home, he is led 'by the Spirit' into the desert to be tested. And here we hear echoes of another people at another time and in another place who were led by this same Spirit into a similar desert for the same purpose: Who are you? What ultimately matters to you? What will characterise your kingdom? Are you entertaining an illusion – even a religious illusion – or facing the truth about yourself, your God, this world and your calling in it? His journey into this desert is no accident; it is a vital element of the experience and journey of all God's people at all times. Even God's Son is not exempted from the hunger, pain and tortured self-examination of it.

Following this experience, Jesus goes back to his home town of Nazareth. It might have been easier for him to preach his first sermon where people did not know him so well and where he could have got away with being more 'perfect' than those who had watched him grow up might wish to allow. But, no, Jesus returns to Nazareth and goes to the synagogue, where he reads the set lesson for the day (from Isaiah), sits down and preaches his inaugural sermon: 'Today,' he says with a completely straight face, 'this scripture has been fulfilled in your hearing'. The particular scripture involved here speaks of the chosen one of God being anointed to be the ultimate liberator and healer of God's people and, therefore, the world. To claim to be the subject of the divine text is almost blasphemous. And the sermon goes down so well with the people that they drag him out and try to throw him off a cliff. So much for affirmation from the people of God; so much for the people of God having ears to hear and eyes to see what doesn't appear to fit their pre-packaged theology and prejudiced biblical religiosity.

Jesus' friends

And this leads us to the point of this partial and selective reading of the story of God's pilgrim people, constantly being called to embark on a journey which leads them into the unknown future with the sole certainty that the God who calls them and beckons them to move out will never leave them or abandon them – even though this journey will lead them to their deaths. Jesus meets strangers and invites them to leave what is familiar to them and go with him on a journey, the end of which they cannot possibly imagine. It will be a journey in which they will be introduced to people and situations that will make them uncomfortable. Their religious and social presuppositions will be challenged to their roots. Their world view will be threatened, disturbed and reshaped. They will find themselves completely out of their depth and discover resources within themselves which they would never have believed were there. They will be invigorated, enthused, emboldened and excited – but they will also be horrified, frightened, disillusioned and humiliated.

However, all this will be done gently and in due time. Jesus does not dump on them what they cannot possibly bear. Rather, he leads them one step at a time, allowing them to live a little longer with their theological misconceptions and cultural prejudices, giving them the space to witness, experience, try out for themselves, and question all he does with them and for them. This Jesus knows the clay with which he is working and neither lumps it together in a blandly uniform pot, nor discards what appears to be insignificant or hopeless; indeed, he shapes the individually distinguished, yet flawed, pieces that together make a full set.

Called to walk with Jesus

The new friends of Jesus probably had little or no idea what Jesus had in mind when he asked them to go with him. They surely had little understanding where all this was going to lead them in the end. But, in asking them to accompany him, leaving behind some of the familiar things of life, he was inviting them to embody what had always been the calling of God's people: to travel light and be re-shaped along the way. It is a brave calling because it promises pain and loss. It is not for the fainthearted or the romantic. It is only for those who know their need of God and his words and who are prepared to put one foot in front of the other in order to see where it will all lead. It is essentially only the curious who will go with Jesus, those who are not satisfied that 'this' is all there is, those who refuse to accept that the apparent way of the world is the only way the world can be.

The disciples of Jesus followed him with mixed motives and a variety of fantasies. But follow him they did. In one sense, that was all Jesus required of them: start the journey with me, and we'll see what happens along the way. He did not examine their theological soundness or doctrinal purity. He did not criticise their ethics or demand changes in their eschatology before they could come with him. He did not make sure that they would ultimately last the course before inviting them – they would have to choose for themselves whether or not they would go with him to the bitter end. Jesus let them be the people they were, with all their strengths and weaknesses, bringing with them the totality of their personality and character and bearing their own particular life story. They only had to be willing to walk – the rest would follow in due time.

Jerusalem, Jerusalem

For these friends of Jesus, as for the gospel-writers, the significance of one particular place in the story cannot be overstated. Jerusalem was at the heart of the religious establishment of Israel, the locus of all the people's nostalgia for a theocratic past glory and their hopes for a glorious ideal future in which their faith would be vindicated by the victory of their God over the unbelieving and idolatrous pagan nations. It was the place where God himself was present to the people, resident in the Holy of holies in the Temple, the guarantor of this people's vindication. It was the city where God's purposes had been and would be worked out in the sight of Israel's enemies. Roman imperial rule would not last for ever, and the occupying forces would be turfed out by the chosen one of God, thus ushering in the new age of God's almighty and ultimate reign. The history of this city would bear witness to the power of Israel's God exacting revenge for past humiliation and establishing a permanent throne from which he would preside over a new world order.

But Jerusalem was even more than this. It was the metropolis, the capital city of the nation, the locus of administrative order and political power. It may have been an obscure part of the great Roman Empire, but it was also the place where different peoples and economies met. When people spoke of Jerusalem, they evoked a concept that embraced political, economic, historical, religious and psychological power. The name itself represented and symbolised power, order and control. Here the rulers of the Empire were acknowledged and obeyed – albeit reluctantly – by the religious and political power-brokers of Judaism. When Rome was opposed, even in hopeless gestures of desperate rebellion, it was not the religious leaders who were leading from the front. Jerusalem was a place of despair, humiliation, hope and aspiration, a place of seething resentment alongside resentful compromise and collaboration with the Empire.

And it was to Jerusalem that Jesus and his friends ultimately set their faces. According to Luke's account, the pivotal point – the point of no return, as it were – came on the top of a mountain where three of Jesus' friends had an experience that they didn't fully understand. A little earlier, Peter had affirmed Jesus as the 'Messiah of God', the anointed one who would set Israel free. It is not clear just how Peter himself would have explained what he meant by this. But soon after, he went with James and John, and together they witnessed Jesus being shrouded in radiant light and conversing with two other men whom they took to be Moses and Elijah. Now, however, Jesus began to prepare them for the inevitable fate awaiting him. Resisting their desire to enshrine the religious experience of the moment, Jesus pulled no punches in telling them that they must now descend from the mountain and confront the principalities and powers on their own territory. 'He set his face to go to Jerusalem.'

The company Jesus keeps

Couldn't Jesus have done it differently? Couldn't his journey have been less suicidal and deliberately confrontational? And why did he have to take these poor innocents with him, knowing what would lie ahead for them and imagining the pain it would cause them and many others? Was it all really so inevitable, or could it have been avoided?

Jesus faced these questions at the outset of his public ministry when, after his baptism, he was led by the Spirit into the desert to be tested. What sort of kingdom was his to be? One that would play the world's power games by the world's rules? One in which material well-being and the satisfaction of personal need take precedence over a right way of living? One in which the image of spirituality matters more than the reality of what takes place in the hidden places of the body and soul? Or a kingdom in which God can be taken for granted and whose love can be abused – all for the sake of spiritual entertainment or titillation? Or one in which the painful path of integrity and faithfulness to God can be traded for power – a pain-free short-cut to glory in which the end bears no relation to the means?

The so-called 'temptations of Jesus' in the desert at the beginning of his public ministry were not the last time he was tested in this way. In Gethsemane, on the cross itself, and many times on the journey that preceded them, Jesus faced these awesome and awful choices. Whom would he heal, and where and when? Would he compromise his vision of God's character and kingdom in order to avoid pain and suffering for himself? Could not this cup pass him by? Was there no other way? And what if he had got it all wrong and this was all just a terrible waste, the delusion of a maniac? No, Jesus was not a superman impervious to the agony of doubt and the fear of pain; rather, he was fully aware of what this meant – for him, for his friends, for the world, and for God. And he set his face to go to Jerusalem.

Who goes there?

What is intriguing about all of this is just how risky the whole enterprise was. The friends of Jesus were not the sort of people every leader would want to have around them. Indeed, Jesus himself must have been free to choose not to walk the path laid out before him, but to seek an easier way to live and to die. The mere fact is that, if this is truly God's story and the story of God's people at a pivotal point in history, then we must be prepared to consider the fragile risk that God himself took in coming among us in this man, walking with these particular friends to these particular places, at this particular point in history in that particular part of the world. This book is an exploration of that story, of these people at that time and place; but, as we shall find, it is also peculiarly my story and our story together. If God still calls people to journey with him, we must begin with the journey he himself took with people like us; only then will we be able to hear the echoes of eternity resonating with our own experience and our own vocation to be God's people in and for God's world.

Jesus

Leith Anderson

Here is a great introduction to the greatest man who ever lived for those who don't know much about Him, and a fascinating read for those who have grown up in the church and are very familiar with the Gospel accounts. Leith Anderson's conversational storytelling style makes the book appealing to a wide range of audiences and ages.

Bethany House Publishers
PB / 0 7852.7636 x

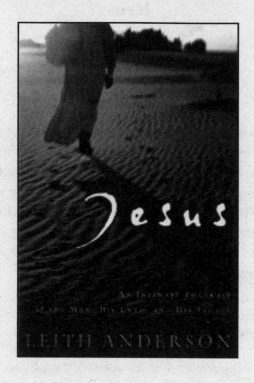

1

Circa 4 BC✝

There was no good way to hurry the pregnant young bride as she traveled the caravan route from Nazareth to Bethlehem. Her husband, Joseph, may have wanted to encourage her to greater speed, but she already was doing her best.

> ✝Calendar calculations based on solar or lunar (365 days vs. 360 days per year) make some variables on the year of Jesus' birth.
>
> The Gregorian calendar of 1582 put that year at AD 1, but since Jesus was born during the reign of King Herod who died in March or April of 4 BC, the year is most likely 4 BC.

They needed to make it to Bethlehem before the baby arrived or their tax would increase by fifty percent. The Roman government required all Jewish citizens to register in the town of their family of origin, and Joseph already could ill afford this head tax. It was difficult enough to pay for the two of them, but three would stretch him to the limit. It certainly would help if they could reach the village and register with the Romans before the baby was born. And every day on the road was a day away from his carpenter shop. No work meant no income. If all went well, they could travel to Bethlehem, register with the Romans, and soon return to Nazareth. Maybe the baby would wait until they got home to make an appearance.

Nazareth was not a particularly important place. A frontier town, it was located in northern Palestine and set in a high valley not far from major caravan trade routes. Because the government didn't always have political control over the area, an independence of style of life and perspective marked many of its citizens. The mainstream of Jewish culture tended to look on those from Nazareth with disrespect and contempt because it was in Galilee and not Judea, but this probably suited Joseph just fine. It was a good place to live, far from the larger cities with their inherent problems.

As the couple traveled southward, Mary must have thought about her cousin Elizabeth. She was married to a priest named Zechariah, and they were exempt from the travel part of this oppressive census. The priests' heritage didn't include "ancestral homes" like everyone else. So Mary was struggling to make this journey, difficult in the best of times but many times worse at nine months pregnant. She needed to rest, her feet were swollen, and where could she relieve herself? All this while Elizabeth was no doubt sitting comfortably at home nursing her new baby

But Elizabeth had lived with many years of infertility. There wasn't a greater burden any woman could bear than never to have children. Once Elizabeth had passed menopause, she and Zechariah had given up and accepted their destiny from God.

Zechariah, a direct descendant from the first high priest of Israel, Aaron, was part of an honorable but crowded profession. There were so many priests that they were separated into divisions and assigned to duty in the Jerusalem temple on a rotating schedule.

The honor of a lifetime came to old Zechariah while his division was serving at the temple. As part of the liturgy, he was selected for the sacred assignment of burning incense to God. Filled with awe and nervous beyond description, Zechariah carefully lit and burned the incense at the altar while thousands of Jews worshipped in the outer courts of the temple.

And then, multiplying Zechariah's already heightened anxiety, an angel appeared at the right of the altar. But the angel told him, "Don't be afraid, Zechariah. God has heard your prayer. Your wife, Elizabeth, is going to have a son, and you are to name him John. He will be a joy and delight to you as well as many others. He will be great in God's opinion. Your son will be filled with the Holy Spirit from the day he is born. He is never to drink wine or other alcohol. He will restore many of the people of Israel to the Lord their God. Your son will walk before God in the spirit and power of the prophet Elijah, turning the hearts of fathers and children back to each other and leading people who are disobedient back to right living. He will prepare his people for the coming of the Lord."

Genuinely wanting proof of this incredible announcement, Zechariah recovered from his fright enough to ask, "How can I be sure this is really going to happen? I'm an old man, and my wife is past her child-bearing years."

The angel's answer surprised Zechariah again. "I am Gabriel. I am the angel who stands in the presence of God waiting for his instructions. God himself sent me to tell you this good news. Let me give you some proof – you are going to lose your ability to talk so you won't be able to speak until the day John is born. Every silent day you will remember that you didn't believe my words, right up until the day you see them come true." Meanwhile, those thousands of worshippers waiting outside wondered about the priest's delay. When Zechariah came out, he indeed was unable to speak and tried to communicate with a quickly improvised sign language. The audience sensed that something supernatural had happened, but they didn't know they were eyewitnesses to the beginnings of a miracle with implications far beyond a priest who had suddenly become mute.

As for Zechariah, he did his best without speaking during the rest of his priestly tour of duty. When he returned home to the hill country of Judea, sexual intimacy with his wife, Elizabeth, resulted at long last in conception. While the angelic encounter was the significant event for Zechariah, the pregnancy itself was the dream come true for his wife.

Elizabeth didn't leave her house for the first five months of her pregnancy. Expecting a child was difficult to explain at her age, but she was not ungrateful. Her constant thoughts and words were that "the Lord has done a miracle for me. He has blessed me and removed the disgrace of my life that everyone knew about."

What a memorable day it must have been when Mary's family first heard of Elizabeth's pregnancy. We can almost see Mary's smile behind her hand and her mother's reproving look at her. Who could remember anyone that old having a baby?

Elizabeth's extended family eventually learned that this late-in-life pregnancy culminated in the normal birth of a son. The neighbors and relatives shared in the excitement and celebrated the birth with joy while Zechariah celebrated in silence, still unable to speak. When their boy was eight days old, his parents took him to the synagogue for his circumcision and naming in accordance with ancient Jewish traditions.

The custom was to name a son after his father, and the expectation was that he would be named Zechariah. Elizabeth surprised everyone and announced that his name would be John. Objections were voiced because there was no one else by that name in the family, and mothers didn't normally name their sons. Everyone turned to Zechariah to overrule his wife's choice of a name. Zachariah wrote, "His name is John."

Breaking traditions was fodder for gossip in rural villages, and the story of this unorthodox naming spread around the countryside. Not that the people of the hill country were critical. On the contrary, it was the beginning of a growing sense that something unusual was happening and that the baby John was destined for greatness. They of course could not have known the boy would grow to enormous fame and influence that would someday impact their nation and history.

As Mary thought about all that had happened to her cousin, she must have wondered what her own labor and delivery would be like. At least Elizabeth was at home with family and a midwife to help. What was she going to do if her water broke and the baby started to come here during the trip? What could she expect from Joseph? After all, it wasn't his baby.

She thought back to how she had become pregnant thirty-six weeks earlier. It certainly hadn't been something she, who had never been intimate with a man, had anticipated. She had fully intended to come to her wedding night as a virgin – the alternative was unthinkable and the stigma would have been unbearable.

Almost two years earlier, Mary had been engaged to marry Joseph. In their culture it was common for parents to make the arrangements. When the engagement moved toward the formal betrothal, a girl might consider backing out, but that was unlikely because it would bring shame to her family.

If theirs was a typical engagement, Mary may have met Joseph only a few times and never had been alone with him.✝

✝There is a tradition saying that Joseph was older than Mary and that he may have lost a first wife through death, though there is no historical evidence for such a theory.

If her parents believed he was the right man for her to marry, it wasn't a young woman's place to ask questions about her future husband's personal history. Truth be told, a girl in Mary's situation may have worried about his sexual experience in contrast to her innocence, but that wasn't the kind of thing she could talk about to anyone else. Mary certainly knew of married couples who loved each other, and that's what every bride wanted and prayed for.

Betrothal was serious – equivalent to marriage without living together. The day they were betrothed, she was referred to as Joseph's wife and he as her husband, and it would take a legal divorce to end their relationship. A year would pass before they would actually marry and she would move in with Joseph and his family. Brides in every century and culture have dreams about their weddings, and Mary would have known what to expect. The wedding, which would include the whole community, would last for a week, and the celebration would be a joyful time of eating and dancing around the "king and queen."

A smile curved Mary's lips as she remembered the wedding, but she quickly sobered as she acknowledged there had been no wedding night intimacy with Joseph. Her thoughts went back even further to the most defining moment of her young life. As had happened to Zechariah, an angel had appeared to her and identified himself as Gabriel. "Greetings, favored one!" he said. "The Lord is with you."

Gabriel's greeting began in the typical manner, but the rest of his declaration was upsetting and troubling to the teenager. Recognizing her fear, Gabriel added, "Don't be afraid, Mary. God has specially favored you. You're going to become pregnant, give birth to a son, and name h m Jesus. He will grow up to be famous and will be called the Son of the Most High. The Lord will give him the throne of his forefather David, and he will reign over the house of Jacob forever. His kingdom will never end." In less than a minute, she was told of an imminent pregnancy that would produce a son of divine origin, and he would have a royal position and power that would last forever.

Mary probably blushed every time she relived the angelic encounter, remembering how she had immediately cut to the most practical part of the prediction. She had asked, "How is this going to happen, since I'm a virgin?" The obvious and expected answer: that she would marry Joseph and immediately become pregnant. But that was not the explanation Gabriel gave. He said, "The Holy Spirit of God is going to make this happen. In the shadows of the supernatural, you will experience the power of the Most High God. You are going to give birth to a holy child who will be called the Son of God. And this isn't all. Your relative Elizabeth, the wife of Zechariah, is sixth months pregnant even though everyone thought she would never have a baby. You see, nothing is impossible with God."

Mary had been taught from childhood that nothing was impossible with God, but all this went far beyond her understanding. The angel had said that the Holy Spirit was going to do this. But how?

Anticipating Mary's need for some accreditation of this extraordinary prediction, Gabriel had included Elizabeth's miraculous pregnancy in the announcement. Since conception was unlikely for a woman past menopause and impossible for a teenage virgin, if the first proved true then Mary could expect that the second was the "divine impossibility" the angel had revealed to her.

Now walking down the caravan road with the full-term baby inside her, there must have been a thousand questions swirling through her mind. As she struggled to make sense of all that was happening, she held onto the words she had told Gabriel: "I am the Lord's servant. May everything happen to me just as you said."

Many events had occurred during the previous year since the angelic visitation. She had hastily announced a trip to see Elizabeth, who lived south of Nazareth. Whatever explanation she had given to her parents, they must have accepted it and let her go. Mary wanted to verify the first half of the prediction. If her relative Elizabeth was indeed pregnant, then Mary could know what to expect.

When Mary arrived unannounced at Elizabeth's house and greeted her, Elizabeth had a supernatural experience of her own. She felt her baby suddenly move inside of her and at the same time had a sense that her whole body was filled with the Holy Spirit of God. She was so thrilled that she called to Mary, "Blessed are you among women, and blessed is the child you will bear! But why am I so special, that the mother of my Lord should come to visit me? The moment you said hello, my baby jumped for joy inside of me. God bless you, Mary, for believing that God is going to do what he said!"

Mary responded in poetry, words very much in the style of the Old Testament prophets she heard quoted each Sabbath in the synagogue:

"My soul glorifies the Lord!
My spirit rejoices in God my Savior, who has paid
  attention to the simple life of his servant – me!
Every generation from now on will know my name and call me
  blessed,
because the Mighty God has done great things in my life.
Holy is his name!
God is merciful to every generation of those who fear him.
Look at the miracles he has done.
He has scrambled those with proud hearts; he has even
  crumbled the thrones of monarchs.
At the same time God has honored the humble.
He has filled the stomachs of starving people and sent the rich
  away hungry.
God has specially blessed his servant
Israel, keeping his promises of mercy to Abraham and his
  descendants forever. ✝

✝"Mary's native language was Aramaic. When her poetry was later
translated into Latin, this poem was titled 'The Magnificat," the Latin
would for *glorifies* in the first line.

Certainly this expressed her own heart as she reflected on the
greatness of God to her Jewish people and particularly to her. Mary
was deeply humbled by the honor of bearing a supernatural child,
and her words were reminiscent of the famous Jewish mother
Hannah, who rejoiced over the birth of her son Samuel, one of
Israel's greatest spiritual and political leaders. But more than Mary's
feelings and her familiarity with Hannah's words, God had divinely
inspired Mary. Here was far deeper meaning and greater significance
than she could have realized at the time.

It was not a brief visit to the home of Elizabeth and Zechariah.
Mary stayed there for three months, the remainder of Elizabeth's
pregnancy. She may have been there to hold Baby John when he was
only a few hours old.

There was no way Mary could have known then that John would turn out to be such an unusual man. He left home at adulthood and lived in the desert, part of his personal journey to especially connect with God and prepare him to become one of Israel's greatest prophets.

∽∾

As the couple from Nazareth was nearing their destination, Bethlehem, just a few miles south of Jerusalem, Mary had to know that the baby would be born very soon. Calculating from when her periods stopped, Mary would figure it was around the time she returned home from visiting Elizabeth that she became pregnant.

The facts had been clear: she was pregnant and she was still a virgin. Her emotions ranged from awe to embarrassment. How had God done what had never been done before? How did she explain this to her family and friends and to Joseph? The obvious assumption by everyone would be that shed been unfaithful to him and had had an affair with some man during her three-month journey to visit Elizabeth. The only explanation she could give was what Gabriel had told her – that the Holy Spirit of God performed some inexplicable miracle inside her uterus, producing an unprecedented and clearly supernatural pregnancy.

Pregnancies are hard to keep secret for very long. When Joseph found out, he had faced an agonizing moral choice. That probably was the worst part so far for Mary. She had seen the hurt in his eyes and heard the anger in his voice. He justly had felt betrayed, and she no doubt felt guilty for his anger and sorrow even though she had done nothing wrong.

Under Jewish law he could accuse her of adultery, which was a capital offense, since engaged couples were considered legally married even though they had not yet had their wedding or sexually consummated their relationship. ✢

✝In practice, few if any women were actually stoned to death for sexual immorality.

There were too many legal hurdles to overcome, and who would want to kill a pregnant woman anyway? Yet it wouldn't be an easy life for a single mother or for her child. In their male-dominated society, she was disgraced, had few prospects for marriage, and could even be forced into prostitution in order to survive.

But Joseph cared for Mary. He was a good man. He decided that a quiet divorce was best least humiliating for her and least awkward for everyone.

Mary would never forget the day Joseph changed his mind. In the midst of his agonizing and wrestling with what he should do, he had a dream. An angel told him, "Joseph, son of David, don't be afraid to marry Mary. The baby she is carrying was conceived in her by the Holy Spirit. She will give birth to a son and you are to name him. Call him Jesus, because he will save his people from their sins."

Like most of his generation, Joseph believed in dreams and heeded them, since dreams were one of the ways God communicated with humans. Not that it was an easy dream to obey – he was being asked to believe that Mary was still a virgin, that God had initiated the pregnancy, and that her child was to be the savior of Israel. Joseph was told to wed Mary and raise the boy to be named Jesus, as if he were his own. Only an angel could ask this much of someone.

Since that never-to-be-forgotten night, Joseph may have done some research of his own and learned that his dream was consistent with an old prophecy from Isaiah, who had predicted: "The virgin will be with child and will give birth to a son, and they will call him Immanuel, which means 'God with us.' " However, it's one thing to hear ancient words read from a scroll in the synagogue and quite another to discover that these words from God apply specifically to you and to your family.

When he awakened the next morning, Joseph made a life-changing decision to obey the dream. Soon after this he moved the wedding date forward and married Mary in accordance with the angel's instructions. The pregnant young girl he married remained a virgin throughout her nine months of pregnancy. How unusual was that? Married for almost nine months without sleeping by his wife's side?

Then it turned out late in Mary's pregnancy that the Roman government ordered a census of the area that included Nazareth.✝

✝Officially, the order came from Caesar Augustus in Rome. Locally it was under the authority of Quirinius, the Roman consul since 12 BC (he later became governor of Syria in AD 6). Lacking other historical references to this particular census, it may be that it was actually conducted by King Herod with Roman approval. Such a census was not unusual in the Roman Empire, for purposes of taxation, military recruitment, or political districting.

The Romans used census and taxes as a tool for controlling conquered nations.

This particular census required that people return to their communities of family origin. Because Joseph was a descendant of the famous king David, he and his immediate family were required to register for the census in David's hometown of Bethlehem. There were no hardship exemptions for pregnancy. Joseph had no choice but to transport his nine-months-pregnant wife more than sixty miles from the lowlands of Nazareth in the north to the higher elevation of Bethlehem in the Judean hills to the south. Inns were few and crowded, although they couldn't have afforded to stay in one even if rooms had been available. Roads always had bandits. Bethlehem was an out-of-the-way obscure village.✝

✝Its claim to fame was that King David was born and raised near Bethlehem. He left as an adult and eventually established the capital in the nearby city of Jerusalem.

So why Bethlehem?

"Ephrathah" was an additional point of reference because this was not
the only Bethlehem (which means "House of Bread" in Hebrew): it had
always been and still was "small among the clans of Judah," the tribal
district in which both Jerusalem and Bethlehem were located.

Centuries earlier the prophet Micah had predicted that Bethlehem
would be the birth place of the Messiah. "But you, Bethlehem
Ephrathah ✝ though you are small among the clans of Judah, out of
you will come for me one who will be ruler over Israel, whose origins
are from of old, from ancient times."

Since he was a distant descendant of David and technically had
royal blood, Joseph and his family must have often talked about their
ancestral hometown. Travel to Bethlehem normally would have
been too far and too expensive, but now they had to go under orders
from their Roman masters. As they neared the village, they would
have known there were many other pilgrims coming for the same
reason and housing would be a problem. They found temporary
lodging in the animal quarters of one of the Bethlehem homes. Not
long after their arrival, Mary went into labor and soon delivered a
baby boy, whom they immediately named Jesus. For a typical
delivery of the times, only women were present. Far from her
Nazareth home, Mary did not have the support and presence of her
mother and other familiar women kinfolk, and maybe the woman of
the house delivered the babe. The infant was wrapped in long strips
of cloth resembling the Egyptian mummies of that neighbor nation.
One of the animal feeding troughs, a manger, was used as a
makeshift crib for the bundled newborn baby.

Bethlehem was sheep country. The hills served as pastureland
where sheep were raised for wool, for food, and for sacrifice at the
not-too distant Jerusalem temple. Shepherds tended community
flocks. In the social order of the culture, they held a low status. ✝

✞So many shepherds were considered untrustworthy that many courts
would not permit their testimony in civil or criminal cases.

So it was a huge surprise when an angel appeared to a group of
shepherds in the hills outside of Bethlehem. A brilliant heavenly
light illumined him while he told the terrified shepherds, "Don't be
afraid. I have great, joyful good news for everyone. Today in the
town of David a Savior has been born to you; he is Christ the Lord.
This will be the sign for you: you will find this baby wrapped in
cloths and lying down in a manger." Then a large number of angels
joined the first angel and spoke to the shepherds in unison: "Glory to
God in the highest heaven. Peace to everyone on earth who pleases
him."

It would have been the angels' appearance out of nowhere more
than the instructions they gave that most stunned the shepherds.
After all, even though it was somewhat unusual that a baby would
be cradled in a manger, it was common for a baby to be wrapped in
cloths.

Recognizing they were in the middle of a supernatural event, they
consulted with each other in great excitement and agreed, "Let's go
into Bethlehem and see what the Lord has told us about." In town
they found Mary, Joseph, and the baby exactly as had been described
to them. When they left the manger, they told of their experience
throughout the village, though many found shepherd stories far-
fetched. But the shepherds knew what they had witnessed and
accepted it as being from God. They worshipped and praised him for
including them in the events surrounding the birth of the special
child.

Mary and Joseph without doubt were trying to understand it all. It
would be years before they began to truly grasp the implications and
meaning of the extraordinary events surrounding the birth of the
baby Jesus.

A baby born to a virgin is truly an amazing occurrence, but there was even more going on behind the story in Bethlehem. Though Jesus was not biologically related to Joseph, he was Joseph's legal son through adoption. Because Joseph was a descendant of King David, Jesus was lawfully in the line of royal succession. Although he had a supernatural birth, his family tree documents the humanity of Jesus. ✞

✞Two different family trees are given by Matthew and Luke in the New Testament. Scholars have long debated the significant differences. Some think that Matthew traces Joseph's lineage and Luke traces Mary's lineage.

Others say that Matthew gives Jesus' legal line of descent from King David while Luke gives Jesus' physical line of descent from Adam. (The two genalogies of Jesus are found in Matthew chapter 1 and Luke chapter 3.

Jesus was born into a community with important religious and cultural traditions. As had happened to his relative John, the first significant ceremony after Jesus' birth was his circumcision when eight days old. This marked him as a Jew in the tradition of Abraham. ✞

✞Circumcision literally cut to the essence of life and reproduction but also was the physical symbol of God's covenant with Israel as his specially chosen people.

It was at the circumcision ceremony that he was formally given the name assigned by the angel before he was conceived, *Jesus*.

The next milestone required a journey to the temple in Jerusalem for a ceremony where the first-born male of every family was consecrated to God. Jewish law required the presentation of a sacrificial lamb as part of the ceremony, although the poorest families were allowed to substitute two young pigeons. Away from home and probably low on money Joseph and Mary presented pigeons for sacrifice when Jesus was consecrated. God had supernaturally and dramatically intervened in their lives. They held a baby they loved with the same passion as parents all through history. For them, one of the highlights of their lives was their baby's dedication at the temple, but they couldn't afford the normal sacrifice. While others brought expensive lambs, they held a pair of pigeons. It was at least humbling possibly embarrassing.

Such consecrations were everyday occurrences at the temple. There were many parents and babies, and the liturgy was predictable and routine. Joseph and Mary would have been simply part of the crowd. But they were surprised by the words and actions of two elderly people who spent every day at the temple. The first was Simeon, a devout and righteous man whose life focused on expectation of the Messiah.✟

✟Messiah is the term used to identify the person Jews have looked for to free their land from bondage and lead them to political power.

Few parents welcome the touch of a complete stranger on their baby, but Simeon took Jesus in his arms and spoke a prayer of gratitude: "Great God, you have fulfilled your promise to me, your servant. Now you can let me depart in peace because I've seen your gift of salvation with my own eyes. I've seen the Savior for all people, both Gentiles and Jews."

Simeon's lifetime dream was now fulfilled. He looked at Mary and spoke a prophecy that was at the same time wonderful and troubling: "This child's destiny is to bring failure and success to many people in Israel. Many will criticize him, and the inner thoughts of many people will be revealed by him. And – " Simeon paused to search Mary's eyes – " someday he will pierce your own soul too."✟

✟Sons can indeed bring pain to their mothers' hearts, but none quite like the pain that would pierce Mary's heart when Jesus died.

Then came an 84-year-old named Anna. She was an acknowledged prophetess who virtually lived at the temple. When she
approached Jesus and his parents, she publicly declared that Jesus
was the one whom everybody was expecting to bring redemption to
Jerusalem.

All of this was strange and unfamiliar to two rural visitors from
Nazareth. They were seeing further confirmation from a wide
assortment of people and circumstances – confirmation that this was
no ordinary child; confirmation that he was the long-predicted and
expected Messiah.

The trip to Bethlehem and Jerusalem was supposed to be brief –
just long enough to register, pay the tax, and return to Nazareth. But
Joseph and Mary decided to make their home in Bethlehem, possibly
because of the ancient prophecy from Micah. Before settling in, they
returned to Nazareth to show off their new baby to family and
friends and to pack up their belongings.

So Bethlehem became their new home. Joseph was a carpenter.
Mary nursed and raised her son. New friends surrounded them. But
just when those first years seemed as if they would become the
peaceful norm, another unexpected encounter forced them to flee the
country as refugees.

Around the time of Jesus' birth, there were Magi a thousand miles
east in the land of Persia (modern Iran who diligently studied the
stars. They belonged to a caste of priests who specialized in interpreting life and predicting the future through astrology. While modern scientists would classify them as superstitious, those scientists
would have to acknowledge that their ancient celestial studies and
records were disciplined and detailed.

The Magi were drawn to a star in the western sky that beckoned
them toward Jerusalem. Combining the star with the cultural expectation of a coming king of the Jews, they decided to form a caravan
and make the long journey to see for themselves. Upon arrival in
Jerusalem, they explained to all who would listen that they were
seeking the king of the Jews in order to worship him. Word of the

search of the Magi soon reached King Herod at his family palace just inside the western wall of the city. Herod was threatened by any hint of competition for his throne and its power, and when Herod was upset, everyone was upset.✝

✝Herod was part Jew and part Idumean – which was a source of consternation to Jews, who wanted a fully Jewish king. Further, Herod was really a vassal king of the Romans and therefore an agent of Roman authority among a people who yearned to be independent.

Herod ordered a gathering of religious scholars and asked them where the Messiah was to be born. They quoted the prophet Micah and pointed the way to Bethlehem. In his paranoia, Herod secretly met with the Magi in order to manipulate them into helping him find the baby who was prophesied to be king. He asked when they first saw the star, calculating the baby's age at two years or less. Then he asked the Magi to report back to him when they found the child so he "could join them in worship," he told them.

With the beckoning of the star and the directions given by Herod and his scholars, they headed out and found the house of Joseph, Mary, and Jesus. Delighted to reach their goal, they worshipped Jesus, presenting him with expensive gifts of gold, incense, and myrrh. Joseph and Mary were encountering new wonders: visitors from a distant empire and gifts worth a small fortune for their family. What they didn't realize then was that they and their son were in mortal danger from their own king.

The Magi often dreamed and interpreted the dreams of others, a standard medium for hearing from their gods. So they weren't surprised by the dream that followed their encounter with Jesus. It instructed them not to report back to Herod and to find a different route back to Persia instead of returning through Jerusalem.

An angel again visited Joseph. The angel warned him to "get up, take the child and his mother, and escape to Egypt. Stay there until you hear from me, because Herod is going to search for the child to kill him." The threat was imminent and they responded immediately. The small family made the very long trip to northeast Africa, where they remained as foreigners until King Herod died. Such an expensive journey would not have been possible without the resources from the Magi's gifts.

As soon as Herod realized that the Magi had deceived him, he ordered a massacre of all baby boys aged two and younger in the town of Bethlehem, his way of making sure he killed any boy who might someday seek his throne. What he did was an atrocity that took innocent lives, bereaved loving parents, and impacted Bethlehem for an entire generation.

Herod died in 4 BC. Since his death wouldn't have been common news in distant Egypt, an angel informed Joseph in another dream, "It's time for you to take Mary and Jesus back to Israel, because those who were trying to kill him are dead." Joseph planned to return to Bethlehem but then evaluated the possible locations for residence upon return and decided that their old hometown of Nazareth in the Galilee area was safest. Thus Nazareth became their long-term home, where Jesus grew up and where Joseph made his living in carpentry until his death.

∽∼

Little is known about the rest of Jesus' early childhood. Unconfirmed legends report childhood miracles and supernatural powers, but these stories appeared long after Jesus' death and are historically unsubstantiated. What we do know is that his childhood was positive: he grew strong, became wise, and evidenced the grace of God on his life.

The Feast of the Passover that commemorated the escape of the Hebrew people from Egyptian slavery nearly fifteen hundred years earlier was an annual event. Jews gathered in Jerusalem for the Passover from around the Mediterranean world, and the city's population swelled by hundreds of thousands. It was the dream of every

Jew to go to Jerusalem for Passover at least once in a lifetime. Although the distance from Nazareth was a not-so-easy sixty miles, Mary and Joseph made the annual pilgrimage with Jesus. The year when Jesus was twelve, they made the journey as they had in previous years. Because of bandits and other dangers, it was normal for them to travel in a caravan for protection. When they began their trip to return home, they didn't know they had left Jesus behind in Jerusalem. Assuming him to be with other traveling families and friends, they didn't realize he was missing until they had traveled a day's journey toward home. They faced the same worries and panic shared by all parents of missing children. Perhaps their fear was greater because they realized he was a special child who had been entrusted by God to their care.

It took them three days after returning and searching the streets of Jerusalem before they finally found him. Jesus was sitting in the temple courts asking questions and listening to the answers of the religious leaders and teachers of Judaism.

It takes great knowledge, experience, and wisdom to ask a profound question. Besides that, the young Jesus was giving answers to his own questions, often providing insights that were beyond the ability of the professional scholars. A crowd gathered. Everyone was amazed at his level of understanding, his questions and his answers.

When his parents finally found him and saw what he was doing, they were astonished. They lived with him every day but did not realize he was capable of such interaction and dialogue with the spiritual leaders of the country.

But in typical parental reproach, Mary recovered from her amazement and said, "Son, why have you treated us this way? Your father and I have been worried sick looking for you." But this wasn't about them. This whole episode was another step toward Jesus' destiny and another step away from being an ordinary young man growing up in Nazareth.

Jesus answered his mother, "Why were you looking for me? Didn't you know I would be in my Father's house?" Jesus was saying to his adoptive father that his true father was God and that the temple in Jerusalem was God's house and therefore a very natural place for Jesus to be. This idea went right over the heads of Mary and Joseph. They didn't understand what he was talking about. They just wanted to get him back home to Nazareth.

Jesus did return home with them. It wasn't time yet for him to go public. Eighteen more years of ordinary human life in the obscurity of the province of Galilee lay before him. At home, Jesus filled the role of an obedient son, working with his carpenter father, while Mary kept pondering all these things in her heart.

Prayers for People Under Pressure

Jonathan Aitken

In this new book, Aitken expounds his own view of the Psalms, the fruit of much prayer, study and reflection. He has busy, stressed modern men and women at the forefront of his mind as he writes. This book is designed to be kept in the top drawer of a businessman's desk, the satchel of a student, or the briefcase of a top flight lady executive.

Continuum Books
£8.99
PB/0 8264.7639 2

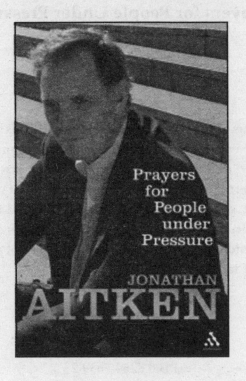

Prayers
for
People
under
Pressure

JONATHAN
AITKEN

Published in the UK in 2005 by Continuum,
The Tower Building, 11 York Road, London SE1 7NX

Part 1: Journey Into Prayer

'I know you're having a terrible time. Can I come in and pray with you?' said the man standing on my doorstep. It was the summer of 1997 and I was under tremendous pressure from media stakeouts and scrutiny. So I hesitated, fearing that this might be yet another ingenious ploy by a reporter to get inside the house. After some suspicious peering at the entryphone screen I recognised the man on the doorstep. He was a distant acquaintance, Mervyn Thomas. I remembered that he had recently written me a sympathetic letter about the disastrous collapse of my libel action against *The Guardian*. I did not have many sympathisers in those dark days. So, on impulse, I let him in.

In the conversation that followed Mervyn Thomas made it clear that what he had really meant on the doorstep was that he wanted to pray *out loud* with me. Belonging as I then did to the church reticent wing of Anglicanism I would rather have gone to the dentist without an anaesthetic. However, the combination of my terrible times and my guest's sympathy weakened my resistance. So Mervyn did pray aloud and I half-heartedly joined in the 'Amen'. It was my first experience of one-on-one extempore oral prayer.

'Would you like me to come again?' asked Mervyn Thomas.

'Well … er … yes … no … I don't think this kind of thing is really my scene … Alastair Burt is now Parliamentary Private Secretary to the Rt Hon Michael Howard MP, Leader of the Opposition. I mean, I wouldn't like to do it too often,' I muttered.

'But I think you do need regular prayer support,' was the gentle response.

Regular prayer support. It was the second time the phrase had crossed my horizon in the past few days. Its first appearance came in a letter from a political acquaintance offering to convene a group of 'friends from Parliamentary and public life' who would meet once a week to give me 'regular prayer support'. The writer of this letter was Michael Alison. Good, solid, dependable old Michael. Eton, Cambridge, the Brigade of Guards, Tory MP, junior Health Minister, Willie Whitelaw's No. 2 as Minister of State for Northern Ireland, Margaret Thatcher's Parliamentary Private Secretary, Privy Councillor, Church Commissioner and a quintessentially loyal senior backbencher. I was on friendly terms with him but not close. A few months earlier I had asked him if a press story saying that he had refused a knighthood was true. 'Well, yes, I didn't really feel worthy of it', was his reply, which I thought bordered on the eccentric considering how many far less worthy parliamentary colleagues collect their 'Ks' with the rations.

I knew Michael was a practising Christian because he was a regular attender at the Communion service for MPs held monthly in St Margaret's, Westminster, followed afterwards by breakfast in Speaker's House. However, there were no clues from his self-effacing conversation at these events to suggest that Michael could be into 'praying out loud' or any other deviations from traditional religion, such as forming groups to provide fallen sinners with 'regular prayer support'. It sounded a step too far from the C. of E. that I knew. So I stayed cool and reticent about the idea.

In their different ways, Mervyn Thomas and Michael Alison stayed warm and persistent. They had an unexpected American ally in Charles Colson, with whom I was exchanging deeply personal letters that summer. Notorious for being Richard Nixon's 'hatchet man', who had served a jail sentence for Watergate-related offences,

Colson had been a valuable source of new material for my 1993 biography of the 37th President of the United States. In my historical interviews with Colson about the goings-on in the Nixon White House he had barely mentioned his post-Watergate conversion to a life of Christian faith and ministry. Even so, we struck up a good rapport and he reviewed my book generously in the American press. However, we were no longer in touch with each other until, by chance, Colson was staying in a London hotel on 21st June 1997, the day when I became front-page news as public enemy number one after being caught out telling a lie on oath in the *Guardian* libel case.

Colson immediately wrote me a letter urging me to take the Christian path of repentance. Filled with remorse for my wrongdoing, I was receptive to his suggestion. However, I had no real understanding of the concept of repentance. I did not know the deeper meaning of the Greek word for it, *metanoia*, which translates as 'a change of heart and mind'. I thought repentance consisted of saying sorry, preferably as quietly and as privately as possible, and then getting back to business as usual.

As my correspondence with Colson developed, he seemed to be suggesting a far less convenient approach to repentance. He recommended that I should 'get a group of praying friends' around me to whom I should 'become accountable'. He mentioned his own experiences described in full in his 1976 autobiography, *Born Again*, of belonging to a group which consisted of a Senator, two Congressmen and a Washington DC pastor. This quartet breakfasted together once a week, 'shared everything as brothers' and 'had fellowship' – whatever that was. This formula of Born Againers sharing coffee, croissants, sins and Bible reading had no appeal for me. My religion was private and was going to stay that way.

For some weeks there was a tug-of-war in my spiritual life between privacy and fellowship. It was resolved not by Evangelical Protestants but by Roman Catholics. Long before I was in any kind of trouble I had developed a friendship with Father Gerard Hughes SJ, the author of *God of Surprises*. We had met when my political star was in the ascendant and the skies of my ambition seemed cloudless. At that time I was so keen on worldly success that I was not particularly receptive to what he called 'spiritual direction'. However, there must have been the seeds of a latent spiritual hunger buried somewhere deep within me. For against my natural instincts and in defiance of the pressures of a Cabinet Minister's diary, Father Hughes somehow persuaded me to participate in the first ever parliamentary retreat in Lent 1994, a commitment which meant setting aside several hours a week for the various activities this involved.

During the retreat we talked a lot about prayer, which Father Hughes defined as 'daring to make the inner journey'. Later he added that there were times in the journey when one needed companions and there were times when one needed to pray alone. On that basis there was no need for any tug-of-war between what my self-defence mechanism called 'private religion' and what Messrs Colson, Alison and Thomas variously called 'fellowship', 'prayer partnership' or 'prayer support group' religion. Even so I was still equivocal about getting involved with such novel (for me) activities, until one night I was reading a retreat on prayer by Evelyn Underhill who quoted some advice from a 16th-century Catholic mystic, St Teresa of Avila. The advice was, 'when you start to pray, get yourself some company'. This sentence hit me like a killer punch, knocking out my already fading resistance to Michael Alison's proposal of 'a prayer support group' to help me through my troubles.

The group that duly convened for breakfast, Bible reading and prayer every Thursday morning consisted of what appeared to be a gathering of reserved, cautious and determinedly non-intrusive Englishmen. In alphabetical order we were: Jonathan Aitken, Michael Alison, Tom Benyon (all ex-MPs); Alastair Burt, a sitting MP[1]; Anthony Cordle, the son of a former MP; Michael Hastings, a senior BBC executive; James Pringle, a retired businessman; and, later on, Mervyn Thomas. How Michael Alison got this lot together

---

[1]Alastair Burt is now Parliamentary Private Secretary to the Rt Hon Michael Howard MP, Leader of the Opposition.

remains something of a mystery. I myself knew none of them well and three of them not at all. The only common denominator was that they were all willing to turn up once a week to pray for someone in trouble.

Although my troubles were getting steadily worse, unfolding into the nightmare scenario of defeat, disgrace, divorce, bankruptcy and jail, the dynamics of this prayer group soon took on a life that went deeper and wider than the Aitken dramas.

Until I joined this group my idea of praying was to say the Lord's Prayer, occasionally adding one or two 'Lord, help me!' mumbles of an entirely self-centred nature. On a bad day I might possibly open the 1662 Book of Common Prayer and read whichever of its versicles, responses, prayers or collects seemed particularly appropriate to my circumstances. Although some of the BCP's liturgical creations have great power and beauty, such a formal style of prayer can easily become stilted and depersonalised. So I was ready to enlarge my prayer horizons even if the new prayer techniques to which I was being introduced came as quite a surprise.

The most regular of these techniques was to go round the table at our Thursday breakfasts, asking: 'What are your prayer needs?' Once we had broken through the barriers of British reserve with each other, this question brought to the surface all manner of replies in areas such as family worries, job or money pressures, personal relationship problems and so on. 'What are your prayer needs?' may sound a mundane question, but the oral prayers that flowed from it were sometimes remarkable, as were the answers to those prayers.

We were fortunate that our group included some experienced believers with great gifts of prayer. For example James Pringle, who had a voice like a cello and an encyclopaedic knowledge of the Bible, had rare skills in linking our prayer requests to passages of scripture. Mervyn Thomas, an experienced Baptist pastor, brought a fervour to prayer that I had never before experienced. Michael Alison changed from a pillar of the Anglican establishment into a sage of Reform theology (a subject he had studied at Ridley Hall, Cambridge), using his learning to lead our Bible readings with great expertise. The rest of us joined in with far less scriptural knowledge and devotional experience but, even so, the totality of the group's prayerfulness somehow felt powerful.

These Thursday breakfasts made two important impacts on me. The first was that the word 'Brothers', or in its longer form 'Brothers in Christ', took on a real meaning. Although we were very different characters our unity of purpose turned us into a fraternal group of loving prayer partners within a matter of weeks. Jesus' words: 'When two or three are gathered together in my name, there am I in the midst of them,' cast their own mantle over us all, so much so that there were times during our prayers when I felt his presence to be near. This strong feeling of being part of a brotherhood of Christ's followers had its effect on my prayers. I stopped asking for God's holy electrical energy to come down from the skies to solve my problems, to stop me from being prosecuted, going to jail, losing my house and so on. Instead, I prayed for my brothers (whose private troubles sometimes seemed almost as needful as my public torments) and for the requests they had made on behalf of their families, their friends and their situations. This seismic shift away from self-centred prayer towards praying for others was swiftly followed by the second impact of belonging to the group. The more I heard about Jesus Christ from our Bible studies and prayers, the greater became my desire to learn more about him. I felt his powerful attraction, perhaps even his call (though I did not recognise it at the time) and so I prayed to get to know him better.

This new shift towards God-seeking prayer met with an unexpected response from Michael Alison. He told me that he had been a former churchwarden of a leading evangelical church in London: Holy Trinity, Brompton, which ran classes in Christian teaching called Alpha courses. He said I should do one. At that time I had heard neither of the church, nor of the course. But I trusted Michael so, at his instigation, I went to see the Vicar of Holy Trinity, Brompton. He was not the rabid hot-gospeller I had somehow been expecting to meet. He was a reassuringly avuncular figure, the Revd Sandy Millar whom, 40 years earlier, I had thought of as an icon because when I was a small boy at Eton he had been a school prefect or Member of Pop. As the heroes of one's youth can be the heroes of one's life it did not seem as strange as it might otherwise have done for me to be sitting in Sandy's vicarage study receiving his godly wisdom, which seemed to come down to: 'If you're serious about having a relationship with Jesus you should come and do an Alpha course here at HTB.'

When I found out what an Alpha course was, I did everything I could to avoid it. A cover story in *The Spectator* by Christine Odone on Alpha was published a week before the 1997 autumn course began. It was a hatchet job, caricaturing Alpha as an extremist sect for the Hooray Henrys and Henriettas of Chelsea and Kensington who enjoyed swooning in the aisles, confessing their sins in groups and empowering themselves with the Holy Spirit to make more money. I promptly tried to back out of the course I had signed up for, but a surprisingly steely Michael Alison persuaded me to stick to the plan. As I was still wavering on the night the Alpha course began, his persuasion took the form of physically escorting me to Holy Trinity, Brompton, where I felt out of place, uncomfortable and unpleasantly notorious. The only reason I could think of for being there was that I had made a bad call of judgement out of good manners to Michael Alison and Sandy Millar.

I found the Alpha course far more orthodox, interesting and congenial than I had expected. These reactions had much to do with the quality of the talks given by the Alpha chaplain, Nicky Gumbel, and the normality of the people who were in our group, which was led by Bruce Streather, a solicitor and amateur golfing champion who in time was to become one of my closest friends. However, despite the good preaching of Gumbel and the good company of Streather, I do not think I would have lasted for the duration of the ten-week course had it not been for the fifth talk, entitled 'How Do I Pray?' It was given, not by an ordained clergyman, but by a young

woman in a mini-skirt called Jo Glenn. It was her message rather
than her mini-skirt which captivated me, for by the end of the
evening my searchings had taken a new turn towards something my
spiritual life had sorely lacked – prayer discipline.

Your Best Life Now

Joel Olsteen

In this inspirational self-help guide, Joel Osteen, the pastor of Houston's Lakewood Church, offers a seven-step program, based on spiritual principles, to make life more meaningful and rewarding on a daily basis.

Kingsway
£8.99
PB/0 4465 3275 4

1. Enlarging Your Vision

I heard a story about a man on vacation in Hawaii with his wife. He was a good man who had achieved a modest measure of success, but he was coasting along, thinking that he'd already reached his limits in life. One day, a friend was driving the couple around the island, showing them the sights. They stopped to admire a gorgeous house set high on a hill. The property was replete with beautiful palm trees and lush green gardens in a picturesque, peaceful setting with a panoramic view overlooking the ocean.

As the man gazed at the magnificent home, he commented to his wife and friend, "I can't even imagine living in a place like that."

Right there, something inside him said, *Don't worry. You won't. You will never live in a great place like that.*

Startled at his own thoughts, he asked himself, *What do you mean?*

As long as you can't imagine it, as long as you can't see it, then it is not going to happen for you. The man correctly realized that his own thoughts and attitudes were condemning him to mediocrity. He determined then and there to start believing better of himself, and believing better of God.

It's the same way with us. We have to conceive it on the inside before we're ever going to receive it on the outside. If you don't think you can have something good, then you never will. The barrier is in your mind. It's not God's lack of resources or your lack of talent that prevents you from prospering. Your own wrong thinking can keep you from God's best.

Your own wrong thinking can keep you from God's best.

You, too, may have assumed that you've already peaked, that you've reached your limits in life, that you will never be more successful. *I'll never achieve significance, do something meaningful, or enjoy the good things in life that I've seen others enjoy.*

Sad to say, you are exactly right ... *unless* you are willing to change your thinking. That's why the first step to living at your full potential is to *enlarge your vision*. To live your best life now, you must start looking at life through eyes of faith, seeing yourself rising to new levels. See your business taking off. See your marriage restored. See your family prospering. See your dreams coming to pass. You must conceive it and believe it is possible if you ever hope to experience it.

To conceive it, you must have an image on the inside of the life you want to live on the outside. This image has to become a part of you, in your thoughts, your conversation, deep down in your subconscious mind, in your actions, in every part of your being.

Envision Your Success

From the time she was a little girl, Tara Holland dreamed of becoming Miss America. In 1994, she entered the Miss Florida pageant and won the title of first runner-up. She decided to try again the following year. She entered the same contest, and once again, won the prize as first runner-up. Tara was tempted to get down and discouraged, but she didn't do that. She stayed focused on her goal.

She decided she needed to change her environment, so she moved to Kansas, and in 1997, she entered the Miss Kansas pageant and won the title. That same year, she went on to be crowned Miss America. Tara Holland saw her dream come to pass.

In an interview after the pageant, someone asked Tara the secret to her success. She admitted that after she had lost twice in a row at the state-level competitions, she had been tempted to give up, but instead she went out and rented dozens of videos of local pageants, state pageants, Miss Teen, Miss Universe, Miss World – whatever she could find. She rented hundreds of videos of various pageants and watched them over and over again.

As Tara watched each young woman crowned a winner, she pictured herself in that situation. She pictured herself receiving the crown. She pictured herself walking down the runway in victory. Time and time again she envisioned herself winning. Seeing herself as a winner, said Tara, was the key to her success.

Another reporter asked her if she was nervous walking down the runway in front of millions of people watching on television and with the announcer singing the famous Miss America song.

Tara's response was interesting. "No, I wasn't nervous at all," she said. "You see, I had walked down that runway thousands of times before."

Have you ever walked down that runway? Have you ever seen yourself accomplishing your dreams? Do you keep that vision of victory in front of you? Tara Holland knew she would never be a winner until she first saw herself as a winner. She had to reprogram her mind, to rid herself as much as possible of the hurtful memories of losing. She had to replace that vision in her mind of herself as Miss Runner-up. She had to develop a can-do attitude. She saw herself stepping onto the winner's platform. She saw herself walking down that runway in victory. She created an environment of faith and success.

What you keep before your eyes will affect you. You will produce what you're continually seeing in your mind. If you foster an image of defeat and failure, then you're going to live that kind of life. But if you develop an image of victory, success, health, abundance, joy, peace, and happiness, nothing on earth will be able to hold those things from you.

Too many times we get stuck in a rut, thinking we've reached our limits. We don't really stretch our faith; we don't believe for anything bigger. But God wants us to constantly be increasing, to be rising to new heights. He wants to increase you in His wisdom and help you to make better decisions. God wants to increase you financially, by giving you promotions, fresh ideas, and creativity.

The Scripture says that God wants to pour out "His far and beyond favor." God wants this to be the best time of your life. But if you are going to receive this favor, you must enlarge your vision. You can't go around thinking negative, defeated, limiting thoughts. *Well, I've gone as far as my education will allow. Or, I've had this sickness for years. I guess it's my lot in life.*

To experience this immeasurable favor, you must rid yourself of that small-minded thinking and start expecting God's blessings, start anticipating promotion and supernatural increase. You must conceive it in your heart and mind before you can receive it. In other words, you must make room for increase in your own thinking, then God will bring those things to pass. Until you learn how to enlarge your vision, seeing the future through your eyes of faith, your own wrong thinking will prevent good things from happening in your life. God will not pour fresh, creative ideas and blessings into old attitudes.

You must conceive it in your heart and mind before you can receive it.

Get Rid of Those Old Wineskins

Centuries ago, wine was stored in leather wineskins rather than bottles. Animal skins were dried and cured until the leather could be shaped into containers to hold the wine. When the wineskins were new, they were soft and pliable, but as they aged, they often lost their elasticity; they wouldn't give anymore. They would become hardened and set, and they couldn't expand. If a person poured new wine in an old wineskin, the container would burst and the wine would be lost.

Interestingly, when Jesus wanted to encourage His followers to enlarge their visions, He reminded them, "You can't put new wine into old wineskins." Jesus was saying that you cannot have a larger life with restricted attitudes. That lesson is still relevant today. We are set in our ways, bound by our perspectives, and stuck in our thinking. God is trying to do something new, but unless we're willing to change, unless we're willing to expand and enlarge our vision, we'll miss His opportunities for us.

The fact that you are reading this book, however, says that you are ready to go to a higher level; you want to reach your full potential. The good news is, God wants to show you His incredible favor. He wants to fill your life with "new wine," but are you willing to get rid of your old wineskins? Will you start thinking bigger? Will you enlarge your vision and get rid of those old negative mind-sets that hold you back?

One fellow whose marriage was on the verge of dissolution told me, "Joel, I've been this way for a long time. Nothing good ever happens to me. I don't see how my marriage could be restored. We've always had these problems."

"That kind of thinking will keep you from receiving the good things God wants to pour out in your life," I told him. "Those wrong attitudes will block the flow. You must stop dwelling on negative, destructive thoughts that keep you in a rut. Your life is not going to change until you first change your thinking."

Early in our marriage, Victoria and I were out walking through our neighborhood one day when we came upon a beautiful new home in the final stages of construction. The doors were open, so we stepped inside and looked around. It was a fabulous home, much prettier than any of the other homes in that community. Most of the other homes around us were one-story, ranch-style homes that were forty to fifty years old, but this house was a large two-story home, with high ceilings and oversized windows providing an appealing view of the backyard. It was a lovely, inspiring place.

When we came out of the house, Victoria was excited. She turned around, looked back at the home, and said, "Joel, one day we're going to live in a beautiful home just like that!" At the time, we were living in an extremely old house that had experienced some foundation problems, preventing all of our doors on the inside from closing properly. We had stretched our faith and spent everything we had just to buy that home and get into that neighborhood. Thinking of our bank account, and my income at the time, it seemed impossible to me that we'd ever work our way up to a home like the one we had toured.

Being the "great man of faith" that I am, I said, "Victoria, that home is so far beyond our reach, I don't see how we could ever afford something like that."

But Victoria had much more faith than I did, and she would not give up. We stood out in front of that house for thirty minutes and debated. She told me all the reasons why it could happen. I told her all the reasons why I doubted.

She said, "No, Joel; I feel it deep inside. It is going to happen."

She was so filled with joy, I didn't want to burst her bubble, so I let the matter drop. But Victoria didn't! Over the next several months, she kept speaking words of faith and victory, and she finally talked me into it. She convinced me that we could live in an elegant home like the one we saw. I got rid of my limited thinking and I started agreeing with her. I started believing that somehow, some way, God could bring it to pass. We kept on believing it, seeing it, and speaking it.

Several years later, we sold our property, and through another real estate deal, we were able to build a house just like the one we had viewed. We saw it come to pass. But I don't believe it ever would have happened had we not first conceived it on the inside. I don't believe it would have happened if Victoria had not talked me into enlarging my vision.

God has so much more in store for you, too. Start making room for it in your thinking. Conceive it on the inside. Start seeing yourself rising to a new level, doing something of significance, living in that home of your dreams. If you want to see God's "far and beyond" favor, then you must replace those old wineskins.

"I've gone as far as my parents were able to go," Steve said to me. "I've gone as far as anybody else in my family. That's good enough, isn't it?"

"No," I told him. "You don't have to be bound by the barriers of the past. God wants you to go further than your parents. I'm sure your parents were fine, hardworking people, but don't fall into that trap of just sitting back and accepting the status quo. You need to make a decision that you are not going to live an average, mediocre life. When you get up in the morning you need to have the attitude of: *I'm going* to do something great. *I'm going to excel in my career. I'm going to enthusiastically serve other people. I'm going to break out of this mold and rise to new heights.*

I tell my children all the time, "You're going to go much further than Daddy. You have so much potential. You're going to accomplish great things!"

I'm not simply trying to instill pride in our children; I want them to have a big vision. I want them to conceive great possibilities at an early age. I want them to grow up expecting God's favor, expecting to be leaders, expecting to excel in whatever they do. And I know they must have it on the inside before God can ever bring it to pass on the outside.

One day, I was driving through Houston with my eight-year-old son, Jonathan. As we drove down the freeway we came upon the Compaq Center, the sixteen-thousand-seat arena that was the former home of the Houston Rockets professional basketball team, and soon to be the home of Lakewood Church. I slowed down and pointed. "Jonathan, look over there. One day, that's where you're going to be preaching."

He said, "Oh, no, Daddy. When I get old enough, I'm going to preach in Reliant Stadium!" (Reliant Stadium is Houston's seventy thousand-seat home of the Houston Texans football team.)

I thought, *I like the fact that he's got a big dream.* When I first told that story at Lakewood several years ago, after the service a lady came up and handed Jonathan a check for one hundred dollars toward that new stadium. He was so excited. He said, "Daddy, I wish you'd talk about me more often in your sermons!"

Even if you come from an extremely successful family, God still wants you to go further. My own father accomplished great things in his lifetime. He inspired people all over the world. But I'm not going to be satisfied to do merely what Daddy did. I don't want to simply hold my ground and maintain. No, I want to press on toward new heights.

If you look carefully, you will see that God has been trying to encourage you. He's allowed people to cross your path who are far more successful than you are, who have much stronger marriages, who are enjoying His favor in marvelous ways. When you see or hear about other people succeeding or doing what you want to do, be encouraged rather than jealous. Don't say, "That could never happen to me. I'm not that talented. I'll never get those kind of breaks. I'll never have that much money."

Get rid of those old wineskins. Change your thinking. Get beyond the barriers of the past and start expecting God to do great things in your life.

"Do You Not Perceive It?"

Understand, God is constantly trying to plant new seeds in your heart. He's constantly trying to get you to conceive, to give up antiquated ideas and spawn new bursts of creativity within. The key is to believe, to let the seed take root so it can grow.

What if Victoria had acquiesced concerning that new house, and said, "Yes, Joel; you're right. We're just young people. We'll never afford this. That house is way out of reach."

We'd probably still be living in our original crooked house. Thankfully, she enlarged her vision and conceived what God was saying to her. Perhaps, God has been speaking to you, as well, trying to move you to a new level. He's put people in your life as examples to inspire you. When you see their accomplishments, their joys, their victories, something inside you should say, "Yes, God! I know You can bless me in a similar way. I know I can have a great marriage. I know I can be that happy. I know I can go to those new heights."

There is a seed within you trying to take root. That's God trying to get you to conceive. He's trying to fill you with so much hope and expectancy that the seed will grow and bring forth a tremendous harvest. It's your time. You may have been sick for a long time, but this is your time to get well. You may be bound by all kinds of addictions, all kinds of bad habits, but this is the time to be set free. You may be struggling financially, in all kinds of debt, but this is the time for promotion. This is your time for increase. Friend, if you will get in agreement with God, this can be the greatest time of your life. This can be the time that God pours out His immeasurable, far and beyond favor.

God says, "Behold, I am doing a new thing. Do you not perceive it?" Notice, God is always ready to do new things in our lives. He's trying to promote us, to increase us, to give us more. Yet, it's interesting that God asked the question "Do you not perceive it?" In other words, are you making room for it in your own thinking? Are you believing for increase? Are you believing to excel at your job? Are you believing to be a more effective leader, or a better parent?

It's time to enlarge your vision.

Maybe God wants to improve your marriage, restore your family, or promote you at work. But that seed of opportunity can't take root because of your doubts.

"How could my business ever take off and begin to flourish? I've got so many obstacles. It's just impossible."

God is saying to you something similar to what He told the Virgin Mary and others throughout Scripture. It's not going to be by your might. It's not going to be by your power. God said it's going to be by His Spirit. The power of the Most High God shall come upon you and cause it to happen. With God on your side, you cannot possibly lose. He can make a way when it looks as though there is no way. He can open doors that no man can shut. He can cause you to be at the right place, at the right time. He can supernaturally turn your life around. Jesus said, "If you believe, then all things are possible."

My question to you is: Will you believe? Will you allow that seed to take root? The angel told Mary that she would conceive without knowing a man. In other words, God was saying it could happen through supernatural means. It can happen without the bank loaning you the money. It can happen without having the right education. It can happen in spite of your past. It can happen despite what the critics are telling you. With God, all things are possible.

When we got the news that the Compaq Center might be coming available, some of my initial thoughts were similar to Mary's. *How could this be? How could we ever get that facility? It's going to be too expensive. The city will never let a church use that. It's much too prominent.* But this time, I expanded my vision. I let the seed take root. I conceived it on the inside. I began to "see" our congregation worshiping God in the Compaq Center in the heart of Houston.

Over the next few months, plenty of people told members of our congregation, staff, and me, "It's never going to happen. You don't have a chance. You're wasting your time."

That didn't matter. The seed was growing on the inside. When it looked impossible, and we faced all kinds of challenges, I just said, "Father, I thank You that You are fighting our battles for us. I thank You that You're going to show us some of that immeasurable, far and beyond favor." The seed kept growing, getting stronger and stronger. Sure enough, three and a half years later, against strong adversity, God turned the situation around, and He brought us out with the victory.

God wants to do big things in your life, as well. Don't settle for a small view of God. We serve the God that created the universe. We've got to eliminate this barely-get-by mentality. "God, if You'll just give me a fifty-cent raise, I think I'll make it this year." "God, if You'll just help me endure this marriage ..." "God, all I want is a little happiness."

Get rid of those old wineskins. Get rid of that small-minded thinking and start thinking as God thinks. Think big. Think increase. Think abundance. Think more than enough.

Years ago, a famous golfer was invited by the king of Saudi Arabia to play in a golf tournament. He accepted the invitation, and the king flew his private jet over to the United States to pick up the pro. They played golf for several days, and enjoyed a good time. As the golfer was getting on the plane to return to the United States, the king stopped him and said, "I want to give you a gift for coming all this way and making this time so special. Anything you want. What could I get you?"

Ever the gentleman, the golfer replied, "Oh, please; don't get me anything. You've been a gracious host. I've had a wonderful time. I couldn't ask for anything more."

The king was adamant. He said, "No, I insist on giving you something so you will always remember your journey to our country."

When the golfer realized that the king was resolute, he said, "Okay, fine. I collect golf clubs. Why don't you give me a golf club?"

He boarded the plane, and on his flight back home, he couldn't help wondering what kind of golf club the king might give him. He imagined that it might be a solid gold putter with his name engraved on it. Or maybe it would be a sand wedge studded with diamonds and jewels. After all, this would be a gift from the oil-rich king of Saudi Arabia.

When the golfer got home, he watched the mail and the delivery services every day, to see if his golf club had come yet. Finally, several weeks later, he received a certified letter from the king of Saudi Arabia. The U.S. professional thought that rather strange. *Where's my golf club?* he wondered. He opened the envelope, and to his surprise, inside he discovered a deed to a five-hundred-acre golf course in America.

Sometimes kings think differently than you and I think. And friend, we serve the King of kings. We serve the Most High God, and His dream for your life is so much bigger and better than you can even imagine. It's time to enlarge your vision!

The Prayer That Changes Everything

Stormie Omartian

Intimate conversations with God often focus on immediate needs, concern for others, and direction regarding His will, but praise requires believers to look beyond themselves and their circumstances and place their attention solely on God. Stormie shares personal stories, biblical truths, and practical guiding principles to reveal the wonders that take place when Christians offer praise in the middle of difficulties, sorrow, fear, and, yes, abundance and joy

Harvest House Publishers
£7.99
PB / 0 7369.1468 4

Also by the same author

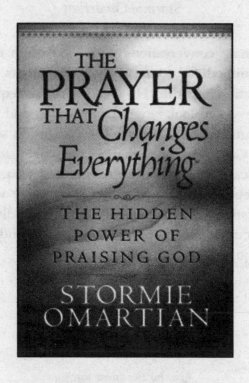

THE
PRAYER
THAT Changes
Everything

THE HIDDEN
POWER OF
PRAISING GOD

STORMIE
OMARTIAN

What Is the Prayer That Changes Everything?

Proclaim the praises of Him who called you out of darkness into His marvelous light.

1 Peter 2:9

If you're like me, you don't want to live a lukewarm, mediocre, "barely making it," sad, lonely, hopeless, miserable, frightened, frustrated, unfulfilled, meaningless, ineffective, or fruitless existence. You don't want to be imprisoned by your circumstances or chained to your limitations. You want to live an *extraordinary* life. A life of peace, joy, fulfillment, hope, and purpose. A life where all things are possible.

The kind of life I just described can only happen when we enter into a close relationship with God.

I mean *really* close.

There are many people who *believe* in God. Some of them live their lives with a sense of God in the back of their mind. Others do religious things for God. Still others love God and serve Him to the best of their ability, but they long for more in their relationship with Him. Yet not many are *really* close to Him.

You may be thinking, *How close is really close exactly?*

It's close enough to know Him intimately. Close enough to communicate your whole heart to Him on an ongoing basis. Close enough to be able to direct your attention away from yourself *completely* and place it on Him *entirely*. Close enough to understand who *He* really is and then allow that knowledge of Him to define who you really are. It's loving Him with all your heart and letting Him love you with all of His.

You know how it is when you fall in love. That special person occupies your every thought, and it's hard to focus on other things. You experience a constant wellspring of joy bubbling up from within you that seems as if it could never run dry. You long for that person when you're not with them, and you can't wait to be in their presence again. Being near them takes your breath away. You love them so much it sometimes makes your heart hurt. You delight in all you see in them, and you seek to know everything there is to know about them. You want to wrap your arms around them as tightly as you can and never let go. You want your souls to intertwine until you can no longer tell where that person ends and you begin. And every time you embrace, new strength and fulfillment flow into your being. You feel as though you have finally connected to someone at a depth you always dreamed about. You complete each other. Your heart has found a home. The world is wonderful. And all is good.

It's a *glorious* way to feel.

This is also the way God wants us to feel about *Him*.

All the time.

When you are in love you wish you could feel that way forever. But if you did, then your heart would hurt every day and you would never get anything done. So as the *extreme intensity* of your love fades – which it must do or we would never live through it – the *depth* of it must grow. It must be watered and fed and nurtured and become like a beautiful oak tree that cannot be shaken because the roots have gone down so deep.

That's what God wants to happen in your relationship with *Him*.

I'm not saying that your first love for God needs to fade. I'm saying that it needs to grow. After that beginning rush – that initial spiritual high – your relationship with God needs to be nurtured and deepened.

But how does all this happen? How do you develop that kind of love for God? What should you do to make your relationship grow deeper? How do you get *really* close to Him?

One way is to read His story. The Bible. It reveals who He is. It shows how He works. It tells us of His desires and plans for our lives. It speaks of His great love for us.

Another way is to receive His Son, Jesus. And then spend every day for the rest of your life trying to fathom love so great that He would willingly lay down His life in brutal torture and crucifixion on a cross, just so you could always be close to God.

Another way is to pray.

My definition of prayer is simply *communicating with* God. It's a love relationship first and foremost. Prayer is baring your soul to the One who loved you before you even knew of Him and letting Him speak to your heart.

Far too often prayer becomes a complicated issue for people. In fact, there can seem to be so many aspects to it that many people become intimidated. They fear that they can't pray well enough, or right enough, or long enough, or eloquently enough. They are afraid that their prayers won't be heard because they themselves are not good enough or holy enough or knowledgeable enough. In all the books I have written, I have sought to dispel that kind of fear and intimidation and make prayer accessible to everyone.

In this book I want to focus on one very important form of prayer – or *communicating with God* – and that is worship and praise. (I know that worship and praise can be considered as two separate ways we honor God, but they are so interconnected that I'm going to refer to them as one expression.) Worship and praise is the *purest* form of prayer because it focuses our minds and souls entirely away from ourselves and on to Him. What it communicates is pure love, devotion, reverence, appreciation, and thankfulness to God. It's exalting God for who He is. It's communicating our longing for Him. It's drawing close to Him for the sake of being close. When we worship God, we are the closest to Him we will ever be. That's because praise welcomes His presence in our midst.

One of the most wonderful things about God is that He lives in our praise. He inhabits the praises of His people. "But You are holy, enthroned in the praises of Israel," the Bible says (Psalm 22:3). When we worship Him, it's not like worshiping some cold and distant deity. He's a loving God who *wants* to be with us. And when we worship Him, He is.

Isn't that amazing?

What an awesome gift! *When we praise and worship God, His presence comes to dwell with us.* And the most amazing thing about that is when it does, things change. Always! You can count on it. Hearts change. Situations change. Lives change. Minds change. Attitudes change.

Every time you praise God, something changes within you, or your circumstances, or in the people or situations around you. We cant see all that is being affected, but we can trust that it is, because it is impossible to touch the presence of God and there not be change. The reason for that is you are coming in contact with all that *God* is, and that will affect all that *you* are.

Praise is the prayer that changes everything.

Enough About You, Let's Talk About Me

When I first came to the Lord, I didn't understand the power of praising God. I thought praise was something you did on a Sunday morning in church while waiting for all the people to get there who were coming in late. It was a prelude to the main event – the sermon. That's what we were there for, wasn't it? It seemed a little like when the appetizers are served at a dinner party, during which time all the guests arrive. And once everyone is present, the dinner is served.

After I received Jesus into my life, however, I started going to a new kind of church. One where worship and praise was a priority. I had never seen anything like it.

Growing up as a child, I didn't go to church much. Just Christmas, Easter, funerals, and one extended visit to a relative's house, when my mother left my dad, where that family went to church every week! Of course they *had* to, since the father in that home was the pastor. It was the family business, after all. But even with going to church every week, I never found much life in it. I don't remember any real worship time, except for a hymn or two. The choir performed what music there was. It was nice, but I was always with the adults and didn't understand much of what was going on or being said. Plus, I was with my mother, and she had a completely distorted view of God, church, and the Bible. It made me never want to go any further into it.

My mother was mentally ill. Only no one understood it back then or knew what to do about it. And there was a social stigma attached to it, so that if anyone found out you had a mentally ill relative – especially a parent – you were suspect from then on and socially ostracized. Not that we were all that socially accepted in the first place. We lived isolated lives. But the few people who had anything to do with us would have been reduced to zero at first knowledge of something like that. So my mother's problem was swept under the rug.

My dad always loved my mother in spite of how mean she was to him. He wouldn't have her committed, even at the urging of her own family, because he always hoped she would "someday snap out of it:" He said he first realized something was wrong on their honeymoon when she thought people were following them and trying to kill her. Because of that, they couldn't go to the hotel they were supposed to stay in. They had to travel to three different hotels before my father finally put his foot down and said," This is it. We are staying here!"

Untreated, my mother's mental illness grew worse throughout the years. The way she coped with me as a child was with violence and abuse and keeping me locked in a closet for many hours at a time. I never knew *exactly* why I was put there, but I thought I must have done something really bad. And then at other times, she seemed so far away in her own world that she wasn't aware I existed.

So the pendulum would swing, with no predictability, from physical abuse to abandonment.

As a result, I grew up with serious feelings of rejection, fear, depression, anxiety, hopelessness, painful loneliness, and a sadness that planted a perpetual lump in my throat. It was the kind of lump you get when you have a constant ache in your heart and you must continually choke back a lifetime of uncried tears. You have kept them back for so long that you know they have become a torrential flood building up behind a dam. You learn to keep that dam from breaking at all costs because, if it ever did, it might destroy everything in its path. The kind of tears I'm talking about can only be released in the presence of unconditional love and acceptance. And where on earth can you go to find that?

My dad never went to church that I recall except the day of his funeral. My family and I had a simple service for him and buried him the way he had requested. He always said his dad *never* went to church, but his mother made him go twice on Sunday and once in the middle of the week to sit for four hours at a time on hard benches while the preacher screamed about going to hell. He said he knew there was a God and he believed in Jesus, but he was never going to enter a church again as long as he lived. As far as I know, he kept his promise.

After I grew up and was out of the house, I tried everything I could get my hands on to be rid of the emotional pain I had inside. It was unbearable. I apologize to anyone reading this book who knew me during those years, because there must have been times when you wondered what was wrong with me. I could *appear* normal for a while, but I just couldn't keep it up. And then I would break down, suddenly withdraw, clam up, or be distant. It was all about hiding who I really was. It was all about holding back the tears.

One of the ways I coped was to drink way too much alcohol. I drank until I was giddy, but I wouldn't stop there. I had to keep going until I was drunk and passed out on someone's couch. I took drugs until I nearly killed myself many times. I went into the occult determined to make contact with some kind of spiritual being who could help me because I knew no human could. I did make contact with a spiritual being, all right, and whatever it was frightened me to death. My fear and depression continued to increase. I explored Eastern religions, but their gods were cruel, distant, and cold. If I wanted cruel, distant, and cold, I could go back and live with my mother. At least she was familiar, and by this time I understood where she was coming from.

In my twenties I had a number of relationships with men. But that old spirit of rejection was always in control. As a result I made sure I rejected *them* before they could reject *me*. There were several young men who were quite wonderful, but they didn't know the *real* me. The broken, hurting, sad, anxious, desperate, suicidal me. And I could never risk letting them see that side. If I were to tell them the truth about my life and my emotional state, rejection was a sure thing. So I ended the relationships while everything was still good. The young men were baffled about why I left with no explanation. It was because my situation was beyond explanation. At least I couldn't explain it.

Out of all those relationships I ended up getting two abortions. One in the back room of an old rundown house in Tijuana where the doctor who performed it told me if I died during the operation, he would have to dump my body in the desert. He apologized in advance just in case that happened. The other abortion happened in a hotel room in Las Vegas with no anesthetic. I was blindfolded and gagged, and another man, the doctor's "assistant," laid across my body with his full weight and put his hand over my mouth so I could not move or scream. It was worse than a nightmare because there was no hope of waking up from it. During both of those times, killing a child never entered my mind. Staying alive another week was always my only goal.

Finally, when I was 28, I couldn't keep up the front anymore. Everything in my life failed. I had a career as a singer, dancer, and actress on television, but all the shows I had been doing were canceled. There was a major industry transition away from musical variety and comedy shows. That was okay with me because I no longer felt like singing and nothing was funny to me anymore.

I had a short first marriage which I expected to fail. And it did. My health, mind, and emotions failed right along with it. I couldn't keep up the front anymore. All of my attempts to find a way out of the pain had come to nothing, and I could no longer fight the suicidal thoughts I had battled every day for as long as I could remember.

I planned my suicide. I began collecting enough sleeping pills and various drugs from friends to do the job right. I did not want to wake up in a hospital somewhere after having my stomach pumped. I didn't want to wake up at all. I wanted to be rid of the pain forever. I knew I had become what my mother had often predicted – a worthless failure who would never amount to anything. All the degrading profanity she used to describe me summed up how I felt about myself and my life. And I couldn't bear it anymore.

At this crucial time my friend Terry came to me and told me about Jesus. She had talked about Him before in a gentle way, but I wasn't listening then. She was more insistent this time because she could see I was in bad shape. We were singing together on a record session, and she took me aside on a break and gave it to me as straight as anyone could. She said she had been praying for me for the past four years we had been working together in television. She extended the love of God to me like a lifeline and begged me to come with her to meet her pastor. It wasn't as much *what* she was telling me as it was the love and concern with which she said it that convinced me to say yes.

We met Pastor Jack Hayford at a popular restaurant close by, and he spent two hours talking to me in a way I could understand about who Jesus really was. His words were compelling. And if what he said was true, I wanted the life Jesus promised. He gave me books to read, one of which was the Gospel of John, and asked us to meet him again the following week. While reading the books during that week, my eyes were opened to the truth and reality of the Lord.

When we met with Pastor Jack again, he asked me if I wanted to receive Jesus and find the life God had for me. I said yes, canceled my suicide plans, and he and Terry prayed for me. I wasn't sure what I was getting into, but I could sense the love and peace of God in these two people, and I wanted what they had.

Immediately my life began to change. I started going to Pastor Jacks church, and the minute I walked in, the love of God was so strong it brought me to tears. The dam was starting to break. And I wasn't the only one. Everyone else felt the same way. The saying that went around at the time was that you shouldn't go to this church without Kleenex and waterproof mascara.

The first thing I learned in church was the importance and power of worship and praise. Pastor Jack led worship, but he didn't just lead the music. He also taught us *how* to worship God and *why* God was deserving of all the praise we were giving Him. He taught us about how much God loved us, and how we could love Him back through our praise and worship.

In every service I attended, the worship was life-transforming. Even though we were all there to praise God, we were the ones being blessed, empowered, enriched, fulfilled, and changed. Each time I was in a worship service, I was changed. I came to worship *God*, but in the process God changed me. That happened years ago, but I remember it as though it were yesterday. That's because it changed my life completely.

I attended that church for 23 years before my family and I moved to a different state. From then on, every time I have gone into a church the first thing I look for is that kind of life-changing worship. The kind that changes everything every time you do it. The kind that changes you. Changes your perspective. Changes your mind, your life, and your circumstances.

Formed by the Desert

Joyce Huggett

Joyce Huggett draws upon the stories of Abraham and Sarah, Moses and Miriam, Elijah, the palmists, Hosea and his wife, John the Baptist and Jesus himself – to explore how God worked mightily through them and how their experiences can be an inspiration for our own lives.

Kevin Mayhew
£6.99
PB/1 8441 7277 5

Other titles by the same author

Published in 2004 by Kevin Mayhew Ltd.,
Buxhall, Suffolk, IP14 3BW

Elijah: Like Moses – Like Us
(extract)

For years, it would seem, Elijah, had endured the desert of oppression, watching and waiting and wondering and praying the prayer of listening to God. In time, this man whose name testifies to the kind of person he is – 'Elijah' is variously translated 'The real God is Yahweh' or' The Lord is my God' – knows intuitively that the time has come for his pin-prick of light to pierce the prevailing darkness. The time has come to speak, to challenge, to cajole, to woo God's people back to himself. Appearing out of the blue, as it were, like a well-aimed arrow, he heads straight for his target, King Ahab, and makes this startling God-inbreathed claim: 'In the name of the LORD, the living God of Israel, whom I serve, I tell you that there will be no dew or rain for the next two or three years until I say so' (1 Kings 17:1 GNB). Just that. Having delivered his one short, pithy prophecy, Elijah returns to the obscurity of the desert. He returns at the command of God: 'Leave here, turn eastward and hide in the Kerith Ravine, east of the Jordan. You will drink from the brook, and I have ordered the ravens to feed you there' (1 Kings 17:4).

The Desert: A Place of Hiddenness

God sends Elijah into the desert of hiddenness for at least two main reasons: to hide from the wrath of Jezebel and to be personally transformed. God knows what Jezebel will infer from Elijah's prophecy – that the forthcoming drought is a sign of God's displeasure, even of his judgement on a nation that has so wantonly disobeyed and forsaken him in favour of foreign gods. God knows that she will be infuriated by the implied challenge to the popular belief about Baal – that he is not only the fertility god but also the lord of the rain clouds. He knows that, consequently, she will set up a witch-hunt for Elijah leaving no stone unturned until he is found and killed. He must therefore hide his servant in some safe place, protect him for his own good and because his public ministry is not yet finished; it has only just begun.

God also knows that, if Elijah is to be effective for him, he needs the refining and the empowering that is the desert's gift to us. Albert Osborn puts this well: 'Before speaking publicly about God, we ought always to be sure that God's Word is in our very bones, burning for expression. Thousands of our words will not equal a few of God's words.'

Among other things, Elijah needs to be certain that God and not Baal is the Lord of the elements; that his promises are true: 'If you follow my decrees and are careful to obey my commands, I will send you rain in its season, and the ground will yield its crops' (Leviticus 26:3).

So he wends his way, through one thicket after another, through one narrow pass after another, to a narrow glen overhung with a tangled wood where a brook bubbles its way between the gaunt, rocky masses. There in this gorge God has selected as his hiding place, he sits camouflaged by his hairy cloak, listening to the silence that enshrouds this place – a silence that is disturbed only by the cry of the solitary bittern, the raucous racket made by the ravens, the occasional hissing of a snake, the distant roar of a lion or two, the incessant chuckle of the brook, the still, small, voice of God – and his own reflections.

What are Elijah's thoughts and feelings here in the desert of hiddenness? Does he sometimes feel full of frustration as he thinks of Ahab's blatant disobedience, Jezebel's ruthlessness, the apostasy of his people and their need of a leader? Is he champing at the bit, desperate to return to rescue the nation from the current crisis? Does he feel jealous of the prophets who have not been forced to flee? Does he feel de-skilled, forgotten, overlooked, worthless, shunted into a siding? Does he sometimes cry out, like the psalmist, 'How long, O Lord?'

Or does he relish the silence? As he sits or strolls, as he gazes and beholds, as he listens and learns, as he marvels at the regular meals delivered to him by the ravens, does his heart thrill to the language of creation? Do the towering rocks speak of God's greatness and his own littleness – of God's grandeur and his own ordinariness? Does the solid mass of rock with its countless nooks and crannies and protective caves testify to the protective part of God's nature that provides shelter, not only from enemies like Jezebel but also from the relentless glare of the Middle Eastern sun? Does he learn to 'read God's other book', the book of nature as he examines every petal and sepal of each tiny opening spring flower: the crocuses, the anemones, wild cyclamen, miniature irises and narcissi that appear, as from nowhere, in this part of the world?

Does the vastness and the brightness of the night sky fill him with awe and wonder: the inky blackness of it with its myriad of stars and its sometimes cheese-coloured, sometimes blood-orange moon so clearly seen in this place where no other lights vie for attention? Does he take time to contemplate every bubble and droplet of the brook? Does he tune in to the music of the flowing stream? Does he contemplate the crags of the granite walls, the lichen that grows on its great, gaunt face as well as in its cracks and crannies, the towering, poker-straight pine trees, the play of the sun on the sometimes friendly, sometimes frowning forests? Does he relish the pure, unpolluted nectar God provides for his sustenance – water from the stream? Does he befriend every pine cone, become acquainted with every butterfly, study the spaces between things like the gentian sky peeping between the evergreens? Do the shapes of the rocks and shrubs and pieces of bark intrigue him? Does the texture of the pine needles, water, birds' feathers and insect wings delight him? Do the colours of God's world soothe his soul: the brown of the parched earth, the unbroken blue of the sky the greens of the forest, the buffs and blondes of the grasses, the greys of the granite rocks, the mauves and lilacs, creams and pinks, lemons and paper-whites of the wild flowers and butterflies? Does he find himself lost in wonder, love and praise as he sits musing outside his cave, alone, watching the silvery light of a full moon transform the grotto he now calls home? Possibly. As James reminds us, Elijah 'was a man just like us' (5:17). In silence, away from the noise and the pressures, the frustrations and tough questions life poses, we see more clearly, understand more fully, and hear more distinctly. Stillness is the school all would-be listeners to God must attend for a long, long time if they would learn the art and enjoy the privilege of focused listening and focused loving.

Sometimes this silence is an alive silence – full of the chatter of birds, the rustling of the wind through the trees, the urgent hum of bees and the discernible still, small voice of God. At other times it is the powerful kind of silence David Runcorn experienced in the desert:

> The intensity was alarming. There was an almost physical quality to it. It pressed upon me like the heat of the sun above … Like an uncompromising but faithful companion [it], pursued me, questioning, probing, seeking truth … At other times, in the early morning or in the evening, the silence softened and yielded in a stillness that wove its presence round me like a seamless robe. There seemed to be no part of life that it didn't touch and influence.

The Desert: A Place of Temptation

Camping there, month in and month out, like most desert dwellers, Elijah lurches from one extreme to the other: from the quiet ecstasy of knowing himself drawn by the gravitational pull of God's love to the boredom with it all that Andre Louf describes so well:

Solitude is an easy thing only for the beginner who is still thoroughly sick and tired of the noise and pressure of the modern world which he has just recently left. But the desert is not only a place of relaxation, even if God is being sought there. In next to no time it begins to weigh like lead. It can engender boredom. And one gets fed up with it. It fairly quickly presents itself as both inhospitable and uninhabitable. The moment comes for every recluse when he finds himself on the point of running away from solitude and giving up prayer. This is the hardest moment, on which everything depends, the classic temptation of *accidie*, boredom, dreariness. This temptation we can only withstand in the power of the Spirit.

Is Elijah tempted to run away? This temptation surely tugs at him from the first day onwards. After all, he's been brought up to believe that ravens are to be avoided at all costs. Had not God decreed: 'These are the birds you are to detest and not eat because they are detestable: the eagle, the vulture ... any kind of raven' (Leviticus 11:15; Deuteronomy 14:14).

Ravens feed on carrion, offal and on rotting matter. Yet God clearly said that these birds that Elijah has been conditioned to dismiss as repulsive would feed him. Does Elijah feel nauseous as, morning by morning and night by night, ravens carry in their big, soiled beaks meat and bread, meat and more bread, more meat and yet more bread? Does prejudice against these 'detestable birds' tempt Elijah to run away? Does the unvaried diet add fuel to the flames of temptation? Does he panic as he watches that energetic, laughing, frothing stream turn into a trickle and then become a mere puddle whose meagre water supply is greedily sucked up by the sun? Does fear that he is being condemned to die a slow, lingering death tempt him to leave his hideaway prematurely? Does the very isolation of his hiding place become increasingly irksome as the weeks become long, lonely months? Does loneliness prompt him to flee? Quite possibly – particularly on long, cold winter nights when clouds hide the moon and stars and he sits and stares into a space of total darkness. 'Elijah was a man just like us ...

If such temptations come, Elijah seems to manage to snuff them out quite quickly. In doing so, the desert becomes the chisel in the hand of God with which the Creator reshapes and remoulds his servant. As each temptation is confronted and rejected, Elijah becomes more and more like the trees in the forest that frame his cave: slowly but surely he pushes strong, sturdy, tenacious roots of trust down and out until the part of him that is not seen, his inner self, grows as healthy as his outer self. Unable to fend for himself in any way, he abandons himself to God and discovers him to be the Trustworthy One. As he trusts, he learns lessons that he needs to learn experientially – to acknowledge his own nothingness, his own poverty, his own defencelessness, his own limitations, his own need of help. Consequently, he learns to allow God to be God, he learns to listen and to wait. Eventually, these lessons learned, Elijah hears God's voice: 'Go at once to Zarephath … and stay there. I have commanded a widow in that place to supply you with food' (1Kings 17:9).

The Desert: A Place of Miracles

Elijah goes. Does he leave readily or reluctantly? We are not told. Neither are we told what thoughts fill his mind as he walks the 73 miles north to Zarephath in present-day Lebanon. We are told that 'Zarephath' means 'a smelter's crucible.' In this crucible, God's prophet is to be further changed. Stripped now of all resources, Elijah ventures into another kind of desert – the desert of difficulty. The prophet who is renowned for so fearlessly confronting Ahab emerges from his hiding place with nothing to give, nothing to say. Unable to offer the widow anything, he can only hold out empty hands and beg. What is more, he, an Israelite, is forced to beg from a Lebanese woman – a gentile. How humiliating! Here, in the 'desert' of Zarephath, he learns the lesson of humility. Do it surprise God's chosen one that the prophetic gift has not died? It is as pertinent and powerful as ever: 'The jar of flour will not be used up and the jug of oil will not run dry until the day the Lord gives rain on the land;

(1 Kings 17:14) he promises the widow. Does it amaze him that she believes him – even perceives that he is a 'man of God'?

How humiliating, then, to watch the widows son fall ill, lie languishing and then die. Is this the way God rewards her for her generosity and trust? Elijah knows what to do. Taking the child from his mother's arms, he carries him to his 'prophet's chamber' and, movingly, stretches himself on the Gentile boy's body – touching the child's entire body despite the instructions in Numbers 19:16: Anyone out in the open who touches someone who has been killed with a sword or someone who has died a natural death, or anyone who touches a human bone or a grave, will be unclean for seven days.'

Elijah's prayer is desperate, urgent, bold, to the point: 'Let this boy's life return to him!' (1 Kings 17:21) he cries three times. 'The boy's life returned to him … He lived.' Like many other desert-dwellers before and since, Elijah learns that the desert is the place where God delights to do miracles. And what a miracle! As Lance Pierson observes:

> This is the first resurrection in the Bible. Elijah was asking God to do something new. There is good reason to think that God gave Elijah assurance that he was praying in the right direction. His prayer outreaches his earlier experience. It is the stretching of faith to cross frontiers, to conquer new territory and occupy it for God. He prayed big and complimented God.

Surely Elijah is ready now for the challenges ahead? 'Not yet; God says. 'After a long time, in the third year, the word of the Lord came to Elijah: "Go"' (1 Kings 18:1). '*After a long time* … 'Does Elijah grow tired or resentful of the waiting? Or does he realise that, when we wait, we allow God to be God? Does he realise that God is purifying and refining him in the crucible, that God will not permit him to emerge from that crucible prematurely; if he is removed too soon, he will remain immature, incomplete, malformed? Instead of removing his prophet from the furnace, God gives him the grace to stay until the moment is ripe: for him and for the nation. And, as Lance Pierson rightly reflects, 'Effective work for God takes years of preparation.'

It would appear that, in the hiddenness of Kerith, Elijah's ability to hear God has been sharpened, that he has been further filled with the very fullness of God. God speaks through him and God's healing power now flows through the prophet but the accolades are given to Elijah rather than to God.

Does pride wriggle into his soul? Is that why God kept him in Zarephath for so long? Possibly. 'He was a man like us' and we find it so easy, when God uses us, to pat *ourselves* on the back, to congratulate *ourselves*, to assume that we have arrived spiritually. We find it so easy to forget to give the glory to God. We may pay lip-service to God's part in the miracle but, in the secret places of our hearts, pride finds a niche.

Could it be that pride is one of Elijah's weaknesses? Do we find a hint of this in the rather arrogant prayer that he prays when begging God to restore life to the dead little Lebanese boy? Is he not here, in effect, berating God, asking him: 'What are you playing at, God?' – 'O Lord, my God, have you brought tragedy also upon this widow I am staying with, by causing her son to die?' (1 Kings 17:20).

Did he want God to resuscitate the child for the child's sake, the mother's sake, to save his own face – or a mixture of all three? Are we to catch another glimpse of this same tendency to self-aggrandisement when Elijah climbs Mount Carmel and boasts: 'I am the only one of the Lord's prophets left, but Baal has four hundred and fifty prophets' (1 Kings 18:22)?

Does God keep his prophet in the smelting furnace of Zarephath until humility becomes part of the warp and woof of his life? We learn humility from pondering the vast chasm that lies between us, our fallen desires and our habits on the one hand and God's purpose for our life on the other: When humility becomes a part of us, when things go well, we take a little bit of encouragement for ourselves but give all the glory to God.

Or does God continue to keep Elijah in the furnace until he is purified and refined from other 'besetting sins' – until he is ready to be further empowered by God for the unenviable challenge that lies just around the corner?

We are not told. Neither are we told whether Elijah was content to wait or whether he was resentful. What we are told is that 'after a long time, in the third year [of the drought], the word of the Lord came to Elijah: 'Go and present yourself to Ahab, and I will send rain on the land' (1 Kings 18:1). Elijah goes.

The Desert: A Place of Overstimulation

There are many kinds of desert: the deserts like Kerith where, in the stillness, we know ourselves loved, not for anything we have done nor for anything we can do but because of who we are. There are deserts like Zarephath where, as we interact with others, our own imperfections rise to the surface and demand to be dealt with: where we are purged and purified before we are empowered. And there is the desert of overstimulation where events insist that we act and react rather than reflect; where we are bombarded with words, expectations (other people's and our own) and challenges – maybe with conflict. Perhaps the desert of overstimulation is the most difficult to negotiate – at least for some personality types – the most dangerous to the soul because it often feels like fulfilment or success rather than the remorselessness and lostness that it very often is.

Into this desert of overstimulation Elijah is now sent by God. There has now been no rain for three years. Drought has given rise to severe famine. The situation is so desperate that Ahab, the king, and Obadiah, the faithful prophet of God, scour the land, visiting personally every spring and valley in search of enough blades of grass to keep their horses and mules alive. If they fail, a mass slaughter of their livestock will become necessary. Elijah learns this news through Obadiah himself. He also learns that, while he has been in hiding, Ahab has had every nation and kingdom searched in the hope of unearthing Elijah's whereabouts, Jezebel has massacred

God's prophets, while God's people are dying of starvation. As though this was not enough, he receives a personal slap in the face from Ahab who accuses him of being 'the troubler of Israel'.

Ahab's accusations trigger Elijah's righteous rage: 'I have not made trouble for Israel but you and your father's family have. *You* have abandoned the Lord's commands and have followed the Baals' (1 Kings 18:18, my italics).

Elijah springs into action, masterminds 'the epic of Mount Carmel', wins a landslide victory for God through his prayer, massacres one thousand prophets of Baal, releases rain, races miles through a cloudburst – and then collapses in a heap in the terrifying desert of fear, perceived failure and despair where he begs God to take away his life complaining bitterly, 'I've had enough' (1 Kings 19:4).

The Desert: A Place of Despair

No one can even begin to assess how fast the adrenalin flowed as Elijah made his way to Ahab's palace, what it cost him to mount the massive, public demonstration of God's power on Mount Carmel and to order and oversee the murder of nearly one thousand men. A man of his temperament who survived, even thrived on three years of solitude can project extraversion, can cope magnificently while doing so, but at very great cost to himself. He then needs reassurance and affirmation. If, after being overstretched in this way, he is condemned rather than applauded, he is in danger of collapsing because, in order to operate in this extravert way, he has to don a mask, a *persona* – that front we put on when we prepare to meet people and relate to the world. As John Sanford explains:

> The persona has a double function. One function is to help us project our personality effectively into the world. The other function is to protect us from the outer world by enabling us to assume a certain outer posture but at the same time keep other aspects of ourselves hidden from others. The persona is often useful and necessary. It

enables us to be effective in our dealings with the world, but also to protect ourselves when that is necessary.

Although the persona is therefore invaluable, there are certain dangers inherent in relying on it for too long. When we resort to functioning frequently through the persona and when the persona is so far removed from the genuine personality that it camouflages the person we really are, then a serious problem occurs – an inevitable energy loss. Operating through the persona consumes a great deal of energy so our energy level becomes seriously depleted whereas when we are being genuine our energy level is topped up. James Houston sums up the situation succinctly when he makes the claim that, 'the bigger we grow, the less authentic we become'.

Energy seeped, then poured, from Elijah as he worked for and won that super-human victory for and in the name of God. Consequently; when confronted by Jezebel, like an inflated balloon that has been deliberately slashed, he collapsed – not physically, at first. The physical collapse happened after he had put some 120 miles between himself and Jezebel. It was preceded by an emotional nose-dive into the abyss of despair, desolation and self-rejection: 'He came to a broom tree, sat down under it and prayed that he might die. "I have had enough, Lord," he said. "Take my life; I am no better than my ancestors"' (1 Kings 19:4).

God, the God of the desert, the Tender One, who wooed Elijah into the desert in the first place does not abandon his 'suicidal saint'." He guides the exhausted prophet's faltering footsteps to that tree that is so attractive to the desert-dweller: the broom tree. Was it covered with its white, perfumed blossom? Did its fragrance fill the evening air? Did its silvergrey branches fan Elijah's feverish face as, thankfully, he curled up in its shade? We are not told. We are told that God's weary one sank into a long, deep, much-needed, refreshing, God-given sleep. We are also told, by implication, that God was watching, caring and acting on Elijah's behalf. No rowdy ravens now carry him food. They are replaced by God's own angel who cooks fresh bread for him, and waits on him personally providing water as well as food.

Does this angel suggest to Elijah that he journeys on to 'the mountain of God', Mount Horeb? Or was Elijah already en route for 'the mountain of Moses', as Mount Horeb was popularly known? Again, we are not told. We are told that it took him forty days and forty nights to make this arduous trip – the Bible's way of indicating that it took a 'very long time'.

Away from the limelight, away from the razzmatazz, strangely strengthened physically by the God-given sustenance, amid some of the most spectacular scenery in the world, Elijah, at last, processes the rebel emotions that have given birth to that soul-destroying death wish. The desert is the place where we can give vent to our seething emotions and, having poured them out, not to a sea of sand, but to the God who cares, to expose the hurt that gives rise to the rage. Here, in possibly the self-same cave where Moses met with God, Elijah rails at his Creator: 'I feel you've let me down; he hints. '_I've_ been really zealous for you because your people have rejected you but _you_ ...'

The anger no longer swirls around inside him. The volcano has erupted. The molten lava pours down the mountainside. 'I'm lonely; Elijah continues. 'I'm the only one left. All the others have either turned apostate or been butchered to death. And I'm terrified. They're determined to kill me now.'

God does not retaliate. He metes out no recriminations, no rebukes, no remonstrating. Instead, he offers his servant concentrated listening and focused love followed by one measured piece of wise, compassionate counsel: 'Go out. Stand on the mountain in my presence.'

Does Elijah recall that it was on this very spot that God had said to Moses, 'There is a place near me where you may stand on a rock (Exodus 33:21)? Does he recall that it was said of Moses, 'The Lord would speak to Moses face to face, as a man speaks with his friend' (Exodus 33:11)? Did such memories give Elijah a glimmer of hope? If so, how does he feel when, for days, maybe weeks, he experiences the seeming absence of God rather than his promised presence? How does he feel as he watches the terrifying tornado rip the mountains apart shattering and hurling stones as it rages round the holy mount? How does he feel as the foundations beneath his feet shudder and shake and threaten to open up and swallow him when the earthquake follows close on the tail of the tornado? How does he feel when even the all-consuming fire, the traditional symbol of God's presence, fails to reveal the Almighty? Do these phenomena confirm his worst fear – that God has, indeed, absented himself? Does he consequently feel even more embittered, angry, resentful, let down? Possibly. 'He was a man like us' as well as 'a man like Moses'.

The desert is a place where God appears to abandon us, where his apparent absence confuses and distresses us. It confuses us because, having served him faithfully, we feel he owes us a reward. Like petulant children, when no reward appears, or when the desired reward fails to appear, we feel peeved. It distresses us because, deep down, we know that God is our pearl of great price. For his sake we would sell everything. Life without him is no life at all. Our hearts long for him, cry out for him, yearn for him. When he returns, we respond to his faintest whisper – like Elijah.

Trust

Steve Chalke with Anthony Watkis

This book shows how people can work together to repair the damage caused in the last few decades by the loss of trust. Steve Chalke examines practical ways through which trust can be built in 21st century society

Authentic
£4.99
PB/1 8507 8586 4

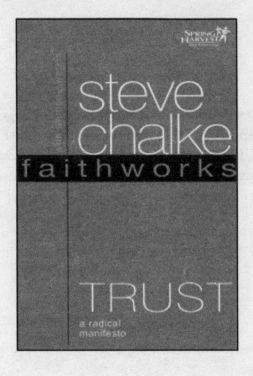

First Published in 2004 by Authentic Media, 9 Holdom Avenue,
Bletchley, Milton Keynes, MK1 1QR

1. A Radical Manifesto

'Our distrust is very expensive.'

Ralph Waldo Emerson

Trust – it's a little word but a big concept. Trust was once in abundant supply; generously given and freely received. Politicians, policemen, doctors, journalists and vicars; all were seen as pillars of the community who could and should, by virtue of their office, rely on being invested with great trust and respect.

Today things are different. The government, the media, the royal family, the church, the police, the law lords and many more have tumbled from their pedestals. Politicians, we reckon, are probably lying to us – covering up the truth in order to serve their own ends. Policemen are likely to be corrupt, brutal racists. Journalists are hooked on sales and sensation rather than truth and integrity. And vicars! Vicars are either rather wet simpletons who don't even really believe the message they earn a living from, or sexual deviants preying on the more vulnerable members of their flock.

It is small wonder, therefore, that trust, or the lack of it, is now the focus of countless column inches, news reports, chat shows and documentaries, not to mention pub conversations. The problem is that much of what is said is nothing more than a pointless commentary on the fact of trust's disappearance; bemoaning the situation we find ourselves in and expressing a yearning for things to

be different – a kind of 'If only we could turn the clock back'
mentality. However, as a wise man once explained, 'Stupidity is
doing tomorrow what you did yesterday and expecting a different
result.' Trust won't just reappear out of thin air – we need to adopt a
more constructive approach to our problem.

'I think we may safely trust a good deal more than we do.'
Henry David Thoreau

We would all like to live in a world filled with trust, but we don't.
The important question, therefore, is what are we going to do about
it? We have a stark choice. Trust won't just happen because we want
it to. Therefore, we can either keep behaving as we are now and get
used to the way things are, or take some action designed to reverse
our plight. And if action is going to be taken, then it's high time to
take the first steps.

For the Church, at least, much of this journey is about what it
means to live out our faith in the new context in which we find
ourselves at the start of the twenty-first century – a minority group
in a postmodern, post-Christendom culture. The challenge of this
is to learn to live (as many Old Testament biblical characters, such
as Daniel in Babylon, had to do) with the shift from a culture where
we had power, to one in which we need to work hard to find
influence.

In the end, to say that our society no longer trusts its big
institutions is simply another way of recognising that it has lost faith
in them. The Church can no longer demand that society automatically believes it to be faith-worthy. Instead it must learn how to work
hard to win favour as it demonstrates a faith that works.

Hard Talk
Building trust is a difficult and time-consuming business that
requires a lot of hard and sustained work. Trust can be encouraged or
eroded by our behaviour. It evolves over time and with experience. It

can't be rushed or hurried. It has to be earned. But, as expensive as it is to develop, trust is vital to every aspect of life; not just publicly but privately, not just collectively but individually. The task of this book is, therefore, to analyse the key components on which trust is built and so consider the processes by which it is either developed or destroyed. It will explore the benefits of being trusted. It will examine practical ways in which trust can be built. It will then specifically ask hard questions of both government and Church as they both strive to become more trusted by the public and each other.

There are countless commentaries, some very good, some superficial, on the reasons for the erosion of trust in society today. The primary aim of this book is not to add to them. Rather than a catalogue of reasons for failure, this book is a manual for reconstruction. Any analysis of the past that we engage in is to enable us in our real task – to answer the all-important question of where should we be heading now. In a world where trust has been eroded, is it possible to become agents of change – building trust instead of laying blame?

The title of this book is *Trust – A Radical Manifesto.* What is our radical manifesto concerning trust? It is simply this. Rather than spending our time worrying about and bemoaning its loss, we commit ourselves, as individuals and institutions, to become those who demonstrate a new trustworthiness. For the challenge of the moment set before us all – from government to Church, media to business leaders and ordinary individuals to royal family – is simply this: consistently to adopt behaviours that rebuild trust. Or, if we will not, to watch as our society slowly disintegrates.

Though the title of this book is *Trust* (in fact, *because* the title of this book is *Trust)*, its content is more accurately about something else, something closely related, but something subtly different – trustworthiness. The reason is simple. The key question we all face is not so much 'Why don't people trust me?' as 'What can I do to become worthy of their trust?'

Ebb and Flow

In generations past a person was to be trusted unless they proved themselves to be unworthy of it – trust was society's default setting. Today, however, most people want to be safe rather than sorry. Trust is no longer automatic. The new rule is 'guilty until proven innocent'. Trust has to be earned the hard way.

'Who would rather not trust and be deceived?'

Eliza Cook, 19th century poet.

Trust is never a simple 'on' or 'off' affair. Though once established it can survive great disappointments, when it is abused, even where it has been developed over years, it will be damaged. Trust is like money in the bank. While one withdrawal will not necessarily take you into the red, if over time funds only flow out, eventually even the richest account will be emptied. However, the reverse is also true: the more deposits we make (however small), the more credit we collect. The building or breakdown of trust, then, is normally incremental. Though, in some cases, an act of betrayal is enough to destroy it immediately, most of the time its ebb and flow are gradual. Which means that, for trust to have become such a scarce commodity in our society, we must perceive ourselves to have been disappointed and let down very often.

Brave New World

There are many reasons why, for instance, trust in the government and politicians in general has diminished over the years. No doubt the behaviour of specific individuals and groups of politicians who have not lived up to the trust bestowed upon them has significantly impacted the situation. The actions of characters such as Lord Jeffrey Archer, Dame Shirley 'homes for votes' Porter and the scandal surrounding Dr David Kelly's death and the search for 'Weapons of Mass Destruction' have done little to convince the public to trust our political leaders. However, it is simplistic in the extreme to conclude that the breakdown of trust in politics is entirely the fault of individual politicians. There is no objective means of comparison between those in office today and their counterparts of, say, one hundred years ago, but it would not be unreasonable to assert that the behaviour of our current crop of politicians is no worse than that of generations past. In fact, it is generally far better and they are required to be far more accountable.

Our society is different for all sorts of reasons to the way it was a century ago. We don't want to turn the clock back. We can't turn the clock back – and even if we could it would only read the wrong time! Instead we want to, need to, face the challenges of life in the early twenty-first century; the world of 24/7 media coverage, message management and information overload. And we have to face a new world which poses new challenges for us, requires new skills of us, but also creates new opportunities for us.

'Trust is the watchword for everyone here at the BBC – we're independent, impartial and honest.'

BBC Values Statement

Some have argued that the greatest single reason for the absence of trust in society is the role of the media. Nothing in life today is hidden from its glare. Nothing is private, nothing secure, nothing sacred; everything is vulnerable to being leaked, uncovered or 'outed'. In the past someone had to mess up extremely badly before the public found out. Today, however, there is rarely a single week without an expose of some sort breaking. But though bad news sells papers, the impact of repeated reports of a lack of personal or corporate integrity naturally tarnishes our understanding of people and institutions generally. And each news report telling tales of sleaze, negligence or mismanagement represents another withdrawal from the bank account of trust. Or to put it another way, no single wave will destroy a coastline: however, the repeated crash of thousands of small waves will eventually cause even giant cliffs to crumble into the sea.

'Journalists who used to dine with politicians now dine on them.'

Geoff Mulgan

But if the media has been partly responsible for the decline of trust in society, it has also fallen victim of its own sword. The public no longer considers that the words it reads and the reports it hears carry the weight they once did. For instance, Andrew Gilligan's report of the 'sexed up' 45 minute claim in the government's Iraq Dossier, and the subsequent scandal that emerged, did significant damage to public perception of the media's trustworthiness as well as the government's. A recent MORI poll reported that while 92% of people trust doctors, a mere 20% trust journalists. How can we believe what we are told if there is the suspicion that the writers are inventing or 'sexing up' the stories themselves?

Pointing the Finger

Before pointing the finger at someone else, it is important to remember that when you do, three more point straight back at you. Like it or not, the Church in the UK is hardly in a position to preach any sermons on trust to its surrounding culture. There have been endless tales of the abuse of power by leaders of all denominations. It is a tragic fact that, in the perception of many, Roman Catholic priests are identified with paedophilia and Anglican vicars with repressed homosexuality. But the ministers of the lesser denominations are also viewed with deep suspicion – to the average man on the street, a charismatic or community church and a cult are not far apart.

There is, however, a greater reason why trust in the Church has declined. Over the years the Church's role in society has changed radically. In centuries past we played an important role at the hub of the community. The Church was the sole provider of medical care, education and just about every form of social welfare available. That is no longer the case. Where once our reason for existing was to serve the community and, in so doing, demonstrate God's love and our trustworthiness, the Church has nowadays become principally known for Sunday morning services. We cannot hope to be trusted if our message is not consistent with our actions.

> 'There's clearly quite a lot to that little word trust. And the more you examine it, the more important it becomes to our overall sense of security – the sense that we are standing on solid ground.'
>
> *Rowan Williams*

When Trust Fails

We have looked at some of the ways in which trust has been eroded, but how does its loss affect society?

The cost society carries as a result of the breakdown of trust is extremely high. When we stop trusting we withdraw, we stop participating, we cease to engage. If you don't trust in the Church, you are more than likely to stop being part of it. If you don't believe the reports in newspapers, you are increasingly likely to stop reading them. And if you don't have faith in politicians, you are less likely to vote.

So it was that the 2001 general election yielded the second lowest turnout of voters in the history of modern British democracy (just over 59%, the lowest since 1918). This is alarming for the health of political democracy. It reveals one of two things; either that a huge number of those eligible to vote don't care who is elected to govern them or that, in a world of spin and counter-spin which is all about show rather than substance – a world in which we are all being manipulated anyway – it doesn't really matter who is pulling the strings. Either way, an enormous number of people have lost trust in the political process.

> 'You can't help but think that the sound bite and a scrap for the benefit of Jeremy Paxman don't really do justice to the democratic process.'
>
> *Tony Benn*

In the run-up to the 2002 local elections there were adverts posted all over Croydon (the Greater London borough in which I live) asking

Trust

the question 'What takes just two minutes but lasts four years?' The answer below simply said 'Your vote!' If that is the way in which democracy is advertised, then it is small wonder so few people can be bothered to participate. After all, non-involvement is a vote - a vote of no confidence! If the sum total of our involvement in the political process amounts to putting a cross on a form, surely we are all missing the point of democracy.

Democracy, as the saying goes, is the government of the people by the people. True democracy requires our active involvement; it brings responsibilities as well as privileges. However, by and large, we've left the world of politics to the professionals and sidelined ourselves. But in doing this we have subverted democracy – we have become uninvolved and uninterested and, as a result, society has paid the price.

> 'Man's capacity for justice makes democracy possible, but man's inclination to injustice makes democracy necessary.'
>
> *Reinhold Niebuhr*

Rather than simply blaming others, it is time to acknowledge that central to our problems has been our political acquiescence. We need a new politics of community involvement and engagement. We cannot afford to leave the future of our society to the elite few any longer. Mature democracy demands our active involvement. But what came first, the chicken or the egg? Was it that in stepping back and letting the professionals handle government we lost touch and so lost trust in the system? Or was it that in losing trust we eventually stepped back and lost touch? Perhaps it's a vicious circle.

'I'm not really interested in politics.' Though commonly felt, this is a ridiculous sentiment. Politics is simply about the affairs of the people. It therefore concerns us all because it directly affects all of our lives – we are all on the receiving end of the policy decisions of both Whitehall and the town hall. Some people, of course, still champion our right to vote as if that, in and of itself, gives us democracy. They say that our forefathers fought for it. But what our forefathers and the suffragettes actually fought for was the right to be involved; to have a voice, not just a vote. It's easy to confuse the two, but when a voice is reduced to a vote, you soon lose the will to vote at all.

'We all get the government we deserve.'

Anonymous

The story is told of a government representative who paid a visit to a local farm. The farmer was out in the fields while his wife was working in the house but keeping a close eye on their eight-year-old daughter who was playing in the farmyard. The government visitor asked the girl if her mum and dad were around – but as he was doing this, her mother happened to look out of the open kitchen window and saw her young daughter talking to a stranger. Horrified, she called out at the top of her voice, 'Who are you talking to? Get in here with me, right now!' 'It's OK mummy' came the unconcerned response, 'he says he's from the government.' 'Well, in that case, get in here and bring the cow with you!'

The problem for us all is that the dominant mindset of our culture leads us to believe that there is always an instant, quick-fix, low cost, easy solution to any and every problem. But we are wrong; there isn't. Whether for the government, the Church, the media or big business, breaking the cycle of distrust and rebuilding trust in public life is going to be a long road which will require a deep and ongoing commitment to travel. In the next chapter we turn our attention to exploring how.

Winning with People

John C. Maxwell

Winning with People will provide you with the
tools you need to immediately improve your
existing relationships as well as cultivate strong,
exciting, and new ones. Using a unique blend
of interesting facts, statistics, humor, real life
examples, and questions for discussion, winning
with people reveals twenty-five key People
Principles for true success in Life.

Thomas Nelson
PB/0 7852.7636 x
£7.99

JOHN C.
MAXWELL

WINNING

— WITH —

PEOPLE

DISCOVER THE PEOPLE PRINCIPLES
THAT WORK FOR YOU EVERY TIME

Introduction

What does it take to win with people? Does an individual have to be born with an outgoing personality or a great sense of intuition to succeed relationally? When it comes to people skills, are there haves and have-nots, and we just have to accept whatever abilities God has given us? Can someone who is good at building relationships become even better?

Most of us can tell instantly when we're in the presence of a real "people person." Individuals with excellent people skills connect with us easily, make us feel good about ourselves, and lift us to a higher level. Our interaction with them creates a positive experience that makes us want to spend time with them.

Some people are so skilled at working with people that they ought to be in a relationship hall of fame. People such as Dale Carnegie, John Wooden, Ronald Reagan, and Norman Vincent Peale easily come to mind. Likewise, there are people whose relational abilities could make them candidates for a relational hall of *shame*. Leona Helmsley, Henry Ford (Sr.), Frank Lorenzo, and Dennis Rodman have such reputations.

But you don't have to read the paper or study history to find examples of relational extremes. You have to deal with them in your own life every day: on the street, at church, (perhaps at home,) and certainly at work. Take a look at the following statements that people put on job applications that reveal their deficiency when dealing with people:

- It's best for employers if I don't work with people.
- The company made me a scapegoat, just like my previous employers.
- Note: Please don't misconstrue my fourteen jobs as jobhopping. I have never quit a job.
- References: None. I've left a path of destruction behind me.

You may find yourself thinking that some of those applicants are now working at *your* place of employment!

Some Know the Secret

What kind of price would you put on good people skills? Ask the successful CEOs of major corporations what characteristic is most needed for success in leadership positions, and they'll tell you it's the ability to work with people. Interview entrepreneurs to find out what separates the successes from the failures, and they'll tell you it is skill with people. Talk to top salespeople and they'll tell you that people knowledge is much more important than mere product knowledge. Sit down with teachers and tradesmen, shop foremen and small business owners, pastors and parents, and they'll tell you that people skills make the difference between those who excel and those who don't. People skills are invaluable. It doesn't matter what you want to do. If you can win with people, you can win!

Many people fall into the trap of taking relationships for granted. That's not good because our ability to build and maintain healthy relationships is the single most important factor in how we get along in every area of life. Our people skills determine our potential success. Robert W. Woodruff, the man whose leadership transformed the CocaCola Company from a small, regional beverage producer to a global organization and financial powerhouse, understood the people factor when it came to achievement. In his book *Top Performance*, relationship expert *Zig Ziglar* quotes the former CEO of the Coca-Cola Company. Zig says that Woodruff used to hand out a little pamphlet he had created that read:

Life is pretty much a selling job. Whether we succeed or fail is largely a matter of how well we motivate the human beings with whom we deal to buy us and what we have to offer.

Success or failure in this job *is essentially a matter of human relationships.* It is a matter of the kind of reaction to us by our family members, customers, employees, employers, and fellow workers and associates. *If this reaction is favorable we are quite likely to succeed. If the reaction is unfavorable we are doomed.*

The deadly sin in our relationship with people is that we take them for granted. We do not make an active or continuous effort to do and say things that will make them like us, and believe us, and that will create in them the desire to work with us in the attainment of our desires and purposes.

Again and again, we see both *individuals and organizations perform only to a small degree of their potential success, or fail entirely, simply because of their neglect of the human element in business and life.*

They take people and their actions for granted. Yet it is these people and their responses that make or break them.

It All Starts with People

All of life's successes come from initiating relationships with the right people and then strengthening those relationships by using good people skills. Likewise, life's failures can usually be traced back to people. Sometimes the impact is obvious. Becoming entangled with an abusive spouse, a crooked partner, or a codependent family member is going to cause great damage. Other times the trouble is less dramatic, such as alienating a coworker that you must interact with every day, failing to build a positive relationship with an important client, or missing key opportunities to encourage an insecure child. The bottom line is this:
people can usually trace their successes and failures to the relationships in their lives.

When I think about my personal failures, I can trace most of them to specific individuals in my life. I once picked the wrong person for financial advice and went into an oil deal with him. It cost me $10,000, which it had taken my wife, Margaret, and me a long time to save. Another time I started a business and asked a friend to take charge of it, thinking he could make it go. But my judgment was poor, and after just a couple of years, the business was more than $150,000 in the red.

I'm not playing victim and blaming my failures on others. Rather, I'm saying that my interaction with others is a huge part of the process. In a similar way, I can't take credit for my successes. None of them was a solo endeavor. My interaction with others helped me to be successful. For every achievement, I can look back and see a relationship that made it possible. Without the help of people like Elmer Towns, Peter Wagner, and Jack Hayford, my career never would have gotten this far. Without the help of a whole slew of. people at Thomas Nelson and at my company, the INJOY group, my book *The 21 Irrefutable Laws of Leadership* never would have been a million seller. And most of my financial blessings can be credited to the help and advice of my brother, Larry Maxwell, and my friend Tom Phillippe.

As important as relationships are professionally, they're even more critical personally. My spiritual life can be traced back to my relationship with my father, Melvin Maxwell. The reason I feel fulfilled every day can be attributed to my relationship with my wife, Margaret; she helps me enjoy our successes. And I must give credit for life itself to my relationships with others. If I hadn't met cardiologist John Bright Cage, I wouldn't be writing this right now. The heart attack I suffered in December 1998 probably would have killed me.

More than an Add-on

Have you ever found yourself dealing with someone difficult and thought, *She's talented, but she sure is hard to work with,* or *He's brilliant, but he doesn't seem to get along with anybody?* Such people never reach their full potential because they are able to accomplish only a fraction of what they could if they knew how to win with people. They don't understand that good relationships are more than just the icing on the cake in life. They *are* the cake – the very substance we need to live a successful and fulfilling life.

So what are people to do if they don't possess great relational skills? I must admit, relationship building comes naturally to me. I was born a people person. But I've also worked hard to improve my skills. I've learned a lot of things about others and myself in half a century. And I've translated those ideas into twenty-five People Principles that *anyone* can learn. The most introverted individual can learn them and become more of a people person. And someone with a knack for people can become a master relationship builder.

> Good relationships are more than just the icing on the cake in life. They *are* the cake.

I say that because these People Principles work every time. They apply whether you are young or old, sanguine or melancholic, male or female, employed or retired. I've practiced them for decades, and I've seen them work as I've traveled to dozens of countries on six continents. By following these principles, I've optimized my chance for success with others, and I've built positive, healthy relationships that have brought me professional success and personal satisfaction.

As you read and learn these People Principles, you will see that some of them are common sense. Others may surprise you. Perhaps you may question a few as a bit too optimistic. But I can tell you from experience, they really do work. One People Principle does not a relationship guru make. But practicing all of these principles will improve your life. (And you can be sure that you will never be nominated for Relational Hall of Shame!)

That doesn't mean you will have a successful relationship with every person you meet. You can't control another person's response to you. All you can do is make yourself the kind of person others want to know and with whom they can build a relationship.

In life, the skills you use and the people you choose will make or break you. I've divided the People Principles in this book according to five critical questions we must ask ourselves if we want to win with people.

1. Readiness: Are we prepared for relationships?
2. Connection: Are we willing to focus on others?
3. Trust: Can we build mutual trust?
4. Investment: Are we willing to invest in others?
5. Synergy: Can we create a win-win relationship?

Learn and practice the People Principles, and you will be able to answer each of these questions in a positive way. That will make you relationally successful. You will be able to build healthy, effective, and fulfilling relationships. And you have a chance to become the kind of person who makes others successful too. What could be better than that?

The Devil's Account
Philip Pullman & Christianity

Hugh Rayment-Pickard

Rayment-Pickard examines the multitude of religious and mythological themes that run through Philip Pulman's trilogy which paint a disturbing picture of a corrupt church. In this book Pickard look's at Pullmans literary influences and links these with Pulman's own, very critical, view of organised religion.

Darton Longman & Todd
£7.95
PB / 0 2325.2563 3

The
Devil's Account

Philip Pullman &
Christianity

HUGH RAYMENT-PICKARD

Published by Darton Longman & Todd Ltd, 1 Spencer Court
140-142 Wandsworth High Street, London SW18 4JJ

Introduction

The religious atheist

Student: I'm an atheist!
G.K. Chesterton: I envy you your simple faith.

I am one of Philip Pullman's most enthusiastic and dedicated readers. When I read *His Dark Materials* for the first time, I consumed all three books in almost as many days. Since then I have read them all again twice. But I didn't just *enjoy* these books, I was *intrigued* by Pullman's atheism – an atheism that seemed to me to be so thoroughly *religious*. I had the feeling that Philip Pullman, like many enthusiastic non-believers, was still secretly in love with both theology and the theological enchantment of the world. I wanted to explore the strange underlying paradox of what I am calling Pullman's 'religious atheism'.

After reading the trilogy, I went on to read all of Pullman's adult and teenage fiction. These books are very varied – ranging from magical-realist novels (fashionable in the 1970s) to detective stories and issuedriven 'teen' fiction dealing with race, feminism, adoption and child abuse. Pullman is certainly versatile, but in every book I kept tripping over religious themes: strange priests, diabolical evil, religious searchers, explorations of the real and the unreal, good and evil, spirit and matter, God and the devil, and ideas about ultimate human meaning and destiny. I became even more curious about the nature of Pullman's religious concerns: was he simply hostile to religion, or was there perhaps a religious quest hidden somewhere within his antagonism?

I don't mean to suggest that Pullman is not sincere. He is a passionate and unapologetic atheist, who has no time for the church. But the mystery is: why does he devote so much energy to religious and theological topics? Perhaps the religious questions are important to Pullman, even if he doesn't like the Christian answers.

One upshot of Pullman's 'religious atheism' is that his fiction contains an inner tension between the novelist and the philosopher, between the story-teller and the anti-theologian. As we will see, Pullman is convinced in his own mind that he is just a teller of stories. This in itself is strange, because if there is one thing that can be confidently said of Pullman the novelist, it is that he *never* just writes stories. There is always something more: some message or meaning.

This book is an attempt to explore and understand what Pullman's message is. What is going on – theologically speaking – in his fiction? How does Pullman use his fiction to explore theological issues? What does Pullman mean by story-telling, and what do his stories actually tell us? What is Pullman's case against religion and what are his own religious concerns?

Everyone likes straightforward answers to straightforward questions. But given the paradoxes at the heart of Pullman's writing, straightforward answers may not be forthcoming. Pullman's writing may be the kind that supplies more questions than answers.

Pullman's writing before *His Dark Materials*

Pullman's career as a writer began with an adult novel, *The Haunted Storm* (1972). Pullman does not talk about this book except to describe it as 'a load of crap'. Pullman is too harsh, although *The Haunted Storm is* not a great novel. Lady Antonia Fraser gave the novel an endorsement as 'an honest and enterprising attempt to interweave the eternal – and immortal – longings of youth into the texture of a contemporary story' *The Haunted Storm is* certainly a serious book that reveals the scale of Pullman's literary ambition. The hero refers on one occasion to Dostoyevsky's *The Brothers Karamazov,* and this is the kind of example that Pullman would like to follow: the exploration of fundamental theological and ethical issues. We also see in this book how Pullman likes to take up controversial and transgressive sexual and ethical themes which reappear in his later writing, particularly in *Galatea* (see pp. 27–29 below) and *The Butterfly Tattoo.*

The Haunted Storm is a quasi-religious novel about different kinds of searches for ultimate meaning and security, symbolised in the novel by a mysterious Holy Well, whose significance is unclear. Matthew (the hero) is an edgy searcher, looking for meaning in an array of theologies and philosophies, and his visit to the Well results in his enlightenment. Alan (his satanic brother) is trying to pass the Well off as a pagan symbol of 'the invincible god' in order to promote his vicious fascist politics. The Revd Cole (a Gnostic vicar) sees the Well as a source of goodness in a world shrouded in darkness and corruption. Elizabeth (the hero's girlfriend and the vicar's daughter) is looking for meaning through her relationships with men, and in the end finds them all lacking. The four main characters are contrasted with Harry (the hero's uncle), who has an unshakeable Christian faith in the goodness of God. The novel – like many examples of philosophical fiction – is structured around set-piece conversations in which ideas are exchanged and debated.

Although the novel is a rather confused and unsuccessful attempt to open up a range of sexual, psychological, ethical and religious themes, it does reveal very clearly Pullman's interest in theology. The hero believes in God, but is troubled by God's apparent absence in the material processes of the world, symbolised by 'the storm'. The hero's experiences lead him to the Nietzschean conclusion that the world is 'perspectival': so contradictory views – such as his uncle's and the vicar's – can simultaneously be correct. He realises that there is no hidden depth to the world: 'Things existed: that was it, that was all that could be said: things existed' (HS 235). The hero finds the conviction that he and the world 'are one and the same thing' and that he must create the meaning of his own life, rather than waiting for some revelation. It turns out in the end that the Well is dedicated to 'the unknown god' rather than 'the invincible god'. So the novel ends on an agnostic rather than an atheistic cadence, leaving room for some possible unknown god to appear.

The Haunted Storm shows Pullman's appetite for telling stories that deal with 'big ideas'. The maturation of these big ideas takes place over the 25 years between *The Haunted Storm* and *His Dark Materials*, which is not only an adventure story, but a narrative statement about what Douglas Adams called 'life, the universe and everything'.

The Haunted Storm was followed by another adult novel, *Galatea* (1978), which Pullman still regards with affection. *Galatea* – as we will see later – explores a number of themes that re-surface in *His Dark Materials*. The hero chases after his missing wife though a magical realist dimension of fantastic cities. One of these cities, like Lyra's world in *His Dark Materials*, is an evil theocracy.

Pullman's most important children's fiction before *His Dark Materials* is a quartet of novels based on the adventures of Sally Lockhart and her friends: *The Ruby in the Smoke* (1985); *The Shadow in the North* (1986); *The Tiger in the Well* (1991) and *The Tin Princess* (1994). At the time, these stories must have seemed simply to be accomplished novels of high adventure. In retrospect we can see Pullman experimenting with many of the themes of his later trilogy. The heroine is a plucky young woman, Sally Lockhart, who takes on diabolical enemies. Like Lyra, Sally is fired by personal confidence and basic values of loyalty, courage and honesty.

In the Sally Lockhart novels we see Pullman's interest in ultimate evil and the forces that are required to combat it. Sally's arch-enemy (in *The Ruby in the Smoke* and *The Tiger in the Well*) is Ah Ling, who functions as Pullman's Satan, Moriarty or Fu Manchu: an exemplary enemy who must not only be stopped but *destroyed*. Ah Ling is not a mere criminal who needs punishing or restraining: he represents an absolute evil that must be overcome absolutely. Ah Ling uses many names, including 'Todd' (presumably Sweeney Todd), to indicate his extreme violence and cruelty. He is a polymorphous villain, 'a mysterious figure' (TW 24) who speaks 'without trace of any accent' (RS 193). '*No* one usually sees him because he always travels at night' (TW 26) and he is known only by rumour and folklore. He is the descendant of Chinese pirates, educated in Europe, but operating in Warsaw, Bucharest and London; and he is accompanied by 'a little imp from hell', a small monkey who waits on his every need. Ah Ling, who has agents all over Europe, is also behind a 'conspiracy, organisation, plot, whatever' to persecute the Jews (TW 199).

Ah Ling is contrasted unfavourably with the equally dastardly Axel Bellman, the villain of *The Shadow in the North*. Bellman's crime is the construction of a massive machine gun that can be used by governments to subdue civil unrest. Bellman is a vile character, but Sally explains that he is at least motivated (however perversely) by the noble aim of keeping law and order. But Bellman does not represent the wickedness of society or capitalism or anything else. Bellman's scheme must be destroyed, but Bellman's death is not a moral necessity in the way that Ah Ling's is. Bellman reeks of power and its misuse, but not of evil. Bellman is 'wrong' says Sally because he doesn't understand 'loyalty', 'love' or 'people' (SN 274).

Ah Ling dies for more primitive moral reasons. Just before he dies, Sally takes the opportunity to deliver a speech to Ah Ling on the nature of an evil that contaminates all humanity.

> Listen to me and learn. Evil ... It's what makes a family starve ... And do you know what's at the heart of it all? Eh? The gnawing poison cancer destroying and eating and laying waste at the heart of it all? It's not only you, you poor pitiful man; it's *me* too. Me and ten thousand others ... I didn't know the consequences of things ... We are all connected. (TW 338)

Although he is not personally responsible for all the wickedness in the world, Ah Ling, and his vicious monkey, *symbolise* the evil of the world in which Sally too is implicated – and for that reason he cannot survive.

Just as the dæmons of *His Dark Materials* represent the souls of the characters in Lyra's universe, so Ah Ling's monkey symbolises his heart of darkness:

> 'It's evil', said Rebecca, as she rubbed something pungent into Sally's hair. 'I don't care what they say about animals being innocent, not knowing good or evil, Adam and Eve, the Tree of Knowledge, blah, blah – that monkey is not innocent. It knows evil and it does evil. If I believed in all that folklore stuff about dybbuks and golems and so on, I'd think it was an evil spirit, not an animal of flesh and blood.' (TW 250)

In fact Ah Ling is not killed by Sally (who has already failed to polish him off with a point-blank pistol shot in *The Ruby in the Smoke*) but by a flood that also wipes out his henchmen and, symbolically, sweeps away his entire house. It is a gothic, apocalyptic death that smacks of final judgement. Ah Ling is not subjected to mere human justice but is destroyed by a cosmic force that intervenes to show that history is ultimately on the side of the good.

Ah Ling is also known by the ironic title 'Ttzaddik' which means 'religious one, saint, holy man' (TW 26). This is a hint of what is to come in *His Dark Materials*, where the evil to be overcome is God himself. Ah Ling is given a divine name 'as a way of keeping evil at bay' (TW 26). The religious themes are not developed at all in the Lockhart stories, but Pullman is already suggesting that there might be some coincidence between divinity and evil. Of course, if God is evil, then he too must be swept away. And so the logic of an enemy who *must* be destroyed is repeated in *His Dark Materials*, but this time the enemy is the Authority (God). Lord Asriel's servant Thorold explains to Serafina Pekkala that his master's ambition is not to defeat the church because that would leave the source of the church's power intact. Asriel is 'a-going to find the Authority and kill Him' (SK 48) and this *destruction*, as we learn, is an absolute requirement for the future growth of humanity. In the end, the Authority is revealed as a feeble old man 'crying like a baby', just as Ah Ling is shown as a pathetic figure, paralysed by Sally's gunshot and driven by the petty motives of greed and revenge.

The theme of radical evil is explored in a more direct and theological way in *The Butterfly Tattoo (1992,* also called *The White Mercedes).* Chris, the hero of the novel, is tempted by the evil Carson who has an inhuman face 'illuminated like hell fire' (BT 180). Of himself, Carson says 'I'm a demon, me. I'm a killer. I'm the angel of death' (BT 181). Carson offers Chris a revised version of the Genesis temptation story (for more on this see pp. 70–72 below), arguing that experience is preferable to innocence. But in contrast to *His Dark Materials* or the Lockhart novels, Pullman allows evil to win. Chris's girlfriend is shot dead – with Chris's collusion – and the novel ends not only with Carson going free, but with his dark ideology unanswered. *The Butterfly Tattoo is* Pullman at his very best: ambivalent, morally complex and unsettling.

The religious reception of *His Dark Materials*

Looking back at the reviews of the trilogy, we see that *His Dark Materials* has drawn both the highest praise and the most scathing criticism. Readers seem either to love Pullman's trilogy or hate it, but few are indifferent or lukewarm in their reactions. The reason for this is that most readers recognised Pullman's anti-Christian agenda and either warmed to it or wanted to warn against it. Nick Thorpe, writing in *The Sunday Times,* described Pullman as an 'anti-Christian fundamentalist', and a writer in the *Guardian* called him 'an evangelical atheist'. Whatever reviewers have said about Pullman's writing – and Pullman's story-telling gifts have generally been applauded, even by those who dislike his message – it is Pullman's big ideas that have attracted the most attention.

Predictably, readers from the conservative Christian right found the trilogy offensive. Peter Hitchens, writing in the *Mail on Sunday*, saw Pullman as an atheist messiah: 'He is ... the one the atheists would have been praying for, if atheists prayed.' ('The Most Dangerous Man in Britain'). Hitchens found *His Dark Materials* 'too loaded down with propaganda to leave enough room for the story'. The *Catholic Herald* claimed his work was 'the stuff of nightmares', and a writer from the Association of Christian Teachers said that Pullman was shamelessly blasphemous and had 'wilfully set out to exploit children in order to advance his own atheistic agenda'. At the fundamentalist extreme, internet sites in the US have called Pullman 'satanic'.

More subtle and insightful commentators have noted Pullman's positive religious concerns. John Pridmore, writing in the *Church Times*, said that Pullman's trilogy would be the inspiration for numerous Church of England sermons. Andrew Marr, writing in the *Daily Telegraph*, made a similar point from a secular perspective:

> What he gives me and what excites me is the sense that a post-Christian world can be as intensely filled with pity, the search for goodness, and an acute awareness of evil, as any religious universe.

Rowan Williams, among others, has also noted Pullman's religious relevance. It is this 'relevance' that has intrigued me: how is Pullman's writing *relevant* to religious concerns when he is, apparently, so utterly hostile to any religious system? Why does Pullman attract religious interest, when he never claims to be setting out religious ideas at all? He is, if he is to be believed, just a teller of stories.

The Case For A Creator

Lee Strobel

Lee Strobel investigates the latest scientific discoveries to see whether they form a solid basis for believing in God. But today science is pointing in a different direction. In recent years, a diverse and impressive body of research has increasingly supported the conclusion that the universe was intelligently designed.

Zondervan

£13.99

PB/0 3102 4144 8

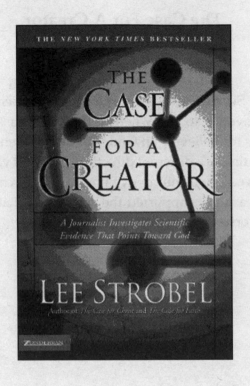

Published by Zondervan, Grand Rapids, Michigan 49530

4. Where Science Meets Faith

I am all in favor of a dialogue between science and religion, but not a constructive dialogue. One of the great achievements of science has been, if not to make it impossible for an intelligent person to be religious, then at least to make it possible for them not to be religious. We should not retreat from this accomplishment.

Physicist Steven Weinberg

Science and religion ... are friends, not foes, in the common quest for knowledge. Some people may find this surprising, for there's a feeling throughout our society that religious belief is outmoded, or downright impossible, in a scientific age. I don't agree. In fact, I'd go so far as to say that if people in this socalled "scientific age" knew a bit more about science than many of them actually do, they'd find it easier to share my view.

Physicist and theologian John Polkinghorne

Allan Rex Sandage, the greatest observational cosmologist in the world – who has deciphered the secrets of the stars, plumbed the mysteries of quasars, revealed the age of globular clusters, pinpointed the distances of remote galaxies, and quantified the universe's expansion through his work at the Mount Wilson and Palomar observatories – prepared to step onto the platform at a conference in Dallas.

Few scientists are as widely respected as this one-time protégé to legendary astronomer Edwin Hubble. Sandage has been showered with prestigious honors from the American Astronomical Society, the Swiss Physical Society, the Royal Astronomical Society, and the Swedish Academy of Sciences, receiving astronomy's equivalent of the Nobel Prize. The *New York Times* dubbed him the "Grand Old Man of Cosmology."

As he approached the stage at this 1985 conference on science and religion, there seemed to be little doubt where he would sit. The discussion would be about the origin of the universe, and the panel would be divided among those scientists who believed in God and those who didn't, with each viewpoint having its own side of the stage.

Many of the attendees probably knew that the ethnically Jewish Sandage had been a virtual atheist even as a child. Many others undoubtedly believed that a scientist of his stature must surely be skeptical about God. As *Newsweek* put it, "The more deeply scientists see into the secrets of the universe, you'd expect, the more God would fade away from their hearts and minds." So Sandage's seat among the doubters was a given.

Then the unexpected happened. Sandage set the room abuzz by turning and taking a chair among the theists. Even more dazzling, in the context of a talk about the Big Bang and its philosophical implications, he disclosed publicly that he had decided to become a Christian at age fifty.

The Big Bang, he told the rapt audience, was a supernatural event that cannot be explained within the realm of physics as we know it. Science had taken us to the First Event, but it can't take us further to the First Cause. The sudden emergence of matter, space, time, and energy pointed to the need for some kind of transcendence.

"It was my science that drove me to the conclusion that the world is much more complicated than can be explained by science," he would later tell a reporter. "It was only through the supernatural that I can understand the mystery of existence."

Sitting among the Dallas crowd that day, astounded by what he was hearing from Sandage, was a young geophysicist who had dropped by the conference almost by accident. Stephen Meyer had become a Christian through a philosophical quest for the meaning of life, but he hadn't really explored the issue of whether science could provide evidential support for his faith.

Now here was not only Sandage but also prominent Harvard astrophysicist Owen Gingerich concluding that the Big Bang seemed to fit best into a theistic worldview. Later came a session on the origin of life, featuring Dean Kenyon, a biophysicist from San Francisco State University, who had co-authored an influential book asserting that the emergence of life might have been "biochemically predestined," because of an inherent attraction between amino acids. This seemed to be the most promising explanation for the conundrum of how the first living cell could somehow self-assemble from nonliving matter.

To Meyer's surprise, Kenyon stepped to the podium and actually repudiated the conclusions of his own book, declaring that he had come to the point where he was critical of all naturalistic theories of origins. Due to the immense molecular complexity of the cell and the information-bearing properties of DNA, Kenyon now believed that the best evidence pointed toward a designer of life.

Instead of science and religion being at odds, Meyer heard specialists at the highest levels of achievement who said they were theists – not in spite of the scientific evidence but because of it. As Sandage would say, "Many scientists are now driven to faith by their very work."

Meyer was intrigued. It seemed to him that the theists had the intellectual initiative in each of the three issues discussed at the conference – the origin of the universe, the origin of life, and the nature of human consciousness. Even skeptics on the panels conceded the shortcomings of naturalistic explanations. Their main response was only to challenge the theists to provide "scientific answers" instead of merely invoking the idea of intelligent design.

That objection didn't make much sense to Meyer. "Maybe the world *looks* designed," he mused, "because it really *is* designed!"

As he walked away from the conference, Meyer was brimming with excitement over what he had experienced. Despite his background in science, he simply had been unaware of the powerful scientific findings that were supporting belief in God. All of this, he decided, was worth a much more thorough investigation.

He didn't know it at the time, but his life's mission had just crystallized.

Interview #2: Stephen C. Meyer, PHD

Already having earned degrees in physics and geology, Meyer went on to receive his master's degree in the history and philosophy of science at prestigious Cambridge University in England, where he focused on the history of molecular biology, the history of physics, and evolutionary theory. He then obtained his doctorate from Cambridge, where his dissertation analyzed the scientific and methodological issues in origin-of-life biology – a field he first got excited about when he heard Kenyon speak at the Dallas conference.

In the past fifteen years, Meyer has become one of the most knowledgeable and compelling voices in the burgeoning Intelligent Design movement. He has contributed to numerous books – including *Darwinism, Design and Public Education; Mere Creation: Science, Faith and Intelligent Design; Signs of Intelligence: Understanding Intelligent Design; Science and Christianity: Four Views; The Creation Hypothesis: Scientific Evidence for an Intelligent Creator; Science and Evidence for Design in the Universe; The History of Science and Religion in the Western Tradition; Of Pandas and People: The Central Question of Biological Origins; Darwinism: Science or Philosophy;* and *Facets of Faith and Science*, and is currently finishing books on DNA and the Cambrian explosion.

He has spoken at symposia at Cambridge, Oxford, Yale, Baylor, the University of Texas, and elsewhere; debated skeptics, including Michael Shermer, editor of *The Skeptical Inquirer*; written for magazines ranging from *Origins and Design* (where he's an associate editor) to *The Journal of Interdisciplinary Studies* to *National Review*; appeared in the *Wall Street Journal*, *Washington Times*, *Chicago Tribune*, and a host of other newspapers; and faced off with Darwinists on National Public Radio, PBS, and network television.

When I flew into snowy Spokane, Washington, to interview Meyer at Whitworth College, where he was an associate professor of philosophy, I wasn't aware that he was in the midst of telling his colleagues that he would be leaving soon to become director and senior fellow at the Center for Science and Culture at the Discovery Institute in Seattle. His impending departure was a poignant time for Meyer, since he had spent more than a decade as one of the most popular professors at the school.

To steal some time alone, we commandeered a nondescript off-campus office, where decorating was an apparent afterthought, and sat down in facing chairs for what would turn out to be virtually an entire day of animated, rapid-fire conversation. In fact, the full transcript of our discussion would top a whopping thirty thousand words – a small book in itself!

At one point, Meyer said, "I was once tested for hyperactivity as a kid. Can you imagine?" Yes, I could. Dressed in a dark blue suit, patterned tie, woolly gray socks, and brown Doc Martin shoes, the lanky Meyer was crackling with energy, speaking enthusiastically in quick bursts of words. His wispy brown hair spilled down onto his forehead, giving him a youthful appearance, but his eyebrows were furrowed in intensity.

His students sometimes faulted him for an absentminded professor's lack of classroom organization, but he made up for it with his infectious passion and disarming sincerity. When he answered my questions, it was in a thorough, systematic, and structured way, almost as if he were reading off invisible note cards. He came off as being brilliant, articulate, and driven.

After swapping some personal stories, we zeroed in on the issue of science and faith. His perspective, not surprisingly, was vastly different from the one I had when I began studying Darwinism in school.

"A Robust Case for Theism"

"We live in a technological culture where many people believe science trumps all other forms of knowledge," I said to Meyer. "For example, philosopher J. P. Moreland described meeting an engineer who was completing his doctorate in physics. 'According to him,' Moreland said, 'only science is rational; only science achieves truth. Everything else is mere belief and opinion. He went on to say that if something cannot be quantified or tested by the scientific method ... it cannot be true or rational.' Harvard geneticist Richard Lewontin claimed science is 'the only begetter of truth.' Do you agree with those perspectives?"

"No, I don't," came Meyer's reply. "Ironically, to say that science is the only begetter of truth is self-contradicting, because that statement in itself cannot be tested by the scientific method. It's a selfdefeating philosophical assumption.

"Beyond that," he continued, "while I certainly respect science, I don't believe scientific knowledge necessarily takes precedence over other things that we know. For instance, Moreland has argued that there are some things we know more certainly through introspection than we know from the sciences. I know I have free will on the basis of my introspection, and no studies in the social sciences will convince me otherwise."

He motioned toward a light switch on the wall. "I know I can turn that switch on, and I refute those who say I was determined thus," he said, leaning over to turn on the light. "In addition, history can tell us much, even though we can't test it by repeated experiment.

"Now, there's no question that science does teach us many important things about the natural world. But the real question is, 'Do these things point to anything beyond themselves?' I think the answer is yes. Science teaches us many true things, and some of those true things point toward God."

I quickly interrupted. "On the contrary," I said, "when I learned about Darwinism as a student, I was convinced that science and faith were at odds – and that science definitely had the edge in the credibility department. What would you say to someone who believes that science and Christianity are destined to be at war?"

"Well, that's certainly one way that people have conceptualized the relationship between science and faith," he said. "Some claim science and faith are fundamentally at odds. Others have said science and faith represent two separate and distinct realms that don't and can't interact with each other.

"However, I personally take a third approach, which is that scientific evidence actually supports theistic belief. In fact, across a wide range of the sciences, evidence has come to light in the last fifty years which, taken together, provides a robust case for theism. Only theism can provide an intellectually satisfying causal explanation for all of this evidence."

"For instance?"

"For instance," he continued, "if it's true there's a beginning to the universe, as modern cosmologists now agree, then this implies a cause that transcends the universe. If the laws of physics are fine-tuned to permit life, as contemporary physicists are discovering, then perhaps there's a designer who fine-tuned them. If there's information in the cell, as molecular biology shows, then this suggests intelligent design. To get life going in the first place would have required biological information; the implications point beyond the material realm to a prior intelligent cause.

"Those are just three examples," he concluded. "And that's just the beginning."

The Problem with Noma

"Isn't it dangerous to mix science and faith that way?" I asked. "A lot of scientists follow the lead of the late Stephen Jay Gould in saying that science and faith occupy distinctly different 'magisteria' or domains.

"He called this philosophy NOMA, which is short for 'nonoverlapping magisteria.' He said: 'The net of science covers the empirical universe ... [while] the net of religion extends over questions of moral meaning and value.' What's wrong with having that kind of strong dividing line between the hard facts of science and the soft faith of religion?"

"I think NOMA is partially true," Meyer said – a concession that surprised me a bit. "There are domains of science that are metaphysically neutral. They answer questions like: 'How many elements are in the periodic table?' Or 'What is the mathematical equation that describes gravitational attraction?' Or 'How does nature ordinarily behave under a given set of conditions?' Questions of this sort don't affect big worldview issues one way or the other. Some people use Galileo's old aphorism – 'Science tells you how the heavens go, and the Bible tells you how to go to heaven.'"

I jumped in. "That sounds trite, but it does make some sense."

"Of course," he said. "There is a sense in which science and religion do have different objects of interest and focus, like the nature of the Trinity on one hand, and what are the elementary particles present at the Big Bang on the other hand.

"However, there are other scientific questions that bear directly on the great worldview issues. For instance, the question of origins. If fully naturalistic models are correct, then theism becomes an unnecessary hypothesis. It's in these instances where science and metaphysics intersect – where worldview questions are at stake – that it's impossible to impose the NOMA principle. That's because what science discovers will inevitably have implications for these larger worldview questions. The only real way to keep the two separate is to subtract from the claims of one or the other.

"You see, NOMA says science is the realm of facts, and religion is the realm of morality and faith. The essential problem is that biblical religion makes very specific claims about facts. It makes claims about the universe having a beginning, about God playing a role in creation, about humans having a certain kind of nature, and about historical events that are purported to have happened in time and space.

"Let's just take the historic Christian creed: 'I believe in God the Father almighty, maker of heaven and earth: And in Jesus Christ his only son, our Lord; who was conceived by the Holy Spirit, born of the Virgin Mary, suffered under Pontius Pilate, was crucified, dead, and buried; the third day he rose again from the dead.'

"Well, Pontius Pilate is situated historically in Palestine in the first century. A claim is made that Jesus of Nazareth lived at the same time. An assertion is made that he rose from the dead. God is called the Creator of heaven and earth. You see, it's inherent to the Christian faith to make claims about the real world. According to the Bible, God has revealed himself in time and space, and so Christianity – for good or ill – is going to intersect some of the factual claims of history and science. There's either going to be conflict or agreement.

"To make NOMA work, its advocates have to water down science or faith, or both. Certainly Gould did – he said religion is just a matter of ethical teaching, comfort, or metaphysical beliefs about meaning. But Christianity certainly claims to be more than that."

This particular statement about Gould seemed vague. I wanted to pin him down by demanding specifics. "Could you give me one concrete example of how Gould watered down Christianity to make NOMA work?" I asked.

"Sure," he said. "In his book *Rocks of Ages*, Gould reduces the appearance of the resurrected Jesus to doubting Thomas to being merely 'a moral tale.' This was necessary for Gould to do under the rules of NOMA because all of Jesus' post-resurrection appearances come from a religious document – the Bible – and NOMA says religion must confine its claims to matters of morality and values. But the Bible clearly portrays Jesus' appearances as being actual historical events. Christianity hinges on the conviction that they really occurred.

"NOMA may try to exclude this possibility by restricting religion to mere matters of morality, but the writers of the Bible did not see fit to limit their claims about God to the nonfactual domain that NOMA has allocated to religion. Now, there might be some religions that can fit comfortably with NOMA. But biblical Christianity – because it's built not just on faith, but on facts – simply cannot."

Law professor Phillip Johnson also has been strongly critical of the NOMA concept. "Stephen Jay Gould condescendingly offers to allow religious people to express their subjective opinions about morals, provided they don't interfere with the authority of scientists to determine the 'facts' – one of the facts being that God is merely a comforting myth," he said.

"So," I said to Meyer in summing up, "while much of science and biblical religion are concerned with different things, they clearly do have some overlapping territory."

"Precisely. And when that happens, either they agree or disagree. The judgment of nineteenth-century historians, who were writing mainly out of an Enlightenment framework, was that where they did overlap, they invariably disagreed – and of the two domains, science was a more warranted system of belief. They believed conflict would continually grow between science and biblical religion."

"What do *you* believe?" I asked.

"My judgment is quite different," he said. "I believe that the testimony of science *supports* theism. While there will always be points of tension or unresolved conflict, the major developments in science in the past five decades have been running in a strongly theistic direction."

He paused momentarily, then punched his conclusion: "Science, *done right*, points toward God."

Creatio Ex Nihilo

Meyer's perspective couldn't be more different from the one I had when I was studying evolution in school. I had concluded that the persuasive naturalistic theories of Darwin eliminated any need for

God. Meyer, however, was convinced that science and faith are pointing toward the same truth. I decided to press him for more details.

"Could you list, say, half a dozen examples of how you believe science points toward theism?" I asked.

Meyer settled deeper into his chair. "I would start," he said, "with the new cosmology – the Big Bang theory and its accompanying theoretical underpinning in general relativity. These two theories now point to a definite beginning of the universe. The fact that most scientists now believe that energy, matter, space, and time had a beginning is profoundly antimaterialistic.

"You can invoke neither time nor space nor matter nor energy nor the laws of nature to explain the origin of the universe. General relativity points to the need for a cause that transcends those domains. And theism affirms the existence of such an entity – namely, God.

"In short," he added, "naturalism is on hard times in cosmology; the deeper you get into it, the harder it is to get rid of the God hypothesis. Taken together, the Big Bang and general relativity provide a scientific description of what Christians call *creatio ex nihilo* – creation out of nothing. As Nobel Prize–winner Arno Penzias said about the Big Bang, 'The best data we have are exactly what I would have predicted had I nothing to go on but the first five books of Moses, the Psalms and the Bible as a whole.'"

Meyer waited, apparently to see if I had any further questions, but I motioned for him to continue with his examples.

"The second category of evidence would be for 'anthropic finetuning.' This means the fundamental laws and parameters of physics have precise numerical values that could have been otherwise. That is, there's no fundamental reason why these values have to be the way they are. Yet all of these laws and constants conspire in a mathematically incredible way to make life in the universe possible."

I asked him for an example. "Take the expansion rate of the universe, which is fine-tuned to one part in a trillion trillion trillion trillion trillion," he said. "That is, if it were changed by one part in either direction – a little faster, a little slower – we could not have a universe that would be capable of supporting life.

"As Sir Fred Hoyle commented, 'A commonsense interpretation of the facts suggests that a superintellect has monkeyed with physics, as well as chemistry and biology, and that there are no blind forces worth speaking about in nature.'

"Well, maybe this looks fine-tuned because there actually is a fine-tuner. In the opinion of physicist Paul Davies, 'The impression of design is overwhelming.' And I thoroughly agree. This is powerful evidence for intelligent design.

"The third example of science pointing toward God is the origin of life and the origin of information necessary to bring life into existence," he continued. "Life at its root requires information, which is stored in DNA and protein molecules.

"Richard Dawkins of Oxford said that 'the machine code of the genes is uncannily computer-like.' If you reflect on that, you realize that computers run on software programs that are produced by intelligent engineers. Every experience we have about information – whether it's a computer code, hieroglyphic inscription, a book, or a cave painting – points toward intelligence. The same is true about the information inside every cell in every living creature."

"Isn't that just an argument from ignorance?" I asked. "Scientists may not currently be able to find any explanation for how life began, but that doesn't necessarily point toward a supernatural conclusion."

"This is *not* an argument from ignorance," Meyer insisted. "We're not inferring design just because the naturalistic evolutionary theories all fail to explain information. We infer design because all those theories fail *and* we know of another causal entity that is capable of producing information – namely, intelligence. Personally, I find this to be a very strong argument indeed."

An Ensemble of Evidence

Continuing on to the fourth example, Meyer said, "Then there's the evidence for design in molecular machines that defy explanation by Darwinian natural selection. These integrative, complex systems in biological organisms – which microbiologist Michael Behe calls 'irreducibly complex' – include signal transduction circuits, sophisticated motors, and all kinds of biological circuitry."

"What's the argument based on this?" I asked.

"You see, these biological machines need all of their various parts in order to function. But how could you ever build such a system by a Darwinian process of natural selection acting on random variations? Natural selection only preserves things that perform a function – in other words, which help the organism survive to the next generation. That's survival of the fittest.

"The problem with irreducibly complex systems is that they perform no function until all the parts are present and working together in close coordination with one another. So natural selection cannot help you build such systems; it can only preserve them once they've been built. And it's virtually impossible for evolution to take such a huge leap by mere chance to create the whole system at once.

"Of course, this forces the question: how did the biochemical machine arise? Behe says maybe these biological systems look designed because they really *were* designed. After all, whenever we see irreducibly complex systems and we know how they arose, invariably a designer was the cause."

"How strong of an argument do you think that is?" I asked.

"I think it's very strong," he replied with a smile. "And you see that in the weak objections that are proposed by Darwinists. And again, that's just one more example. The next one would be the Cambrian explosion, which is yet another striking piece of evidence for design in the history of life."

I told him that in a previous interview Jonathan Wells had already explained the basics of Biology's Big Bang. "He talked about it primarily in terms of being an argument against Darwinism," I said.

"Indeed, it is," Meyer replied. "You have between twenty and thirty-five completely novel body plans that come online in the Cambrian. You have a huge jump in complexity, it's sudden, and you have no transitional intermediates.

"But this is also affirmative evidence for design, because in our experience information invariably is the result of conscious activity. Here we have the geologically sudden infusion of a massive amount of new biological information needed to create these body plans, far beyond what any Darwinian mechanism can produce. Darwinism simply can't account for it; design is a better explanation.

"Think about how suddenly these new body plans emerged. As one paleontologist said, 'What I want to know from my biology friends is just how fast does this evolution have to happen before they stop calling it evolution?' Darwin said nature takes no sudden leaps. Yet here's a huge leap – which is what intelligent agents cause. Consequently, the Cambrian explosion provides not just a negative case against Darwinian evolution, but also a compelling positive argument for design."

"All right," I said, "I asked for half a dozen examples. What would be the sixth?"

Meyer thought for a moment. "I'd say human consciousness certainly supports a theistic view of human nature," he said. "Judaism and Christianity clearly teach that we are more than just matter – we're not a 'computer made of meat,' in the words of Marvin Minsky, but we're made in God's image.

"We have the capacity for self-reflection, for representational art, for language, for creativity. Science can't account for this kind of consciousness merely from the interaction of physical matter in the brain. Where did it come from? Again, I think theism provides the best explanation."

Meyer scooted to the edge of his chair. "So what we have here," he said, wrapping up his impromptu presentation in a tone of urgency, "is an ensemble of half a dozen evidences that point to a transcendent, intelligent cause. This is mind-boggling stuff!

Scientists in the nineteenth century weren't aware of these things when they said naturalism accounts for everything. Thanks to the discoveries of the last five decades, we know a lot more today."

"Based on the evidence you've mentioned," I said, "how do you complete the case for God?"

"First, theism, with its concept of a transcendent Creator, provides a more causally adequate explanation of the Big Bang than a naturalistic explanation can offer," he said. "The cause of the universe must transcend matter, space, and time, which were brought into existence with the Big Bang. The Judeo-Christian God has precisely this attribute of transcendence. Yet naturalism, by definition, denies the existence of any entity beyond the closed system of nature.

"The fine-tuning of the physical laws and constants of the universe and the precise configuration of its initial conditions, dating back to the very origin of the universe itself, suggest the need for a cause that's intelligent. Theism affirms the existence of an entity that's not only transcendent but intelligent as well – namely, God. Thus, theism can explain both Big Bang cosmology and the anthropic fine-tuning.

"Pantheism can't explain the origin of the universe, because pantheists believe in an impersonal god that's coextensive with the physical universe. Such a god can't bring the universe into being from nothing, since such a god doesn't exist independently of the physical universe. If initially the physical universe didn't exist, then the pantheistic god wouldn't have existed either. If it didn't exist, it couldn't cause the universe to exist."

"What about deism?" I interjected, referring to the belief that God created the world but has since let it run on its own. "Can't deism account for the origin of the universe too?"

"Yes, I'll provide that caveat – deism can do the same," he acknowledged. "But I believe the existence of design subsequent to the Big Bang undermines deism as an adequate explanation.

"You see, deism can't explain the evidence of discrete acts of design or creation after the universe was created. The deistic god never intervenes in nature, yet we're seeing evidence of intelligent design in the history of life. For example, the high information content in the cell provides compelling evidence for an act of intelligent design of the first life, long after the beginning of the universe.

"Taken together, what we know today gives us heightened confidence – *from science* – that God exists. The weight of the evidence is very, very impressive – in fact, in my opinion it's sufficiently conclusive to say that theism provides the best explanation for the ensemble of scientific evidence we've been discussing.

"Science and faith are not at war. When scientific evidence and biblical teaching are correctly interpreted, they can and do support each other. I'd say to anyone who doubts that: investigate the evidence yourself."

Meyer's whirlwind tour was exhilarating. At first blush, the cumulative case for God, built point by point from the discoveries of science, seemed staggering. Of course, I had a whole slew of follow-up questions, some of which I intended to pose to Meyer, and others I would save for the experts I planned to interview in each of the categories of evidence Meyer had mentioned. I decided to begin with the issue of just how much evidence for God is needed to establish the case for a Creator.

Follow Jesus

Dave Roberts

Do you feel you have connected emotionally, intellectually, spiritually with the heart, the essence, the magnificence of who Jesus was and is and forever will be? If you don't want to settle for a comfortable religion, then you need to read this book and learn what it means to follow Jesus today.

Kingsway Books
£7.99
PB/1 8429.1215 1

3. Meek and Wild

Gentle Jesus, meek and mild. It's a distortion, but a pervasive one; such is the power of song and poetry. But it's dangerous because it is simply not true.

There were times when He was meek. He was meek the day He walked through a hostile crowd that was bent on throwing Him over a cliff. He was meek when He healed the soldier slashed by the fiery Peter. He was meek when He carried the cross toward His death. He was meek when they placed the crown of thorns upon His head.

Jesus chose not to rise up in anger on these occasions, although He could have called ten thousand angels to His side and destroyed those who taunted Him with one word.

There were times when He chose to be meek.

But He was never mild. He was born into conflict and remained in it for the whole of His life. His family had to flee from a vengeful king; He came from a town that had a bad reputation; He jousted with the devil in the desert; He frequently exchanged words with the religious groups of the day. He risked life and reputation by spending time with housefulls of tax collectors and in the company of known prostitutes. He risked the wrath of thousands of people in Jericho by asking Himself to someone's house. He was not condemned to die on the cross because He was mild. He was sent there because He was wild.

Wild enough to turn over the tables of those who were fleecing the faithful as they came to the temple to worship. Wild enough to embrace the hated neighbors (Samaritans). Wild enough to eat with publicans and sinners. Wild enough to question the laws of the day which said you weren't to heal on the Sabbath. Wild enough to touch the unclean leper.

Jesus was meek and wild. Are you comfortable with that paradox?

It is a challenge to our normal either/or mind-set. Is it possible to believe that Jesus' life was full of both/and tensions? Was He a comforter and a prophet, a tough man with a tender heart, someone who valued tradition but undermined tradition? What does the plain record of Scripture tell us?

I can believe that the life of Jesus was marked by paradox, because His very existence seems paradoxical to the ordinary mind. It's not hard to believe that He was a good man who God "adopted." That keeps Him human. It's not hard to believe He was God. Surely only God could have been as holy, perfect, and wise as Jesus. Surely our earthly humanity could not have soiled His divinity.

Jesus was human – easy to believe. Jesus was God – easy to believe. Jesus was both human and divine – much bigger challenge.

But that's what the scriptural record implies: He laid aside His majesty and came and lived among us.[1] He worked with His father as a carpenter. He fell asleep in boats during storms. He ate, He wept, He cried out in anguish as the time of His trial approached. He was moved with compassion for His friends Lazarus, Mary, and Martha.

Jesus was very human.

But Jesus was divine. His earthly mother Mary was impregnated by the Divine. Jesus was the Son of God. He talked to his Father constantly. He regularly used the term Father to describe God. In the Old Testament, this only happens forty times. In the New Testament, the figure is 260.

Jesus talked to the Father in prayer, using the term in every prayer, except in His cry of anguish on the cross as He lamented being "forsaken."

The record of His baptism suggests that God spoke from heaven and declared "This is my son, whom I love; with him I am well pleased."[2]

The record of His life speaks of His authority over the elements of nature. He walked on the water.[3] He rebuked the wind and the raging waters, and they became calm.[4] He rose from the dead, was seen by more than 500 witnesses, and extended His nail-pierced hands to the doubting disciple Thomas.

How do we reconcile His divinity and His humanity? How could they co-exist? It may be helpful to reflect on the fact that once you concede that this complex universe had a Creator, it's not too hard to conceive of the place of the miraculous and unusual.

One writer in Eastbourne won't resolve the issues that surround that co-existence in the pages of a book such as this. Church councils have debated it for millennia. The exact nature of it is at the heart of the difference between the Orthodox churches and the rest of Christendom. Suffice it to say that the debate has been long because most involved in it want to do justice to the reality of the record of Jesus' life, and to resist the temptation to simply believe that He was either human or divine.

If we allow for the reality of the human/divine in the person of Jesus, what other tensions might we allow?

Jesus loved tradition; Jesus undermined tradition

Everything about Jesus' life spoke of Him being deeply rooted in the culture of the Israelites to whom He spoke. So much of what He said was reflective of His respect for tradition. Here are some snapshots – a small cross-section of a huge body of evidence.

When Jesus was challenged by the teacher of the law as to how he might inherit eternal life, Jesus asked a question designed to remind him of the daily prayer patterns of the Jews, one of which started and ended with passages from Deuteronomy 5 and 6. It was with these that the teacher responded.[5]

As the time of His death approached, He took the disciples to Jerusalem for the Passover meal. This symbolic meal was part of the spoken and acted history tradition of the Israelite people. Jesus was to transform it from the story of a nation's deliverance to a symbol of the deliverance of mankind. But He remained immersed in the tradition.

He told them to look out for a man carrying a water pitcher. The significance of the pitcher relates to the fact that it would signify that the man was devout and was preparing his house for the forthcoming Passover in the traditional way. The extended drama of this meal, lost in our short and minimalist versions, is the symbolic nature of the food, every prayer said, and every action undertaken during the meal.

The lamb had been cooked in the quickest way. Bread was baked without yeast. The Passover meal represented the story of those preparing to leave in haste. The bitter herbs represented the wild vegetables they snatched from the roadside to still their growing hunger. The reddish sauce reminded them of their forced labor under Pharaoh. The wine symbolized the joy of escape, the intoxication of gratitude to the Almighty.

At the end of the meal, the disciples and Jesus sang a hymn from the "Hallel" section of Psalms 114–118. The Passover meal was an acted out memory that helped shape the identity of all who participated in it.

There are many other small clues about Jesus and tradition. Jesus attended the feast in Jerusalem with His parents, spoke in the synagogue, observed the prayer patterns of His time, and participated in the everyday traditions of His time.

He publicly declared that He had not come to destroy the law but to fulfill it.[6] Jesus had no problem with basic commands of God revealed in the first five books of the Bible (Torah). But on the occasions when He clashed with the religious authorities of the day, He was usually ignoring the hedge of laws that the priests had built around the Torah. Jesus healed a crippled woman on the Sabbath, but was criticized for doing so. Jesus reminded the crowd that animals would be tended and rescued from harm on the Sabbath, and human beings deserved the same.[7]

He pointed out that it is always lawful to do good on the Sabbath. Elsewhere He pressed home the point by reminding His listeners that the Sabbath was a means for humankind to rest, and that it had not been instituted to provide a test of holiness.[8]

The Apostle Paul commented on information about the resurrection and the nature of the communion meal by referring to the fact these had become traditions among the early Church.[9]

Tradition kills when it feels like an obligation, but when viewed as a means of service, connection, and remembrance, it can be a joy and a comfort. What role might tradition have in your life? Are there everyday rhythms of friendship that help anchor you in your community – regular meals, gatherings for coffee, sporting events? Are there small rituals of faith that will keep your connection with Jesus alive – prayer, weeks of prayer, and family prayer? Are there annual events that present an opportunity to gather with like-minded people?

There are myriad traditions that will create a sense of belonging in this world for you. I'm loathe to describe them, lest it seems prescriptive on my part.

I encourage you think of tradition as being like a metal frame. It's solid and carefully designed. You can climb inside it and hide and let it become a cage. But you can climb on it, let it give you support, and view the world from the top of it.

And as you'll discover elsewhere in these pages, tradition can be a rich source of wisdom, to be followed because it enriches life, not merely because we feel we ought to.

Jesus loved the wisdom behind the traditions He observed, but shied away from those who sought to ensure they were followed by imposing hundreds of minor rules. Does any of this feel familiar to you?

Jesus, the man of paradox, loved wise tradition, but also undermined the traditions of men.

Jesus was a comforter; Jesus was a prophet

A pattern of hope is in Jesus' dealings with the lost, broken, and marginalized people whom He met.

Jesus had announced His mission in the synagogue by declaring He had come to bring good news to the poor, freedom for the captives, sight for the blind, and the release of the oppressed.[10]

To the woman caught in adultery, who had come so close to death, He said: "Woman, where are they? Has no one condemned you?"

"No one, sir," she said. "Then neither do I condemn you," Jesus declared. "Go now and leave your life of sin."[11]

Jesus took time for those deemed not important even by His disciples. They had rebuked the parents who sought Jesus' touch for their child, but Jesus called the children to Him with the words: "Do not hinder them, for the kingdom of God belongs to such as these."[12]

Jesus was an emotional man. His life was not all cool logic and careful theology. Outside the town of Nain, He met the funeral cortege of a loved son, mourned by his widowed mother. When he saw her, His heart went out to her, and He told her not to cry. He spoke with the authority of one who had been there at the creation of the universe, and life returned to the young man's body.

He also looked at the ordinary detail of people's lives and sought to meet their mundane needs. Aware that those who had spent three days listening to Him might be hungry and would need strength for their journey home, He had compassion on them and performed a miracle with fish and bread that meant four thousand men were fed.[13]

Jesus comforted the afflicted, but He also afflicted the comfortable.

Faced with the harsh judgments of the teachers of the law, He wondered if they would ever be satisfied and whether they would always find fault. In their eyes John the Baptist's abstinence and diet meant He was demonized. But Jesus, who ate bread and drunk wine, was condemned as a glutton and a drunkard. "Wisdom," He warned, would be "proved right by all her children."

He warned His own disciples that following Him would mean daily sacrifice and self-denial.[14] He invited the expert on the law to consider the possibility that a Samaritan, the despised neighbor of the Israelite people, might be the one He was being called to love and emulate. He described the king as a fox.[15]

Jesus seemed to care little for popular opinion, warning healed people not to gossip about what had happened to them, risking the wrath of the whole city of Jericho by visiting the tax collector whom everyone hated, and musing that some of the crowds following were spiritual thrill seekers from a "wicked generation."[16]

This prophetic confrontation was a hallmark of Jesus' words and deeds and will echo throughout every chapter of this book.

Are you ready to confront systems of thought with the challenge of the life and words of Jesus? Are you willing to express an unpopular opinion and face the anger and misrepresentation of your motives that will result? Can you live with the tension of seeking to balance that mental toughness with a gracious kindness to people seeking to make sense of their lives and circumstances?

It is vital that you do. Impatience and a judgmental attitude are the curse of the prophet who doesn't internalize the wisdom of the whole of Jesus' life.

Are you willing to embrace the paradox of grace and justice?

Jesus was tender; Jesus was tough

Jesus' life is a challenge to men. If we have been raised in a culture of emotional concealment and taught that the manly thing to do was hide our feelings, then the emotional transparency of Jesus will be an unsettling irritant. It'll help close the spiritual doors of a man's heart if it isn't balanced with the reality of Jesus' boldness, bravery, lack of compromise, and willingness to stand up to the dominant voices in the culture to which He came.

Standing before the tomb of his friend Lazarus, Jesus wept. Looking over Jerusalem, He once again wept as He told of the pain that would be the lot of the people because they had not heeded the message that would bring them peace.[17]

The heartbeat of God sounds in the steady reminders we get of Jesus' compassion. We see the acts of compassion, but can we begin to feel the deep emotions that precipitated them?

It seems He was feeling their pain and alienation, understanding that they were harassed and helpless, unsure of whom to look to for leadership or protection. He found it impossible to ignore sickness, often making His first task the healing of the sick. He healed two blind men and took the risk of touching the unclean leper as He was moved with compassion in response to their heartfelt requests.[18]

Jesus was a tenderhearted man.

But what kind of toughness did it take to hear people attribute your miracles to the devil, to walk through crowds ready to throw you over a cliff, or to endure the lashes that should never have been given to an innocent man?

What kind of man would drive out those who exploited the poor in the temple courtyards, turning over their tables as He did so? What kind of man would die the slow death of suffocation to which hanging from the cross sentenced you?

What kind of man would endure the wrenching pain as the blood seeped from His side, the strength in His arms failing as his torn wrists shot pain through His body, but still speak words of kindness to a dying thief?

What kind of man would return to a group of men that had betrayed Him and make the most verbal traitor the leader of His new community? What kind of man would step nimbly around the verbal traps laid by His opponents, seeking to get Him to disagree with the law of Moses, or the tax laws of the day?[19]

Not a weak man, not a timid man, not a man who lacked principles, and not a man whose life was held captive by the opinions of others.

Jesus was tough because He was compassionate. One led to the other. He had come to take captivity captive. He had come to release the oppressed.

If we only ever speak of the tender Jesus, we will slip into sentimentality. If we only ever speak of the Jesus who challenged human hearts, we will end up sounding shrill. If we speak of both, we can bring words that will sustain and nourish a spiritually hungry, weary, and brokenhearted generation.

Jesus in the 'hood; Jesus in the 'burbs

God posted the notices about the Messiah to the wrong addresses. He sent three astrologers chasing around Israel looking for a sign in the stars. He dispatched a raucous group of angels to the fields to inspire some dread and wonder among the local shepherd population. They were not the ideal people to start a worldwide movement.

Shepherds had always had a bit of a rough deal. David restored their image a little by writing about them in Psalm 23, but the fact that he had once been one indicated his status as the youngest in the family. Disputes over land gave the shepherds the kind of status often accorded to Native Indians or Gypsies. They were the victims of irrational prejudice, and to have the label was to be condemned. The religious authorities of the day had a list of occupations that were either unclean or borderline. Shepherds were among them.

The wise men came from another culture and possibly from a different religion, although they seemed familiar with the Old Testament. They were savvy enough to know that their dreams were from God and left without telling Herod what he wanted to know about the young Messiah's whereabouts.

God had also let the God chasers of that time know He was at work and alerted Simeon and Anna that Joseph and Mary had come to the temple to consecrate the baby Jesus. Simeon warned Mary and Joseph of the challenges they faced.

The arrival of the Christ was made known to every strata of society, including those deemed to belong to the less fortunate parts of it.

There is also a distinct lack of bias in Jesus friendship choices. Was He a man of the people? With several fishermen and Simon the Zealot among His disciples, He was in touch with the ordinary workingman. But He also had a tax collector, a middle-class man, in the disciples' ranks.

How did Jesus get on with the elite of His day? Nicodemus, a member of the ruling council of the Jews, visited privately to talk.20 Jesus also had friends among the rich, including Joseph of Arimathea, who purchased the place where He was briefly buried. Joseph was also a member of the Council and was prominent enough to be granted an audience with Pilate.[21]

Our vision of Jesus as the champion of the poor or the author of godly free enterprise will always need to be tempered by His unwillingness to conform to labels and neat categories. The hand that touched the leper, blessed the child, and washed the disciples feet was also extended to the rulers of His day.

Whenever a sectarian spirit might try to capture our mind, the obstinate paradoxes of an unprejudiced grace stand guard over our hearts.

Ask yourself, is there something about which I'm a bigot? Then ask yourself, what's my excuse? Then ponder this. Jesus was wronged at some point, by every section of society, but He kept on loving in a relentless fashion, aware of their imperfection, but believing the truth could set them free and restore them to their original purpose – loving God and loving their neighbor.

Jesus, in the world but not of it

Because we read the Bible through faith-tinted glasses, we don't always read it slowly enough to see past the obvious and catch the meaningful detail. Jesus did a lot of very ordinary things amid the miracles, parables, and verbal dust ups with spiritually anxious teachers of the law.

He went out with some of the disciples while they did their work and actually helped them catch more fish than normal. He cooked breakfast for His disciples. He washed their feet. He visited people's homes a lot – even when it was not expedient in terms of his reputation, Zacchaeus the tax collector being a case in point. Even some of His miracles were very down to earth: Changing water into wine wouldn't be the first miracle of choice for the pentecostal-healer-in-training today. He made a social occasion more enjoyable!

At other times He had conversations that were likely to attract rebuke from everybody. He talked, while alone, to a woman who was immoral and a member of a despised group.[22]

Religious men were very wary about their contact with women they did not know. If they were menstruating, the man would be deemed to be ceremonially unclean for several days after their meeting, however innocent it might be. Jesus ignored this and risked contamination by letting the woman draw water for Him. He risked slurs on His reputation, given that the woman had been through five husbands and was living with someone she hadn't yet married.

Jesus expanded the boundaries of grace by sharing His life with her and other Samaritans who flocked to hear what He had to say.

Our initial reading of this story might focus on Jesus' insight into the woman's life and His extension of the Gospel to the Samaritans. If we only dwell there, we miss what to us is mundane. The holy teacher talked to a woman – not mundane in Jesus' day. The teacher asked the woman to give Him water, another physical threat to His spiritual integrity and an undermining, in the eyes of the purity obsessed teachers of the law, of Jesus' claim to be the Messiah, the Son of God. In their eyes, a real holy man would know that God would deliver a pure and holy nation and would not have risked His reputation.

It will be clear, as this book continues to unfold, that Jesus was not "of the world." He had not embraced its way of thinking. But His life is a severe provocation to those who would ask us to contain our lives in a Christian enclave, protected from this world and cut off from the mundane contact with people that allows communication, signals acceptance, and is sometimes countercultural because it crosses boundaries of class, gender, race, and creed.

Jesus didn't send His followers out alone. From the nurture of a strong community, they went out in twos to taint the world with goodness, looking out for each other in every circumstance of life.

Ask yourself these questions: Do I spend time with my neighbors or work colleagues or friends doing mundane, ordinary things? Do I eat with them, talk to them about sports, discuss the nature of our work, reflect on the news together? Do I believe that from their growing trust will flow the chance to talk about Jesus, life, and eternity, maybe next week, maybe next year?

Or is the reality that we are all prone to measure our time with people according to a guilt-related yardstick? "How can I share my faith? I must be careful to avoid talking about unspiritual things."

In Britain we have a social phenomena related to quiz nights. My wife and I are going regularly to one with a couple we have known for nearly twenty years. They're avowed agnostics. At the moment, they're grieving the loss of a close friend and need the comfort of uncomplicated friendship. We often talk of faith in passing – their son is involved at our church – but some nights we don't. It never occurs to me to feel guilty when we don't talk about Jesus, nor to feel that somehow my faith will be undermined by this friendship. It does occur to me that Jesus loves them and that I should love them too. It also occurs to me that He who is in us is greater than he that is in the world.[23]

Jesus asked the disciples to do very mundane things when they went out to the towns around Jerusalem. They were to greet people, eat with them, and then offer to pray for their healing before declaring to them that they were being invited to be part of a kingdom with a new set of values.[24]

Are you ready to be ordinary so the extraordinary can be seen in your life as the Holy Spirit prompts you?

And that's not all

We will return to the tension of Jesus' life again as you read on. Was Jesus pessimistic and optimistic? How did He use the Scripture and listen to the Spirit? What did His disciples learn in the everyday conversations and through the crisis times?

Living with the paradoxes in the life of Jesus doesn't involve compromise. You're not being asked to ignore parts of it. You are being asked to take it all seriously. It won't always be understood when you do.

Earlier in this chapter we remarked that John was accused of being demonized because He led an ascetic lifestyle. Jesus was called a glutton and drunkard because He celebrated the good gifts of His Father with people.

You'll find the same if you stand in God's center, embracing grace and justice, the rich and the poor, the pastoral and the prophetic, tradition and innovation.

But that's the challenge of following Jesus.

(A study guide for this chapter is available at www.followingjesus.co.uk)

1. Philippians 2:6–11
2. Matthew 3:17
3. John 6:16–24
4. Luke 8:22–25
5. Luke 10:25–28
6. Matthew 5:17
7. Matthew 12:11
8. Mark 2:27, 3:4
9. 1 Corinthians 11:2, 11:23, 15:3
10. Luke 4:18–19
11. John 8: 10–12
12. Matthew 19:14; Mark 10:14; Luke 18:16
13. Mark 8:1–8
14. Luke 9:23
15. Luke 10:36–37, 13:31–32
16. Luke 11:29
17. Luke 19:41; John 11:35
18. Matthew 9:36, 20:34; Mark 1:41
19. Matthew 22:17

20. John 3:1–21
21. Mark 15:43
22. John 4:1–26
23. 1 John 4:4
24. Luke 10:5–9

Abundant Life Bible

The Abundant Life Bible helps you dig deeper into God's Word. Accept the challenge and experience the joy of discovering the abundant life through a close relationship with Jesus Christ

Tyndale House Publishing
£8.99
PB/0 8423.8491 X

Index
The Life You've Always Wanted

Stories surrounding the life of multi-millionaire Hetty Green, who lived in the early 1900s, describe her as a wealthy woman who lived like a pauper. She wore the same shabby clothes over and over and lined her threadbare coat with newspapers to keep warm. She frequently traveled a considerable distance to a grocery store that sold broken cookies because they were cheaper.

Hetty's stinginess is reputed even to have cost her son, Ned, his leg. At the age of fourteen, he dislocated his knee in a sledding accident, but Hetty refused to take him to a hospital. Instead she tried to treat the injury herself and by taking him to free medical clinics. In the end, his leg had to be amputated.

When she died in 1916, her estate was worth $100 million, the equivalent of many billions in today's dollars. But she had refused to use her money, instead hoarding it obsessively. She had the resources to live well, but she didn't use them.

When you know God, you have all the resources you need to live the abundant life. But at times, Christians simply do not access all that God has made available in Christ. Like Hetty and her money, we are spiritually wealthy but we sometimes live like spiritual paupers. God promises us the abundant life, but we live like we're homeless and starving in a spiritual sense.

What is the Abundant Life?

The dictionary defines the word *abundant* as meaning *more than adequate, richly supplied, plentiful*. Jesus said, "My purpose is to give them a rich and satisfying life." (John 10:10). So the abundant life is one that is richly supplied with what we need, a life that is available because Jesus came to provide it.

But perhaps we should talk about what the abundant life is *not*. It isn't necessarily a life of wealth, comfort, leisure, or freedom from pain. It's not the "good life" we hear about on TV.

But it is a life of access to untold divine resources, the provision God has made for us to live whole, healthy, and hopeful lives. We have everything we need to live the abundant life, the life we were created by God to enjoy. The secret to the abundant life is a close relationship with God as we follow the truths of Scripture.

But unless we know and understand how God means for us to live, unless we dig deeply into his Word, we could wind up like Hetty, starving while the untouched banquet God has laid out for us goes to waste.

How Do You Live the Abundant Life?

Life requires certain elements to sustain it and provide for growth – nourishment, air, and water. If any of these ingredients is in short supply, the living organism will shrivel, weaken, and even die.

The Bible is the nourishment you need to live the abundant life. Jesus is the Bread of Life and Living Water necessary for living as a Christian, and he is made known to you through this book.

Although the Bible was written hundreds of years ago, its message is timeless, personal, and practical because it is from God. As the number one bestseller of all time, the Bible is the most read book in history! Millions of people have discovered in it answers for their deepest needs – and words of comfort, encouragement, hope, inspiration, and guidance.

The Bible contains the recipe for that which leads to the abundant life: a firm and fulfilling connection to Christ. In 2 Timothy 3:16–17, the apostle Paul reminds Timothy, "All Scripture is inspired by God and is useful to teach us what is true and to make us realize what is wrong in our lives ... God uses it to prepare and equip his people to do every good work."

But the Bible is more than an answer book. It is really a library of books filled with inspiring stories, majestic poetry and songs, direct messages and prophecies, and most important of all, the account of God visiting our earth in the person of Jesus Christ.

Where Do You Begin?

If the Bible is fairly new to you, start your reading in the New Testament with the book of Mark (page 761). This book will give you a dramatic introduction to the events that changed the world and can open the door to the abundant life. It is a short, fast-moving biography of Jesus Christ, written by a young man who probably witnessed most of Jesus' three year ministry. In addition, Mark probably knew Jesus' disciples well and drew on their memories to help write this book.

Then follow the growth of Christianity by reading the book of Acts (page 830). This picks up where Mark ends and continues the dynamic story of the first Christians and how they spread the Good News of Jesus Christ all over the world.

Next read the book of Romans (page 857). This is one of the many letters written by the apostle Paul. It was sent to a group of first-century Christians in Rome. In it Paul clearly tells how selfish, arrogant, sinful humans can find acceptance with God. After you finish Romans, read some of the shorter books in the New Testament before turning to the Old Testament.

In the Old Testament, read the people stories in the book of Genesis. Then continue with some of the other books named after the main characters – Joshua, Ruth, Ezra, Job, Jonah, and others. Be sure to read complete stories instead of stopping at the end of a chapter. For instance, the story of Gideon is covered in Judges 6–8 (pages 192–195). The story of Jonah is covered throughout the whole book (pages 701–702) but it is only four chapters long and can easily be read in one sitting.

Then turn to the Psalms (page 415) and read enough of them to get a sense of what it means to worship God and pour out your feelings to him. Save the longer prophetic books (Isaiah, Jeremiah, and Ezekiel) until last. You may want to set up a pattern of daily reading that includes several Psalms along with a section from either the Old or New Testament.

Mark

John the Baptist Prepares the Way

1 This is the Good News about Jesus the Messiah, the Son of God.*
It began ²just as the prophet Isaiah had written:

"Look, I am sending my messenger ahead of you,
   and he will prepare your way.*
³He is a voice shouting in the wilderness,
'Prepare the way for the LORD'S coming!
  Clear the road for him!'*"

⁴This messenger was John the Baptist. He was in the wilderness and preached that people should be baptized to show that they had turned to God to receive forgiveness for their sins. ⁵All of Judea, including all the people of Jerusalem, went out to see and hear John. And when they confessed their sins, he baptized them in the Jordan River. ⁶His clothes were woven from coarse camel hair, and he wore a leather belt around his waist. For food he ate locusts and wild honey.

⁷John announced: "Someone is coming soon who is greater than I am – so much greater that I'm not even worthy to stoop down like a slave and untie the straps of his sandals. ⁸I baptize you with* water, but he will baptize you with the Holy Spirit!"

1:1 Some manuscripts do not include *the Son of God.*
1:2 Mal 3:1
1:3 Isa 40:3 (Greek version)

The Baptism and Temptation of Jesus

⁹One day Jesus came from Nazareth in Galilee, and John baptized him in the Jordan River. ¹⁰As Jesus came up out of the water, he saw the heavens splitting apart and the Holy Spirit descending on him* like a dove. ¹¹And a voice from heaven said, "You are my dearly loved Son, and you bring me great joy."

¹²The Spirit then compelled Jesus to go into the wilderness, ¹³where he was tempted by Satan for forty days. He was out among the wild animals, and angels took care of him.

¹⁴Later on, after John was arrested, Jesus went into Galilee, where he preached God's Good News.* ¹⁵"The time promised by God has come at last!" he announced. "The Kingdom of God is near! Repent of your sins and believe the Good News!"

The First Disciples

¹⁶One day as Jesus was walking along the shore of the Sea of Galilee, he saw Simon* and his brother Andrew throwing a net into the water, for they fished for a living. ¹⁷Jesus called out to them, "Come, follow me, and I will show you how to fish for people!" ¹⁸And they left their nets at once and followed him.

¹⁹A little farther up the shore Jesus saw Zebedee's sons, James and John, in a boat repairing their nets. ²⁰He called them at once, and they also followed him, leaving their father, Zebedee, in the boat with the hired men.

Jesus Casts Out an Evil Spirit

²¹Jesus and his companions went to the town of Capernaum. When the Sabbath day came, he went into the synagogue and began to teach. ²²The people were amazed at his teaching, for he taught with real authority-quite unlike the teachers of religious law.

1:8 Or *in;* also in 1:8b.
1:10 Or *toward him, or into him.*
1:14 Some manuscripts read *the Good News of the Kingdom of God.*
1:16 *Simon* is called "Peter" in 3:16 and thereafter.

²³Suddenly, a man in the synagogue who was possessed by an evil* spirit began shouting, ²⁴"Why are you interfering with us, Jesus of Nazareth? Have you come to destroy us? I know who you are-the Holy One sent from God!"

²⁵Jesus cut him short. "Be quiet! Come out of the man," he ordered. ²⁶At that, the evil spirit screamed, threw the man into a convulsion, and then came out of him.

²⁷Amazement gripped the audience, and they began to discuss what had happened. "What sort of new teaching is this?" they asked excitedly. "It has such authority! Even evil spirits obey his orders!" ²⁸The news about Jesus spread quickly throughout the entire region of Galilee.

Jesus Heals Many People

²⁹After Jesus left the synagogue with James and John, they went to Simon and Andrews home. ³⁰Now Simon's mother-in-law was sick in bed with a high fever. They told Jesus about her right away.³¹ So he went to her bedside, took her by the hand, and helped her sit up. Then the fever left her, and she prepared a meal for them.

³²That evening after sunset, many sick and demon-possessed people were brought to Jesus.

³³The whole town gathered at the door to watch. ³⁴So Jesus healed many people who were sick with various diseases, and he cast out many demons. But because the demons knew who he was, he did not allow them to speak.

Jesus Preaches in Galilee

³⁵Before daybreak the next morning, Jesus got up and went out to an isolated place to pray. ³⁶Later Simon and the others went out to find him. ³⁷When they found him, they said, "Everyone is looking for you."

³⁸But Jesus replied, "We must go on to other towns as well, and I will preach to them, too. That is why I came." ³⁹So he traveled

---

1:23 Greek *unclean*; also in 1:26, 27.

throughout the region of Galilee, preaching in the synagogues and casting out demons.

Jesus Heals a Man with Leprosy

⁴⁰A man with leprosy came and knelt in front of Jesus, begging to be healed. "If you are willing, you can heal me and make me clean," he said.

⁴¹Moved with compassion,* Jesus reached out and touched him. "I am willing," he said. "Be healed!" ⁴²Instantly the leprosy disappeared, and the man was healed. ⁴³Then Jesus sent him on his way with a stern warning: ⁴⁴"Don't tell anyone about this. Instead, go to the priest and let him examine you. Take along the offering required in the law of Moses for those who have been healed of leprosy.* This will be a public testimony that you have been cleansed."

⁴⁵But the man went and spread the word, proclaiming to everyone what had happened. As a result, large crowds soon surrounded Jesus, and he couldn't publicly enter a town anywhere. He had to stay out in the secluded places, but people from everywhere kept coming to him.

Jesus Heals a Paralyzed Man

2 When Jesus returned to Capernaum several days later, the news spread quickly that he was back home. ²Soon the house where he was staying was so packed with visitors that there was no more room, even outside the door. While he was preaching God's word to them, ³four men arrived carrying a paralyzed man on a mat. ⁴They couldn't bring him to Jesus because of the crowd, so they dug a hole through the roof above his head. Then they lowered the man on his mat, right down in front of Jesus. ⁵Seeing their faith, Jesus said to the paralyzed man, "My child, your sins are forgiven."

⁶But some of the teachers of religious law who were sitting there thought to themselves, ⁷"What is he saying? This is blasphemy! Only God can forgive sins!"

1:41 Some manuscripts read *Moved with anger.*
1:44 See Lev 14:2–32.

⁸Jesus knew immediately what they were thinking, so he asked them, "Why do you question this in your hearts? ⁹Is it easier to say to the paralyzed man' Your sins are forgiven; or' Stand up, pick up your mat, and walk? ¹⁰So I will prove to you that the Son of Man* has the authority on earth to forgive sins." Then Jesus turned to the paralyzed man and said, ¹¹"Stand up, pick up your mat, and go home!"

¹²And the man jumped up, grabbed his mat, and walked out through the stunned onlookers. They were all amazed and praised God, exclaiming, "We've never seen anything like this before!"

Jesus Calls Levi (Matthew)

¹³Then Jesus went out to the lakeshore again and taught the crowds that were coming to him. ¹⁴As he walked along, he saw Levi son of Alphaeus sitting at his tax collector's booth. "Follow me and be my disciple," Jesus said to him. So Levi got up and followed him.

¹⁵Later, Levi invited Jesus and his disciples to his home as dinner guests, along with many tax collectors and other disreputable sinners. (There were many people of this kind among Jesus' followers.) ¹⁶But when the teachers of religious law who were Pharisees* saw him eating with tax collectors and other sinners, they asked his disciples, "Why does he eat with such scum?*"

¹⁷When Jesus heard this, he told them, "Healthy people don't need a doctor-sick people do. I have come to call not those who think they are righteous, but those who know they are sinners."

A Discussion about Fasting

¹⁸Once when John's disciples and the Pharisees were fasting, some people came to Jesus and asked, "Why don't your disciples fast like John's disciples and the Pharisees do?"

2:10 "Son of Man" is a title Jesus used for himself.
2:16a Greek *the scribes of the Pharisees.*
2:16b Greek *with tax collectors and sinners?*

¹⁹Jesus replied, "Do wedding guests fast while celebrating with the groom? Of course not. They can't fast while the groom is with them. ²⁰But someday the groom will be taken away from them, and then they will fast.

²¹"Besides, who would patch old clothing with new cloth? For the new patch would shrink and rip away from the old cloth, leaving an even bigger tear than before.

²²"And no one puts new wine into old wineskins. For the wine would burst the wineskins, and the wine and the skins would both be lost. New wine calls for new wineskins."

A Discussion about the Sabbath

²³One Sabbath day as Jesus was walking through some grainfields, his disciples began breaking off heads of grain to eat. ²⁴But the Pharisees said to Jesus, "Look, why are they breaking the law by harvesting grain on the Sabbath?"

²⁵Jesus said to them, "Haven't you ever read in the Scriptures what David did when he and his companions were hungry? ²⁶He went into the house of God (during the days when Abiathar was high priest) and broke the law by eating the sacred loaves of bread that only the priests are allowed to eat. He also gave some to his companions."

²⁷Then Jesus said to them, "The Sabbath was made to meet the needs of people, and not people to meet the requirements of the Sabbath. ²⁸So the Son of Man is Lord, even over the Sabbath!"

Jesus Heals on the Sabbath

3 Jesus went into the synagogue again and noticed a man with a deformed hand. ²Since it was the Sabbath, Jesus' enemies watched him closely. If he healed the man's hand, they planned to accuse him of working on the Sabbath.

³Jesus said to the man, "Come and stand in front of everyone." ⁴Then he turned to his critics and asked, "Does the law permit good

deeds on the Sabbath, or is it a day for doing evil? Is this a day to save life or to destroy it?" But they wouldn't answer him.

[5]He looked around at them angrily and was deeply saddened by their hard hearts. Then he said to the man, "Hold out your hand." So the man held out his hand, and it was restored! [6]At once the Pharisees went away and met with the supporters of Herod to plot how to kill Jesus.

Crowds Follow Jesus

[7]Jesus went out to the lake with his disciples, and a large crowd followed him. They came from all over Galilee, Judea, [8]Jerusalem, Idumea, from east of the Jordan River, and even from as far north as Tyre and Sidon. The news about his miracles had spread far and wide, and vast numbers of people came to see him.

[9]Jesus instructed his disciples to have a boat ready so the crowd would not crush him. [10]He had healed many people that day, so all the sick people eagerly pushed forward to touch him. [11]And whenever those possessed by evil* spirits caught sight of him, the spirits would throw them to the ground in front of him shrieking, "You are the Son of God!" [12]But Jesus sternly commanded the spirits not to reveal who he was.

Jesus Chooses the Twelve Apostles

[13]Afterward Jesus went up on a mountain and called out the ones he wanted to go with him. And they came to him. [14]Then he appointed twelve of them and called them his apostles.* They were to accompany him, and he would send them out to preach, [15]giving them authority to cast out demons. [16]Here are their names:

Simon (whom he named Peter),
[17]James and John (the sons of Zebedee, but
Jesus nicknamed them "Sons of Thunder"*),

3:11 Greek *unclean*, also in 3:30.
3:14 Some manuscripts do not include *and called them his apostles*.

[18] Andrew,
  Philip,
  Bartholomew,
  Matthew,
  Thomas,
  James (son of Alphaeus),
  Thaddaeus,
  Simon (the zealot*),
[19] Judas Iscariot (who later betrayed him).

Jesus and the Prince of Demons

[20] One time Jesus entered a house, and the crowds began to gather again. Soon he and his disciples couldn't even find time to eat. [21] When his family heard what was happening, they tried to take him away. "He's out of his mind;" they said.

[22] But the teachers of religious law who had arrived from Jerusalem said, "He's possessed by Satan,* the prince of demons. That's where he gets the power to cast out demons."

[23] Jesus called them over and responded with an illustration. "How can Satan cast out Satan?" he asked. [24] "A kingdom divided by civil war will collapse. [25] Similarly, a family splintered by feuding will fall apart. [26] And if Satan is divided and fights against himself, how can he stand? He would never survive. [27] Let me illustrate this further. Who is powerful enough to enter the house of a strong man like Satan and plunder his goods? Only someone even stronger – someone who could tie him up and then plunder his house.

[28] "I tell you the truth, all sin and blasphemy can be forgiven, [29] but anyone who blasphemes the Holy Spirit will never be forgiven. This is a sin with eternal consequences." [30] He told them this because they were saying, "He's possessed by an evil spirit."

3:17 Greek *whom he named Boanerges, which means Sons of Thunder.*
3:18 Greek *the Cananean*, an Aramaic term for Jewish nationalists.
3:22 Greek *Beelzeboul*; other manuscripts read *Beezeboul*; Latin version reads *Beelzebub.*

The True Family of Jesus

³¹Then Jesus' mother and brothers came to see him. They stood outside and sent word for him to come out and talk with them. ³²There was a crowd sitting around Jesus, and someone said, "Your mother and your brothers* are outside asking for you."

³³Jesus replied, "Who is my mother? Who are my brothers?" ³⁴Then he looked at those around him and said, "Look, these are my mother and brothers. ³⁵Anyone who does God's will is my brother and sister and mother."

Parable of the Farmer Scattering Seed

4 Once again Jesus began teaching by the lakeshore. A very large crowd soon gathered around him, so he got into a boat. Then he sat in the boat while all the people remained on the shore. ²He taught them by telling many stories in the form of parables, such as this one:

³"Listen! A farmer went out to plant some seed. ⁴As he scattered it across his field, some of the seed fell on a footpath, and the birds came and ate it. ⁵Other seed fell on shallow soil with underlying rock. The seed sprouted quickly because the soil was shallow. ⁶But the plant soon wilted under the hot sun, and since it didn't have deep roots, it died. ⁷Other seed fell among thorns that grew up and choked out the tender plants so they produced no grain. ⁸Still other seeds fell on fertile soil, and they sprouted, grew, and produced a crop that was thirty, sixty, and even a hundred times as much as had been planted!" ⁹Then he said, "Anyone with ears to hear should listen and understand."

¹⁰Later, when Jesus was alone with the twelve disciples and with the others who were gathered around, they asked him what the parables meant.

¹¹He replied, "You are permitted to understand the secret* of the Kingdom of God. But I use parables for everything I say to outsiders, ¹²So that the Scriptures might be fulfilled:

3:32 Some manuscripts add *and sisters.*

'When they see what I do,
   they will learn nothing.
When they hear what I say,
   they will not understand.
Otherwise, they will turn to me
   and be forgiven.'*"

[13]Then Jesus said to them, "If you can't understand the meaning of this parable, how will you understand all the other parables? [14]The farmer plants seed by taking God's word to others. [15]The seed that fell on the footpath represents those who hear the message, only to have Satan come at once and take it away. [16]The seed on the rocky soil represents those who hear the message and immediately receive it with joy. [17]But since they don't have deep roots, they don't last long. They fall away as soon as they have problems or are persecuted for believing God's word. [18]The seed that fell among the thorns represents others who hear God's word, [19]but all too quickly the message is crowded out by the worries of this life, the lure of wealth, and the desire for other things, so no fruit is produced. [20]And the seed that fell on good soil represents those who hear and accept God's word and produce a harvest of thirty, sixty, or even a hundred times as much as had been planted!"

Parable of the Lamp

[21]Then Jesus asked them, "Would anyone light a lamp and then put it under a basket or under a bed? Of course not! A lamp is placed on a stand, where its light will shine. [22]For everything that is hidden will eventually be brought into the open, and every secret will be brought to light. [23]Anyone with ears to hear should listen and understand."

[24]Then he added, "Pay close attention to what you hear. The closer you listen, the more understanding you will be given* – and you will receive even more. [25]To those who listen to my teaching, more understanding will be given. But for those who are not listening,

even what little understanding they have will be taken away from them."

Parable of the Growing Seed

[26]Jesus also said, "The Kingdom of God is like a farmer who scatters seed on the ground. [27]Night and day, while he's asleep or awake, the seed sprouts and grows, but he does not understand how it happens. [28]The earth produces the crops on its own. First a leaf blade pushes through, then the heads of wheat are formed, and finally the grain ripens. [29]And as soon as the grain is ready, the farmer comes and harvests it with a sickle, for the harvest time has come."

Parable of the Mustard Seed

[30]Jesus said, "How can I describe the Kingdom of God? What story should I use to illustrate it? [31]It is like a mustard seed planted in the ground. It is the smallest of all seeds, [32]but it becomes the largest of all garden plants; it grows long branches, and birds can make nests in its shade."

[33]Jesus used many similar stories and illustrations to teach the people as much as they could understand. [34]In fact, in his public ministry he never taught without using parables; but afterward, when he was alone with his disciples, he explained everything to them.

Jesus Calms the Storm

[35]As evening came, Jesus said to his disciples, "Let's cross to the other side of the lake." [36]So they took Jesus in the boat and started out, leaving the crowds behind (although other boats followed). [37]But soon a fierce storm came up. High waves were breaking into the boat, and it began to fill with water.

[38]Jesus was sleeping at the back of the boat with his head on a cushion. The disciples woke him up, shouting, "Teacher, don't you care that we're going to drown?"

4:24 Or *The measure you givbe will be the measure you get back.*

[39]When Jesus woke up, he rebuked the wind and said to the water, "Silence! Be still!" Suddenly the wind stopped, and there was a great calm. [40]Then he asked them, "Why are you afraid? Do you still have no faith?"

[41]The disciples were absolutely terrified. "Who is this man?" they asked each other. "Even the wind and waves obey him!"